Grounded Theory for Qualitative Research

SAGE has been part of the global academic community since 1965, supporting high quality research and learning that transforms society and our understanding of individuals, groups, and cultures. SAGE is the independent, innovative, natural home for authors, editors and societies who share our commitment and passion for the social sciences.

Find out more at: **www.sagepublications.com**

Connect, Debate, Engage on Methodspace

- **Connect with other researchers and discuss your research interests**
- **Keep up with announcements in the field, for example calls for papers and jobs**
- **Discover and review resources**
- **Engage with featured content such as key articles, podcasts and videos**
- **Find out about relevant conferences and events**

Connecting the Research Community

www.methodspace.com

brought to you by

Grounded Theory for Qualitative Research

A Practical Guide | Cathy Urquhart

Los Angeles | London | New Delhi
Singapore | Washington DC

Los Angeles | London | New Delhi
Singapore | Washington DC

SAGE Publications Ltd
1 Oliver's Yard
55 City Road
London EC1Y 1SP

SAGE Publications Inc.
2455 Teller Road
Thousand Oaks, California 91320

SAGE Publications India Pvt Ltd
B 1/I 1 Mohan Cooperative Industrial Area
Mathura Road
New Delhi 110 044

SAGE Publications Asia-Pacific Pte Ltd
3 Church Street
#10-04 Samsung Hub
Singapore 049483

Editor: Jai Seaman
Assistant editor: Anna Horvai
Production editor: Ian Antcliff
Copyeditor: Michelle Clark
Proofreader: Kate Harrison
Marketing manager: Ben Griffin-Sherwood
Cover design: Lisa Harper
Typeset by: C&M Digitals (P) Ltd, Chennai, India
Printed by: CPI Group (UK) Ltd, Croydon, CR0 4YY

MIX
Paper from
responsible sources
FSC
www.fsc.org   FSC® C013604

Library of Congress Control Number: 2012935548

British Library Cataloguing in Publication data

A catalogue record for this book is available from the British Library

ISBN 978-1-84787-053-7
ISBN 978-1-84787-054-4 (pbk)

Contents

Dedication   ix
About the author   x
Acknowledgements   xi
How this book is structured   xii

Chapter 1 Introduction   1

Introduction   1
What this book does not do   3
Is GTM difficult to use?   3
What is grounded theory method (GTM)?   4
Why is it useful?   10
Summary   11
Exercises   12
Web resources   12
Further reading   13
Frequently asked questions   13

Chapter 2 Grounded theory method (GTM)   14

Introduction   14
The discovery of grounded theory   14
The key characteristics of GTM   15
Evolving coding procedures in GTM   21
Myths about GTM   28
Summary   32
Exercises   33
Web resources   33
Further reading   34
Frequently asked questions   34

Chapter 3 Getting started with coding   35

Introduction   35
Coding – a first example   36

Different approaches to coding – what is and isn't GTM?   37
Coding as theory building – not just concepts
   but relationships, too   41
Coding procedures used in GTM   45
Summary   51
Exercises   52
Web resources   52
Further reading   53
Frequently asked questions   53

Chapter 4 Research design using GTM   55

Introduction   55
Philosophical position   56
Methodology   62
Data-collection methods   69
Ethics   70
Reflexivity   70
Theoretical memos   71
Breadth versus depth in research design   72
Summary   72
Exercises   73
Web resources   74
Further reading   74
Frequently asked questions   75

Chapter 5 Coding and conceptualising   78

Introduction   78
Open coding: Example 1   78
Selective coding: Example 1   88
Open coding: Example 2   91
Selective coding: Example 2   99
A word on software for data analysis   101
Summary   102
Exercises   103
Web resources   104
Further reading   104
Frequently asked questions   105

Chapter 6 Building the theory   106

Introduction   106
What is a theoretical code?   107

Theoretical memos   110
Integrative diagrams   114
Theoretical coding: Example 1   116
Theoretical coding: Example 2   121
Summary   125
Exercises   126
Web resources   126
Further reading   127
Frequently asked questions   127

Chapter 7 Scaling up the theory   129

Introduction   129
Why scale up the theory?   130
Levels of theory   131
Relating the emergent theory to the literature   136
Increasing the scope and generalisability of the theory   143
Summary   144
Exercises   145
Web resources   145
Further reading   146
Frequently asked questions   146

Chapter 8 Writing up a grounded theory study   148

Introduction   148
The writing up process   149
The challenges of writing up a grounded theory study   152
How much context of the study should be presented?   153
Representing the coding procedure   154
Presenting a chain of evidence   159
Presenting findings   162
Presenting the substantive theory   163
Theoretical integration and presenting the literature   169
Summary   172
Exercises   174
Web resource   174
Further reading   174
Frequently asked questions   174

Chapter 9 The contribution of GTM – some reflections   176

Introduction   176
Key insights   177

Guidelines for grounded theory studies   182
The future of GTM   185
Summary   187
Exercises   188
Web resources   189
Further reading   189
Frequently asked questions   189

Glossary   191
References   195
Index   201

Dedication

This book is respectfully dedicated to Barney Glaser and Anselm Strauss (1916–1996) for their gift to the world that is grounded theory.

About the author

Cathy Urquhart is Professor of Digital and Sustainable Enterprise at Manchester Metropolitan University Business School, UK. She has taught qualitative research methods around the world in universities in Australia and New Zealand as well as the UK. She is a senior member of the editorial board of *MIS Quarterly*, the journal with the highest impact factor in the field of business.

Acknowledgements

No book gets written without a lot of help and I am truly grateful for all the support I have had from various people along the way. First, I'd like to thank both my editors at Sage – Patrick Brindle and Jai Seaman. Patrick approved the original book proposal and gave me invaluable support and constructive criticism on the early draft. Jai has provided encouragement, support and the final push to finish the book. I'd also like to thank David Hodge at Sage for his detailed and helpful critiques of early chapters. Anna Horvai, as editorial assistant at Sage, has provided prompt and helpful assistance at every stage. Thanks, too, to the anonymous peer reviewer who provided invaluable feedback on the book. Thanks also to Ian Antcliff, production editor, and copyeditor Michelle Clark at Sage who helped the prose run more smoothly.

I'd also like to thank all those colleagues and students who have debated and discussed grounded theory with me over the years, helping me form ideas about grounded theory method, especially Gillian Reid, Karin Olesen, Antonio Díaz Andrade, Mariyam Adam, Karen Day, Riitta Hekkala, Gary Furash, Muhammad Sulayman, and Darren M McDonald. Special thanks go to Hans Lehmann, Walter Fernández and Gaetan Mourmant for robust conversations about Glaserian grounded theory. Special thanks to Stefan Seidel for his incisive and enormously helpful comments on the draft, provided at just the right time.

Finally, no acknowledgements are complete without heartfelt thanks to those who have sacrificed so much on the domestic front. Thank you to Harry and Hannah for being patient when Mum was working on the book. Thank you to Sheila, Ruth and Helen for being there for me. Last, and most important, thanks to Chris, for taking care of the home front, formatting beyond the call of duty and being a loving constant in my life – I am truly grateful, always.

March 2012

How this book is structured

This book is designed for you to use how you want, and contains three major strands, aimed at not only first-time users of grounded theory method (GTM) but also the more experienced. Each chapter focuses on particular aspects, and ends with exercises, Web resources, further reading and frequently asked questions (FAQs) to extend your knowledge further.

The first strand (Chapters 1 and 2) gives the background and intellectual foundations of GTM. The second strand (Chapters 3, 4, 5 and 6) addresses the practical business of doing GTM by, first, getting started with coding (Chapter 3), then designing a GTM study (Chapter 4) and, finally, providing detailed, worked examples of coding and theorising using GTM (Chapters 5 and 6).

The third and final strand addresses issues of scaling up your emergent theory (Chapter 7), issues encountered when writing up and presenting a GTM study (Chapter 8), then concludes by revisiting GTM, its strengths as a research method and the continuing evolution of GTM (Chapter 9).

Below is a more detailed outline of the contents of each chapter.

- Chapter 1 introduces the purpose of the book, then gives a brief overview of GTM. It discusses the key features of GTM under four different headings – Theory, GTM and the literature, Using GTM in the field, and Data analysis using GTM.
- Chapter 2 gives some further background on GTM and how it has evolved into several different versions. This chapter considers some of the intellectual history of GTM. It also explores some myths about it that you may also encounter along the way.
- Chapter 3 helps the new user to get started with coding. It's important to see how GTM fits within broader approaches to coding, so this chapter discusses the key differences between GTM and other coding approaches. There is also discussion of the importance of distinguishing between description and analysis – a vital skill for the grounded theorist – as well as how coding builds theory. A brief example of how grounded theory approaches theory building is also provided, in preparation for Chapters 5 and 6, where we look at coding in detail.
- Chapter 4 discusses research design using GTM. In this chapter, we look at key first questions about the use of GTM in a research design and how the research philosophy and methodology might be considered when designing a grounded theory study. We also discuss how GTM might fit into various research designs and how theoretical sampling might be built into the research design. We look

too at types of data collection, the notion of reflexivity, the use of theoretical memos in the field and ethics.

- Chapter 5 explains coding and conceptualisation in GTM, using two detailed worked examples. The chapter demonstrates open and selective coding through the two examples. It also discusses when to 'elevate' an open code, and when to decide which codes are dimensions of other codes.
- Chapter 6 explains theoretical coding – the all-important stage in GTM – building on the examples in Chapter 5. Diagramming is introduced as a key tool for understanding relationships. Glaser's coding families and other options for building conceptual relationships are considered in the context of the worked examples. How links at lower levels of coding also help build the theory is also discussed. Theoretical memos, and their key role in theorising, are also discussed.
- Chapter 7 gives some options about scaling up the emergent theory from a grounded theory study. It discusses descriptive, substantive and formal levels of theory and their role in theory building. The chapter also considers how to engage the generated theory with the literature, and why this is important. It also illustrates the process of relating theory to literature using the worked examples from Chapter 6.
- Chapter 8 tackles the issues around writing up a grounded theory study. It considers why the process of writing is important and how we can overcome blocks when writing. The chapter then gives some suggestions on how the theory generated by using the method can be written up in a dissertation or a journal paper. It discusses how to position your use of GTM – is your study a grounded theory study or does it just use the method? The chapter also looks at how the chain of evidence provided by a grounded theory study can be represented in a paper or dissertation and gives examples from various studies.
- Chapter 9 concludes by revisiting GTM, its contributions and its strengths as a research method. Some key insights are considered and some guidelines for grounded theory studies. GTM as a living and evolving qualitative method is the final consideration.

1

Introduction

Introduction

This book aims to provide a simple and practical introduction to grounded theory. I've used grounded theory myself in research for many years and feel there is real need for a book that provides examples and gives as much guidance as possible. This is not to say that this is a prescriptive text – there is no one way to do grounded theory – but the book does aim to be as clear as possible. The idea is to give you the basic techniques to be able to do your own grounded theory study and enough information to then proceed with your own adaptations and exploration in grounded theory. This book:

- explains the grounded theory analysis process through clearly worked examples
- explains how the grounded theory process can lead to new theory and new insights about data
- explains how to engage the findings from a grounded theory study with existing literature
- provides exercises, Web resources, further reading and frequently asked questions in each chapter.

This book largely came about through requests from my postgraduate students about the 'how' of grounded theory method (GTM), due to their perception of a lack of practical guidance and examples in the grounded theory literature. This set me thinking about the best way to explain the 'how' without being prescriptive about the method. Although they were convinced by my passionate advocacy of it as a method of analysing qualitative data and the grounded theory studies they had read, they still faced a real problem with understanding and applying the method. So, this book aims to fill that gap – to explain the 'how', without sacrificing the flexibility of the method in the process. It aims, above all else, to be an *accessible* guide to grounded theory method for first-time users, so I make no apologies for the straightforward tone of this book. While precise terms are sometimes needed to explain complex concepts, I believe it's also important to not hide behind terms that complicate rather than illuminate!

This book is also a highly personal view of grounded theory – it is very much the product of my own experiences and those of my wonderful students. The book aims to be the sum total of the advice I might give a first-time user of grounded theory and distil the experiences of over 15 years of using grounded theory in many contexts.

It has become apparent to me how much knowledge about the actual practice of coding remains opaque, and is not available in either research texts or journal papers. There are probably some good reasons for this. First, it is difficult to explain how the coding process is carried out – the best type of learning in this case is to try it out. So, in this book there are lots of examples and exercises. When I teach grounded theory, I try to get people to apply the method to an example as soon as possible – there is no substitute for simply doing it! Second, journal articles do not afford researchers the space required to explain how they have analysed their data in detail. The process of analysis is often messy and iterative, and this sort of truth-telling does not fit well with the notion of a finished piece of research. So often, researchers do not discuss their processes of analysis for fear of being criticised for not following the right path. What happens in research is real and often untidy and any analysis procedure is prone to be affected by the context, how the data was collected, the circumstances of the field, who was carrying out the analysis and many other factors.

So, this book aims to show the reflexive nature of the coding process and encourage you to embark on it yourself as soon as possible. You'll hear a lot about the 'coding process' in this book. Put simply, this is the process of attaching concepts to data, for the purposes of analysing that data.

My experience with the method in the field of information systems has led me to believe that many researchers use grounded theory as a practical coding method, concentrating on the mechanics of coding, rather than as the theorising device it was designed to be. This is a pity because, in doing so, researchers are using the first part of the method only and neglecting the unique power of grounded theory. This is rather like an artist deciding to paint pictures, but never framing them, exhibiting them or describing what they are doing in the context of current art practice. So, throughout the book, the issue of what a theory is, as well as how it might be built and then engaged with other theories, is discussed. You can read this book to find out about coding procedures in grounded theory and not propose to build any theory yourself, but the examples in this book do show how to do so.

In the book, you'll see the term 'grounded theory method' (or its acronym, 'GTM') used rather than the more commonly seen 'grounded theory'. Antony Bryant (2002) uses this term to make the useful point that grounded theory is a *method* that produces a grounded theory, and this is a helpful distinction to make.

What this book does not do

This book does not claim to be a definitive text on the grounded theory method (GTM), nor stake out particular territory. The method has a history that started in 1967 and there are many views on and variants of it. It is an evolving method, too, as researchers increasingly turn to it as a powerful tool in qualitative work. The book does aim to share some useful rules of thumb about applying GTM, however, and gives a personal view. It does not claim to be applying 'pure' grounded theory as there are many debates about what 'pure' grounded theory might be – it is almost inevitable that I will offend someone with my own view of grounded theory.

This book does not spend a lot of time on the philosophical position of GTM, interesting and important though that issue is. Students often ask me if GTM is 'valid'. What they mean by this is whether or not GTM is seen as a scientific method within the positivist paradigm. These issues are further discussed in Chapter 2, but, for now, suffice it to say that GTM can be used within positivist, interpretivist and critical paradigms of research.

Is GTM difficult to use?

When research students say they wish to use GTM, often they are told that it is difficult to use. This book is written to support those students, and defend their use of GTM. It was a revolutionary method of analysing qualitative data when it was launched in 1967, and it still retains its controversial qualities to this day.

Why should it be controversial and why do scholars still debate, and sometimes criticise, GTM? One reason is found in the chequered history of the method itself. From the time the seminal book, *The Discovery of Grounded Theory,* was published (Glaser and Strauss 1967) there have been countless applications of GTM, but also many adaptations and evolutions of the method. With the publication of Strauss and Corbin's (1990) book came a very real disagreement between the co-originators about the very nature of GTM itself. So, students of GTM have to acquaint themselves with the Strauss and Glaser variants of the method and decide which to use. This book inclines towards the Glaserian strand, for reasons explained later.

Students of the method also have to deal with the fact that many journal articles use the term 'grounded theory' as a blanket term for coding and analysing qualitative data. When we attach a code to data, we are also attaching a concept to that data and it is those concepts that help us build theory, as discussed in Chapter 3. GTM is indeed a method that can be used to analyse qualitative data, using codes attached to data, but it is so much more than that, too. It also builds relationships between concepts informed by the codes, which allow us to build theory. As previously remarked, this is an important and, in my opinion, sadly under-utilised aspect of GTM, especially when you consider that the original aim of GTM was to build theory.

GTM also, in my opinion, is a wonderful method of analysing data and building theory. In this book, I want to share what is, for me, the excitement and passion of doing analysis in this way. For me, the experience of using GTM as a PhD student (Urquhart 2001) was a life-changing one. The features of the method mean that you are so close to the data you gain all sorts of rich insights; these insights almost invariably result in excellent research. I have become an advocate of GTM not so much because I used it for my own PhD, but because experience using the method with postgraduate students has led me to see that it produces strong theory grounded in the data. From a postgraduate perspective, I have found that the use of GTM all but guarantees an excellent piece of research, if applied carefully in all its stages.

Of course, GTM is not for everyone. I have two sorts of postgraduate student – the first sort, when encountering GTM, look as if they wish to run from my office immediately and beg to be able to use a framework or theory from the literature instead. The second sort look somewhat nervous, ask some questions about how long the analysis will take and generally have some unexpected joys along the way as they build concepts from their data and experience theory building. It is to this second sort of student that this book is dedicated – I hope it is a useful companion on your journey. I also hope fellow researchers will find this book a useful reference on grounded theory.

What is grounded theory method (GTM)?

It is perhaps best to start with how the creators of grounded theory defined their method, in their seminal book that launched grounded theory (Glaser and Strauss 1967). They defined it as 'the discovery of theory from data – systematically obtained and analysed in social research'(Glaser and Strauss 1967: 1). The key point here is that the theory produced is *grounded* in the data.

The emphasis on theory in the original book is in sharp contrast to the use of grounded theory method (GTM) today, where it is known primarily as a method of qualitative data analysis. So, one of the emphases in this book (as well as helping with practical issues of coding and data analysis) is on what to do with that coding – how to build the theory from it.

For the record, the following are the key features of GTM as explained by Cresswell (1998) and Dey (1999). They provide a good starting point and we'll discuss them in the next sections.

1 The aim of grounded theory is to generate or discover a theory.
2 The researcher has to *set aside theoretical ideas* in order to let the substantive theory emerge.

3 Theory focuses on how individuals interact with the phenomena under study.
4 Theory asserts a plausible relationship between concepts and sets of concepts.
5 Theory is derived from data acquired from fieldwork interviews, observation and documents.
6 Data analysis is systematic and begins as soon as data is available.
7 Data analysis proceeds through identifying categories and connecting them.
8 Further data collection (or sampling) is based on emerging concepts.
9 These concepts are developed through *constant comparison* with additional data.
10 Data collection can stop when no new conceptualisations emerge.
11 Data analysis proceeds from open coding (identifying categories, properties and dimensions) through selective coding (clustering around categories) to theoretical coding.
12 The resulting theory can be reported in a narrative framework or a set of propositions.

Theory

Let's consider first the statements about theory.

1. The aim of grounded theory is to generate or discover a theory.
4. Theory asserts a plausible relationship between concepts and sets of concepts.
12. The resulting theory can be reported in a narrative framework or a set of propositions.

It's important to appreciate, then, that GTM is all about theory, even though its procedures are often more commonly used to analyse data than generate theories. Chapter 1 of the revolutionary book *The Discovery of Grounded Theory* (Glaser and Strauss 1967), which launched grounded theory, states that the aim of the book is to generate theory based on data, rather than verify 'grand theory'. The authors also contended that the classic theories of sociology did not cover all the new areas of social life that needed exploration. They also discussed the idea of qualitative versus quantitative data and concluded that *both* types of data are needed to generate and verify theories.

So, the very first book on GTM begins by putting forward two major points:

- the need to generate new theories rather than force data into a few existing theories
- the idea that qualitative data and quantitative data are *both* useful.

It is worth, at this point, discussing what a theory actually is.

We all formulate theories in everyday life – for instance, we might say, based on our experience, that people who are good at maths tend to be more introverted (my apologies at this point to all those people who are both fine mathematicians *and* extroverts – this is just an example). This working theory is based on our experience of the world and may not be true. It is, after all, an individual perception, so not really 'grounded', in the true sense of the word, but it has the key components of a theory: some constructs – 'good at maths' and 'introversion' – and a *relationship* between the two.

Shirley Gregor (2006), in her paper on theory, gives some useful building blocks of a theory. Table 1.1 shows how these theory components appear in GTM.

So, the theory discovered or generated as a result of using GTM is often represented by a narrative framework, a diagram or a set of hypotheses. In all three cases of representation, it is important that there be a plausible relationship between the constructs because this is a cornerstone of all theories. In GTM this relationship is not usually causal because, in the majority of cases, it uses qualitative data. The relationships between constructs therefore tend to be more a case of 'A is a part of B' or 'A influences B'.

There is extensive guidance in GTM on how to formulate these relationships between constructs (see Glaser (1978) and Corbin and Strauss (2008)). These are the most controversial aspects of GTM, as we will discuss later. For now, though, the important thing to note is that GTM is a method of generating theories and theories contain relationships between constructs.

Table 1.1   Components of a theory in GTM (adapted from Gregor 2006)

Theory component	Definition	In GTM
Means of representation	The theory must be represented physically in some way – in words, mathematical terms, symbolic logic, diagrams, tables or graphically.	Theories are often represented by a narrative framework, diagrams or statements of hypotheses.
Constructs	The phenomena of interest in the theory (Dubin's 'units'). All of the primary constructs in the theory should be well defined. Many different types of constructs are possible – for example, observational (real) terms, theoretical (nominal) terms and collective terms.	The aim is to get to one or two core categories or constructs. This makes for a more coherent theory. All the constructs in a grounded theory, are, well, grounded in observations; they come from the data.
Statements of relationship	These show relationships between the constructs. Again, these may be of many types – associative, compositional, unidirectional, bidirectional, conditional or causal. The nature of the relationship specified depends on the purpose of the theory. Very simple relationships can be specified, such as 'x is a member of class A'.	Because the theory is often based on qualitative data, relationships are not often causal. There is a lot of guidance about the sorts of relationships that are possible between constructs, in the form of coding families (Glaser 1978) and a coding paradigm (Corbin and Strauss 2008).
Scope	Specified by the degree of generality of the statements of relationships (signified by modal qualifiers, such as 'some', 'many', 'all' and 'never') and statements of boundaries showing the limits of generalisations.	The aim is to produce substantive theories that pertain to the area being investigated. The scope and generalisability can be extended by theoretical sampling (Glaser 1978). The substantive theory can and should be engaged with existing theories – existing theories can also be seen as slices of data that help build the theory.

GTM and the literature

A key feature of GTM is the following point from our list above.

> 2. The researcher has to set aside theoretical ideas in order to let the substantive theory emerge.

Of all the features of GTM, this is the one that causes most difficulty for new users. The idea here is that the literature about whatever you are researching is referenced *after*, not before, you build the theory. Glaser and Strauss recommended this because they wanted the data to speak to the researcher, rather than for the researcher to force theories on the data. To me, this is one of the reasons GTM was revolutionary in its time and still is tremendously relevant, today. The idea that we should seek to see what the data indicates, rather than shoehorn it into a theory that already exists, means there is more chance of discovering something new. It also seems to have more integrity as a research process, because it does not seek to impose preconceived ideas on the world.

Of course, no one enters the research process as a blank slate – we will all have read something about the phenomena. The founders of GTM ask that we put that aside, so we do not influence the coding of our data. In practice, it's quite possible to do a literature review before we enter the field – on the understanding, though, that it does not influence the coding process. Once the theory has been developed, *then* we engage our theory with the existing theories and use them to help with the densification of our emergent theory. The literature review we developed initially may then change.

This is not the barrier to using GTM that people might think. In Chapter 2 I give some more advice and information on to how to deal with the literature, but, for now, suffice it to say that I have seen many students conduct a literature review *and* do a successful GTM study! It's the use to which the literature is put, not the act of searching the literature in itself, that is the key point here.

Using GTM in the field

The following aspects from our original list above all relate to using GTM in the field.

> 3. Theory focuses on how individuals interact with the phenomena under study.
> 5. Theory is derived from data acquired from fieldwork interviews, observation and documents.
> 8. Further data collection (or sampling) is based on emerging concepts.

It is true to say that many GTM studies do focus on how individuals might interact with the phenomena under study – for instance, how a work group might react to a new information system – but the use of GTM is quite flexible and varied. I have seen it applied to all sorts of phenomena, from analysing citation information to the design of software. GTM is perfect for studying micro-phenomena, too, because it involves the close examination of data, but it's worth considering that GTM can be used to study larger units as well, such as firms. This is consistent with the idea of theory building – which is when we build larger theories from smaller, substantive ones. We'll discuss this further in Chapter 4, how the unit of analysis may influence a GTM research design.

As previously stated, GTM builds theory from the data acquired from field-work interviews, observation and documents. All these data sources are qualitative, and the use of qualitative data fits well with the inductive process that GTM is. When we say that GTM is inductive, what we mean is it reasons from the ground up – from specific instances in the data to more general conclusions. How the data is analysed – completely or partially – will, again, depend on the research design (discussed in Chapter 4). As a point of interest, it's worth noting, too, that quantitative data can be used in GTM, as part of a mixed method design (again, we'll look at this option in Chapter 4).

It's also important to note that the use of GTM implies *overlapping data collection and analysis*. This means that researchers analyse the data in the field and use the emerging concepts from that analysis to decide where to sample from next. This process is known as *theoretical sampling*, because the emerging theory directs future data collection. So, for instance, if a particular concept (such the effects of job losses on remaining staff) arises from an interview, the researcher could decide to carry out more interviews (with other individuals who have witnessed such job losses). This strategy may not always be practical, depending, of course, on the amount of access granted to the researcher. Sometimes there may be only a set number of interviews permitted in an organisation. So, one good idea for a grounded theory study is to allow for more than one phase of data collection, as Charmaz (2006) suggests (we will return to this in Chapter 4).

Theoretical sampling does two things:

- it enables researchers to build up justification for concepts in the theory by finding more instances of a particular concept
- it allows researchers to follow an emerging storyline suggested by the data.

Data analysis using GTM

6. Data analysis is systematic and begins as soon as data is available.
7. Data analysis proceeds through identifying categories and connecting them.

9. These concepts are developed through constant comparison with additional data.
10. Data collection can stop when no new conceptualisations emerge.
11. Data analysis proceeds from open coding (identifying categories, properties and dimensions) through selective coding (clustering around categories), to theoretical coding.

These characteristics from our list above are all to do with data analysis – the core of GTM. It is also the aspect most often leveraged independently of theory building. It is certainly true to say that the data analysis procedures are systematic, which is one reason they are so frequently leveraged by those who may *not* be building a theory. These procedures are well-known and described in the literature and, as such, are seen as a very legitimate way of analysing qualitative data.

In a systematic fashion, often analysing the data line by line, categories are attached to the data. This is 'coding' and we will discuss this extensively in Chapters 3, 5 and 6. A category is generally a low-level concept attached to a particular piece of data. So, for instance, we might look at a line of text and decide that, in this line, the person is trying to justify a decision. So, we might call this category 'Justification', then find more instances in other parts of the data we are analysing.

The important thing to note here is that the *connecting* of the categories is as important as the naming of them because, if you recall, an important component of a theory is building relationships between constructs. So, it's helpful to see the data analysis in grounded theory – which concentrates on naming categories and connecting them – as laying the foundation for constructs and relationships. As previously stated, further data collection is ideally based on the concepts emerging from such analysis.

Constant comparison is simply the process of constantly comparing instances of data labelled as a particular category with other instances of data in the same category. This is often described as the heart of GTM. It is no more than a simple rule of thumb, but it is also a way of thinking – to ask yourself, 'How does this instance I have labelled X, compare with all the other instances of X that I have labelled?' It really does work as a method of analysis because it encourages researchers to consider closely what they are analysing.

It is usually quite obvious, in a grounded theory study, when to stop data collection. It is when the researcher finds no new concepts are emerging from the data – all that is happening is there are more instances of existing categories. In this way, *theoretical saturation* is reached – the particular category is seen to be 'saturated', that is, full!

While different versions of GTM use slightly different stages of coding, I find it helpful to think of just three:

1 open coding
2 selective coding
3 theoretical coding.

These are the stages recommended by Glaser (1978) and they have the virtue of simplicity.

Open coding means just that – going through the data, line by line or paragraph by paragraph, attaching codes to the data and very much staying open, seeing what the data might be telling you.

The open codes are then grouped into larger categories in the stage of *selective coding*, on the basis of the key categories that are shaping the theory.

In *theoretical coding*, those categories are related to each other and the relationships between them considered. You may well have spotted that this is the act of building theory – finding constructs, connecting them and considering the nature of that relationship.

Why is it useful?

Let me count the ways! In this book, I am an unashamed advocate of GTM because of my experience in using it for research and with postgraduate students. I can honestly say that every time I have experienced grounded theory research, I have experienced new insights. Why should this be so? I think it is because GTM encourages us to take a close look at the data. Coding line by line or at the paragraph level encourages this close relationship with the data. Of course, critics of the method will tell you that what is produced is a hopelessly detailed theory, but there are, of course, ways you can 'scale up' that theory so it can then be engaged with other theories – and it is this which is a vital part of the process and how we get value from the method.

GTM has an obvious appeal in instances where no previous theory exists, so for new phenomena it's an ideal choice. In information systems – my own discipline – we are constantly grappling with new technological developments that cause something of a rethink, especially when it comes to how people relate to information technology – social networking websites are one such example.

GTM is also said to be good for studying processes (Glaser 1978) and the concept of a process in research is a very useful one. I have found it particularly useful when analysing interview data – probably because paying close attention to what people say is likely to lead to new concepts. Looking at the data line by line, as Strauss (1987) suggests simply encourages more analytical thought. So, while a larger-grained, thematic analysis of interviews might seem superficially attractive, it does not give the results that GTM does. I have seen this many times with postgraduate student projects.

The most innovative and exciting aspects of GTM, in my opinion, are twofold:

- the focus on building theory – as opposed to simply trying out existing theories to see if they hold in a particular instance – encourages scholarship and innovation in all disciplines
- the fact that researchers are encouraged to not think about existing theories helps that innovation.

It should be noted, though, that this does not mean researchers should ignore existing theories – we are all under a strict obligation to engage our emergent theories with existing literature (Strauss 1987). This idea is beautifully put by Dey (1993) when he says that researchers should have an open mind, as opposed to an empty head. So, as we have seen, the literature review is delayed. In practice, most people find a non-committal literature review helpful, but it should be noted that its relevance is completely determined by the emergent theory.

It is perhaps best to conclude with a comment from a former PhD student whom I overheard talking to someone else about his experience with GTM. He said he found it hard and time-consuming, but that it had given him an excellent PhD. So GTM is not for the faint-hearted, but it is for anyone interested in doing academically rigorous and exciting work!

Summary

- This chapter first explained its aims – in short, to be a clear and accessible introduction to grounded theory method (GTM) using worked examples to explain the coding and theory-building process.
- It also pointed out that this is a personal view of GTM, derived from practical experience. GTM has a complicated intellectual history, so I have opted for what in my view is simplest and most flexible, while remaining true to its original ideas advanced in 1967 by Glaser and Strauss.
- The chapter then examined the issue of whether or not GTM is, in fact, difficult. It is true to say that GTM has its fair share of complexity, but at its heart is an elegant and simple method for analysing data and building theory.
- We then had a brief foray into the features of GTM – 12 in all, divided into 4 themes – theory, GTM and the literature, using GTM in the field, and data analysis using GTM.
- When discussing theory and GTM, several points were covered. First, what a theory actually consists of was examined, then, second, discussed in the context of theories produced by GTM.
- The stance that GTM takes towards literature was discussed as being a feature that sometimes causes difficulty for novice users. GTM asks that we put what

we have read on one side when analysing the data and keep an open mind. Though the literature review is, thus, to be delayed, it does not, in my mind, preclude researchers from doing a draft one.

- The chapter then briefly discussed some issues around using GTM in the field. GTM has as a key idea that the emerging analysis should dictate future data collection – a process known as theoretical sampling.
- We then had a brief introduction to data analysis procedures in GTM, where categories are identified in the data and connected to other categories.
- I finally concluded with a section in which I unabashedly put forward the many reasons for my thinking GTM is a wonderful research method. I argued that the theory-building focus of GTM is excellent for scholarship and innovation in all disciplines. The detailed engagement with the data that GTM coding procedures demand, in my view, increases the chance of finding something new that can then be substantiated in other settings.

EXERCISES

1 Type the words 'grounded theory' into a search engine such as Google or Bing. Analyse the first page of results. What academic disciplines do the results come from? Pick any result that has as its subject 'What is grounded theory?' Name three differences between it and the description in this chapter and three commonalities.

2 Now type the words 'grounded theory method' into the search engine. Is there any difference between the search results you got for exercise 1 and the results you have now? Name three key differences. For the research papers in the results, identify which academic disciplines those papers come from. Are they different from those given in the first set of results?

WEB RESOURCES

http://en.wikipedia.org/wiki/Grounded_theory This Wikipedia entry gives a fairly comprehensive overview of GTM. That said, it is weighted towards the Glaserian view of GTM. As you will find, many people also use Straussian GTM. Further discussion of the differences between these two strands of grounded theory can be found in Chapter 2.

www.methodspace.com Methodspace is Sage's community for researchers. It's a good place for novices to find resources, follow certain researchers and post queries. Recommended.

www.mendeley.com This is a free citation manager and social network for researchers. New research students can find it effective in helping them to organise their literature searches and find other colleagues with similar interests.

FURTHER READING

Suddaby, R. (2006) 'From the editors: What grounded theory is not', *Academy of Management Journal,* **49**: 633–42. This is an interesting editorial, directed at the management discipline. Suddaby discusses the characteristics of GTM and tackles the problem of mislabelling grounded theory.

Urquhart, C. and Fernández, W. (2006) 'Grounded theory method: The researcher as blank slate and other myths', *ICIS 2006 Proceedings.* **Paper 31.** At the same time that Suddaby's article was published, though we were unaware of it at the time, a colleague and I considered the myths of grounded theory in a conference paper. It is a simple introduction to GTM and the myths surrounding it from the perspective of someone new to GTM.

FREQUENTLY ASKED QUESTIONS

Grounded theory looks really difficult. Is it more difficult than other qualitative research methods?

Personally, I don't think it's any more difficult than any other method. All require that you invest time to learn how to use them. GTM does differ in several key respects from other qualitative methods, however. First, it has a controversial intellectual tradition. This means that first-time users have to make sure they are familiar with the main issues concerning this tradition and can defend their use of GTM. Second, it is unique in its very detailed examination of data, which can and does result in new insights. Such detailed examination requires patience and an analytical eye, which are both skills that can be acquired. Third, it is interested in building theory, which means you have to understand theory and levels of theory. These three aspects mean that first-time users have to be scholarly – no bad thing and no bad foundation for an academic career if you are just starting out! Generally, a piece of GTM work, especially for a PhD thesis, will yield several good journal articles, so the time invested in learning the method is usually worthwhile.

If GTM is so good, why isn't it used more in my academic department? Why isn't it more popular?

One answer to this question lies in the dominance of quantitative approaches in some academic disciplines. Qualitative research is in the minority in many disciplines and GTM is one method among many. It is alone in qualitative research methods, though, in having an emphasis on building theory. Interestingly, this means that it does actually have the potential to contribute to quantitative research because it should be possible to build a theory using GTM for future testing. As for popularity, the searches you have done for the exercises above should have shown you that it is used widely in many disciplines. Most people who have used the method will tell you that it works and I think this is because it is systematic in its approach. In Chapter 2, we will talk more about defending your use of GTM from an academic perspective.

2

Grounded theory method (GTM)

This chapter:

- explains how grounded theory method (GTM) started in 1967
- explains the key characteristics of GTM
- discusses how GTM has evolved into several strands
- discusses different coding procedures used in GTM
- discusses how various myths have evolved surrounding the use of GTM.

Introduction

This chapter aims to equip you with a thorough overview of grounded theory method (GTM). By the end of this chapter, you should have a good understanding of its key characteristics, its intellectual history and its diverse coding procedures. Because GTM does have such a complex intellectual history, it is necessary to know about it, as it is definitely what Bryant and Charmaz (2007) rightly characterise as a contested tradition. The chapter concludes with some myths about GTM and how to defend your use of the method. Let's now start at the beginning.

The discovery of grounded theory

GTM started with a revolutionary book in revolutionary times. In 1967, Barney Glaser and Anselm Strauss published a book entitled *The Discovery of Grounded Theory*. This book outlined a research methodology that aimed at systematically deriving theories of human behaviour from empirical data.

It was a reaction against the use of 'armchair' functionalist theories in sociology. Glaser and Strauss (1967: 10) claimed there was a trend afoot in sociology, that the 'great men' of sociology had generated enough outstanding theories and all there was left to do was test them. They further charged that the 'great men' played 'theoretical capitalist' to a mass of 'proletariat' testers, so sociologists were trained to only test, not imitate. The book is a strong call to generate and ground theory and refocus on qualitative data rather than quantitative verification of theories.

Many people find it difficult to read the original 1967 book, which is a pity. Melia (1996) says it has some 'near mystical passages', which is true. The book has to be seen in the historical context in which it was written, which was in a decade where many new, ground-breaking ideas emerged and changed society forever. I would highly recommend reading this book at some point during your use of GTM. It is indeed a classic and it is always good scholarship to return to the original source of ideas. I have found myself turning back to it again and again while writing this book. No elaborate procedures are given and there is a focus on what theory actually is, as well as the means of developing it. It also provides the baseline for understanding the many debates that have arisen around GTM.

Several more books and articles by the co-originators followed, which developed, and later debated, the method. Glaser's *Theoretical Sensitivity*, published in 1978, introduced several key concepts that are useful in GTM. First, he talked about the role of the literature and induction. The need to be theoretically sensitive was explained as the need to understand theories and how they are constructed, but without then imposing those concepts on the emergent theory. He also introduced the notion of 'coding families' to help with relating concepts in the data.

In 1990, *Basics of Qualitative Research*, by Anslem Strauss and Juliet Corbin, was published. A long and bitter dispute erupted between Glaser and Strauss and what was at stake was nothing less than the identity of GTM. It marked the start of what are effectively two strands of GTM and these endure to this day. We shall return to the dispute, and why it was so important, later in this chapter.

Following the publication of the seminal work in 1967, GTM spread fairly quickly as a qualitative research method within the social sciences and many other fields. For example, Benoliel (1996) says there was a 70-fold increase in published papers with 'grounded theory' as a keyword phrase in the health field over the previous decade. By the mid-1990s, the methodological procedures of GTM had permeated qualitative research to such an extent that Miles and Huberman (1994) labelled it a 'common feature [of qualitative] analytic methods'.

The key characteristics of GTM

We have already discussed a detailed overview of the features of GTM in Chapter 1, but what are the key characteristics that make it different?

Glaser and Strauss (1967) defined their method as 'the discovery of theory from data – systematically obtained and analysed in social research'. It's interesting to note that the systematic nature of the method was emphasised from day one – and page one – of the very first book on GTM by the founders themselves.

This, of course, makes it attractive to novice researchers. As a novice researcher myself in 1997, I can remember stating that it offered well-signposted procedures for new researchers (Urquhart 1997). This signposting is clearest in Strauss (1987) and the controversial book by Strauss and Corbin (1990). Of course, this can also be the Achilles heel of the method, in that just simply following the procedures without thought can lead to a lack of creativity. One thing I warn my postgraduates about GTM is that it is not a failsafe recipe for research. Even if you do follow all the prescribed steps in GTM, you cannot necessarily turn the handle and expect a theory to drop out. Like any methodology of any kind, it requires flexibility, thought and creativity in its application.

In Urquhart et al. (2010), we identified four key characteristics of GTM:

- the main purpose of GTM is *theory building*
- as a general rule, researchers should make sure that they have *no preconceived theoretical ideas* before starting their research
- analysis and conceptualisation are engendered through the core process of *constant comparison,* where every slice of data is compared with all existing concepts and constructs, to see if it enriches an existing category (by adding to/enhancing its properties), forms a new one or points to a new relation
- *'slices of data'* of all kinds are selected by a process of *theoretical sampling,* where researchers decide, on analytical grounds, where to sample from next.

The first characteristic implies that researchers who leverage GTM only for coding procedures are ignoring the main purpose of the method, which is to build theory. Indeed, that is why GTM was developed in the first place. Glaser and Strauss (1967) make a distinction between substantive theories (pertaining to the phenomena at hand) and formal theories. This distinction is discussed in more detail later in this book. In developing either type of theory, researchers need to be capable of *theoretical sensitivity.* Such sensitivity is based on being steeped in the field of investigation and associated general ideas (Glaser 1978) so that researchers understand the context in which the theory is developed. This concept of theoretical sensitivity is key. How can we build theories ourselves unless we understand what a theory is?

The second characteristic (of having no preconceived theoretical ideas) is often held (erroneously) to imply that researchers should not look at the existing literature before doing the empirical research. According to Glaser (1992), the dictum in grounded theory is that there is no need to review the literature in the substantive area under study and this idea is:

brought about by the concern that literature might contaminate, stifle or otherwise impede the researcher's effort to generate categories ...

(Glaser 1992)

He hastens to add, though, that this applies only at the beginning. Once the theory has been sufficiently developed, researchers then need to review the literature in the substantive field and relate that literature to their own work.

From my experience of working with postgraduates, coding for the first time, it's very hard for them to *not* impose what they have read on the data in front of them. Being faced with the task of looking for emergent concepts in the data without any help from anything other than your own mind is a scary process. Small wonder, then, when looking for patterns in the data, people might want to fall back on what they have read already.

If, however, we privilege other theories rather than looking at the data, we lose what is for me the key delight – and the key edge of the method: what Glaser (1992) calls 'emergence'. The idea of *emergence*, for me, is that we stay true to our data, we look for what the data is telling us. Of course, the idea of whether or not some inherent truth resides in the data depends on your point of view. I prefer to think of constructing meanings about the data, but the idea that you give the data due consideration, due respect, before imposing other theories on it makes perfect sense. It makes even more sense when we are dealing with new phenomena, such as information technology, that have permeated most aspects of social life. For instance, if we base our understanding of how people interact with information technology on psychological theories and those theories are based on large samples of American undergraduate students, how relevant is the theory we are imposing? Far better to allow the data to tell its own story in the first instance, build a theory, then, subsequently, engage your theory with the theory that you thought you might impose initially. You can then see if your emergent theory confirms or challenges existing theories. So, potentially, GTM has a huge role to play in theory building, in all disciplines.

The third characteristic, *constant comparison*, is also a key component of grounded theory. Comparative analysis was a *standard* method in social research long before 1967, but in GTM it is a *key* part of the method. As discussed in Chapter 1, it is the process of constantly comparing instances of data labelled in one category with other instances of data labelled for that category.

It is an incredibly simple, but deceptively powerful, rule of thumb for analysing data. The process of constant comparison, in my view, allows the meaning and construction of concepts to remain under review. Consciously comparing the instances of each concept allows for a fuller and more nuanced understanding of what that category might consist of. It also, I think, allows the formation of the category to be more provisional. It is only when it is fully filled in, as it were, by many instances that we can say exactly what

the meaning of that category is. It is also helpful to use constant comparison if there is overlapping data collection and analysis because then the category can be densified using *theoretical sampling* (where the emerging analysis directs more sampling of data), so, if you like, the emerging theoretical storyline is followed.

The fourth characteristic is the selection of *slices of data*. This phrase was coined by Glaser and Strauss (1967) to reflect the fact that different kinds of data give researchers different views from which to understand a category or develop its properties. This is a liberating and interesting idea that is not always understood, but simply means we should be constantly sampling slices of data from the phenomena in order to build the theory out and upwards. The more diverse those slices are, the better. So, one slice of data could be field interviews, another could be surveys. Although the 1967 book did focus on qualitative data, quantitative data was also seen as a legitimate slice of data. Glaser and Strauss (1967) even go so far as to suggest that a slice of data could be anecdotal or, for instance, using a national meat consumption report for a particular professional group. When the theory is more fully formed, a conceivable slice of data might even be another theory, as long as there is an awareness of the dangers of forcing a category down a particular road, lest that very precious quality of grounded theory – emergence – be compromised.

These are useful characteristics to bear in mind when using GTM because they sum up what is unique about it and give some useful guidance as to how you might use it in the field. All that said, some users of GTM will not recognise the above characteristics because they come from the original 1967 book rather than later versions.

We come now to the history of GTM. This history is fascinating, which is why I include it here. It's also a contested history, which is another reason for discussing it. Researchers using GTM have to be aware of the competing versions of grounded theory and, in particular, the well-known split between Glaser and Strauss in 1990. Each strand of GTM has its adherents, which also makes it difficult for first-time users of GTM, who may not realise what contested territory some of these concepts occcupy. This is especially relevant for postgraduate students who need to position their research in relation to a particular research community. It's important to understand the contested principles and decide what your own position on them might be, as defending the scholarly integrity of our work is something we should all do.

The two strands of GTM

As mentioned, any user of GTM needs to be aware of the fact that it has evolved into two distinct strands – the Glaserian and Straussian – as a result of a cataclysmic dispute between its co-founders in 1990. This dispute went

to the core of what GTM actually comprises and what it does, so understanding the dispute is also key to understanding what GTM actually is.

The dispute was triggered by the publication of Strauss and Corbin's (1990) book. It was written in response to their students' requests for a 'how to' manual of grounded theory and contains clear guidelines and procedures. It was at this point, perhaps, that the founders of grounded theory realised their views of what grounded theory actually is might be different.

> students of Glaser and Strauss in the 1960s and 1970s knew that the two had quite different modus operandi, but Glaser only found out when Strauss and Corbin's *Basics of Qualitative Research* came out in 1990.
>
> (Stern 1994: 212, as quoted by Melia 1996)

Glaser reacted badly to the book and requested that it be pulled from publication. When it was not, he wrote a correctional rejoinder, *Basics of Grounded Theory Analysis: Emergence vs. forcing* (Glaser 1992). For him, the issue was nothing less than the heart and soul of GTM. He felt that Strauss and Corbin's 1990 book was far too restrictive in the way it presented GTM. He felt strongly that to follow the procedures outlined in the book would strangle any emergent conceptualisations and, instead, force the concepts into a preconceived mould. He summed up his critique as follows:

> If you torture the data long enough, it will give up! ... [In Strauss and Corbin's method] the data is not allowed to speak for itself as in grounded theory, and to be heard from, infrequently it has to scream. Forcing by preconception constantly derails it from relevance.
>
> (Glaser 1992:123)

Glaser disagreed on two fundamental issues.

- Strauss and Corbin (1990) suggested breaking down the coding process into four prescriptive steps – open, axial, selective and 'coding for process' – whereas Glaser uses just three – open, selective and theoretical coding, at incremental levels of abstraction.
- Glaser objected to the use of a coding paradigm and the 'conditional matrix' that are designed to provide ready-made tools to assist with the conceptualisation process. Glaser felt that to 'force' coding through one paradigm and/or down one conditional path ignored the emergent nature of GTM (Glaser 1992). This makes sense, given that Glaser had suggested 18 coding families (or coding paradigms) in his 1978 book.

So, this is a disagreement that does cut to the heart of grounded theory. The 1990 book represented a substantial departure from what had gone before, in its insistence that only one coding paradigm be used. In fact,

the 1990 book says, *'Unless you make use of this model, your grounded theory analysis will lack density and precision'* (Strauss and Corbin 1990). The mandatory nature of the paradigm, in retrospect, was quite extraordinary. To claim that there could be only one way of relating categories and this was essential seems, in the cold light of day, to have been an aberration in the history of GTM and one that was not necessarily heeded by researchers.

Interestingly, this advice was modified as early as 1998:

In actuality, the paradigm is nothing more than a perspective taken toward data, another analytic stance that helps to systematically gather and order data in such a way that structure and process are integrated.

(Strauss and Corbin, 1998: 128)

In my own discipline, that of information systems, a colleague and I (Seidel and Urquhart 2011b) could identify only seven papers out of 96 that applied the paradigm. Of the small percentage of papers using the paradigm, we could see that causal relationships between categories were more frequently identified and a substantive theory was more likely to be built than in the papers not using the paradigm.

I can remember vividly a postgraduate student of mine who rushed into my office, waving a copy of Strauss and Corbin's 1990 book, saying, 'This is wonderful! I want to try it!' I did relate my own experiences of trying to use the procedures (Urquhart 1997), when I ended up in despair as I tried to fit the paradigm to what I was doing. We agreed that the student should try it – why not? Well, two weeks later, there was a knock at the door and my student said, 'It doesn't work!' One comment I made at the time was that if the coding paradigm recommended by Strauss and Corbin (1990) for connecting categories is a good match for the research phenomena, it might work. Certainly there are some good examples out there of the use of this particular paradigm (see, for instance, Galal, (2001), but my own feeling is that this only occurs when there is a good match between the paradigm and the phenomena being investigated. Why not take advantage of the flexibility of selecting many different options for relating categories, as provided in the Glaserian version? That way, surely, you get a better match between your research problem and ways of theorising about it. For me, the Strauss and Corbin paradigm represented, and still represents, a narrow way of thinking about what is being investigated.

In Corbin and Strauss (2008, the updated edition of Strauss and Corbin 1998) the role of the paradigm is further weakened in favour of emphasising a broader set of tools, named context, process and theoretical integration. The paradigm is presented as only one of a number of 'analytic strategies' or 'tools'. They write that:

One tool for helping the researcher to identify contextual factors and then to link them with process is what we call the paradigm. The paradigm is a perspective, a set of questions that can be applied to data to help the analyst draw out the contextual factors and identify relationships between context and process.

(Corbin and Strauss 2008: 89)

Throughout the book, the authors are careful to highlight that researchers must choose from a variety of analytical tools and 'make use of procedures in ways that best suit him or her' (Corbin and Strauss, 2008: x, Preface).

It is important, then, to read more than just the 1990 book about GTM, even though it is still widely used and read, possibly because Glaser has self-published his books since 1978. Only when I read the original 1967 book (Glaser and Strauss 1967) and two of the most important of Glaser's subsequent books (Glaser 1978; Glaser 1992) did I realise how complex the intellectual tradition of GTM is. If only the 1990 book is used, novice users run the danger of encountering peer reviewers for whom the type of GTM being used – Glaserian or Straussian – really matters. It matters because understanding the dispute helps us to understand the core principles of grounded theory. Table 2.1 lists what I feel are the key books on GTM, authored by its founders, so that you won't fall into this trap.

Ultimately, which version of GTM is used – Glaserian or Straussian – depends on individual researchers and their own preferences. Certainly, my view is that the Glaserian strand offers more flexibility and is closer to the original formulation of grounded theory as put forward in the 1967 book.

The two books that are worth turning to first are Glaser (1978) and Strauss (1987). These will give you a good sense of the two strands of GTM. Then, once you feel you have a good understanding of grounded theory, it is worth engaging with the seminal 1967 book, despite the fact that some people find it difficult to read. It is the definitive text that started it all and gives a good sense of the original intent and form of GTM. It also helps by elucidating the foundations from which GTM has evolved since 1967. From there, you can explore the later works of Glaser, such as his 2005 book, which is a personal favourite of mine, simply because of the joy and energy with which Glaser explores theory building and theoretical codes.

Let's now look more closely at the different stages of coding in the two versions.

Evolving coding procedures in GTM

Table 2.2 lists a number of different coding procedures and the books about GTM in which they appear, starting with the foundational 1967 text. I'll now

Table 2.1   Seminal books on GTM by its founders

Book	Description
Glaser, B.G. and Strauss, A.L. (1967) *The Discovery of Grounded Theory: Strategies for qualitative research*	Essential reading, despite it not being the most accessible of books. Melia (1996) talks of its 'near mystical passages'. As it was the first book on grounded theory, the principles on which grounded theory is based are obvious and the book is notable for its concern about building theory as opposed to the mechanics of coding. It is also very helpful to see the idea of grounded theory in its historical and disciplinary context.
Glaser, B.G. (1978) *Theoretical Sensitivity: Advances in the methodology of grounded theory*	The first book in the grounded theory canon that gives a lot more detail on how the process of coding might proceed. Introduces the idea of theoretical sensitivity – an important idea, which is that of being aware of other theories and how they are built. This book also discusses spacing, sampling, coding, memos, sorting and writing and provides a very important discussion on basic social processes. It introduces 18 'coding families' to assist with theoretical coding.
Strauss, A. (1987) *Qualitative Analysis for Social Scientists*	Provides advice for first-time users, especially around relating efforts to the technical literature and the process of coding in a group. This book also marks the first divergence into the two strands of grounded theory as only one coding paradigm is proposed in this book.
Strauss, A. and Corbin J. (1990) *Basics of Qualitative Research: Grounded theory procedures and techniques*	Probably the most widely read book on GTM, but also the most controversial. Gives very clear procedures, but, at the same time, offers a narrower view of the method.
Glaser, B.G. (1992) *Basics of Grounded Theory Analysis: Emergence vs. forcing*	This is Glaser's response to Strauss and Corbin (1990). It helps us to understand the divergent views held by Glaser and by Strauss and Corbin. It discusses in detail the significance of the issue of 'forcing' in GTM.
Glaser, B.G. (1998) *Doing Grounded Theory: Issues and discussions*	Covers practical areas of doing GTM research, such as motivation, reading the literature, forcing, generating concepts and more on theoretical sampling, theoretical coding, memoing, sorting and writing.
Glaser, B.G (2005) *The Grounded Theory Perspective III: Theoretical coding*	This book breaks new ground in thinking about theoretical coding and the process of relating categories. It introduces 23 new 'coding families' to complement the original 18 coding families in the 1978 book.

discuss them in turn, in the hope that this will give you enough information to be able to choose the coding procedure that will work for you.

Comparing incidents applicable to each category

The first important thing to note in Table 2.2 is that the original book did not set out procedures as such. It focused more on the process than actual stages and introduced a number of important ideas in the course of explaining it. We can see 'comparing incidents applicable to each category' as introducing one

Table 2.2   Different GTM coding procedures

Book	Suggested coding procedure
Glaser and Strauss 1967	Comparing incidents applicable to each category (includes open coding), integrating categories and their properties (selective coding and theoretical coding), delimiting the theory (selective coding and theoretical coding), writing the theory.
Glaser 1978	Open coding, selective coding, theoretical coding.
Strauss 1987	Open coding, axial coding, selective coding.
Strauss and Corbin 1990	Open coding, axial coding, selective coding.
Glaser 1992	Open coding, selective coding, theoretical coding.
Strauss and Corbin 1998	Open coding, axial coding, selective coding.
Charmaz 2006	Initial coding, focused coding, axial coding, theoretical coding.
Corbin and Strauss 2008	Open coding, axial coding and theoretical coding as distinct stages no longer appear, though open coding and axial coding appear as terms in one chapter. The emphasis is on a broader set of tools named context, process and theoretical integration. Two coding paradigms are used as a foundation for context.

of the most important ideas in grounded theory: constant comparison. Open coding – that is, the initial allocation of ideas to data chunks – is only implied.

It is the idea of constant comparison, so deceptively simple, that gives grounded theorists the edge, in my opinion. Constant comparison has been described as a fundamental rule of thumb in GTM. To make these comparisons between the data you are coding right now and the data you have just coded and ask, 'To what category does this incident or property relate?' is the guideline that prevents inconsistent coding (when one data chunk is coded as one thing and another very similar data chunk is coded as something else). While the advent of data analysis software helps us compare the coding and manage the data, I believe that this guideline is as important as ever. It ensures that researchers make their allocation of concepts to data explicit to themselves and, more importantly, the allocations are compared to the data as a whole. Thus, we can see hermeneutic principles of analysis also being applied to the data.

Open coding

Open coding was first explicitly mentioned in Glaser's (1978) book. It surprises me that many people don't refer to this book as, in many ways, it is the most important of his writings because it elaborates brilliantly on many of the key ideas in the 1967 book.

Open coding is described by Glaser (1978: 56) as 'coding the data everyway [sic] possible'. It is the first step in coding and deliberately 'open' so as not to close down any directions a future theory might take. As such it is, along with constant comparison, a foundational technique of GTM.

The act of open coding is about attaching initial labels to your data. These are subsequently grouped into larger codes, as the aim is to build a theory based on them. What the open codes do is flesh out what is important and point to directions in the analysis that you may not have thought of, directions suggested by the data.

Glaser (1978) recommends coding line by line, as does Strauss (1987), for very good reasons. Charmaz (2006) is also uncompromising in her advice on this. I can only say that the discipline of coding line by line – that detailed consideration of the text in front of us – helps free us of our preconceptions. For example, when I first applied grounded theory to my own PhD work into analysts and clients, I discovered that the analysts very often attempted to frame the problem straight away. This was a unique insight for my discipline, as was the conceptualisation of the strategies and props they used to help their clients. I firmly believe that my work would not have been as original as it was had I used any other method than grounded theory for the analysis.

Line-by-line coding also forces a real intimacy with your data – and means that your findings are easy to defend because you really *know* your data. That said, Glaser (1992) does say coding need not necessarily be line by line – there are circumstances where it may not be appropriate. I do agree, because all datasets are not created equal – some whole paragraphs may not be relevant or the data is secondary rather than primary data. Even so, the benefits of looking at the data line by line, in my view, cannot be overstated.

Selective coding

Selective coding is where the two strands of GTM – Glaserian and Straussian – sharply diverge. The Straussian version requires axial coding (explained in the next section) to be done first. In my view, the Glaserian version is simpler.

Glaser (Glaser 1978) defines selective coding as the stage when coding is limited to only those categories that relate to the core category. Future theoretical sampling also is directed by that core category. In my experience, the point at which selective coding occurs is fairly obvious, as there are no new open codes suggesting themselves and definite themes are emerging. Categories become 'saturated' at this stage – that is, there are plenty of instances.

One point not often discussed is the fact that, at this stage, coders often end up with many multiple categories. This is not surprising, when you consider the detailed level – line by line – that open coding starts from. So, some grouping of categories can take place at this stage and this helps develop the abstraction of the theory.

Charmaz (2006) also makes the valuable point that the selective coding stage (which she calls 'focused' coding) may often prompt a return to open coding, as some interesting avenues are almost bound to occur when we consider and group the themes emerging in the data.

Axial coding

Strauss (1987) and Strauss and Corbin (1990) recommend a stage of *axial* coding following *open* coding. The way I tend to think about axial coding is that it combines selective coding with the use of a coding paradigm. The single coding paradigm recommended by Strauss and Corbin (1990) is causal conditions, context, intervening conditions, action/interaction strategies and consequences.

Strauss says that, first, the codes need to be dimensionalised by laying out the properties. We can see this as being similar to the process of selective coding, when we figure out what might be the important categories and which of our open codes need to be elevated or otherwise combined to form those categories, as well as which of these codes might be properties of other categories.

Strauss (1987) then says that the second element of axial coding is to hypothesise about conditions, contexts, interactions, strategies and consequences. We can see this as a process of relating the categories theoretically, or, *theoretical coding*, which is explained in the next section.

My feeling is that it is hard to simultaneously figure out both the properties of a category and then how it might relate to other categories. This is possibly why students in particular come unstuck at this point. I would not dismiss it as a viable coding option, however, especially if researchers consider it in two stages, to simplify the process. There are some examples of the successful use of axial coding in the paradigm, such as Galal (2001), and, if you are interested, I suggest you search out this and other examples cited in Seidel and Urquhart (2011).

There is an extensive description of axial coding in Strauss (1987), which, in my opinion, is better than that contained in Strauss and Corbin (1998). They define axial coding as the act of:

> relating categories to subcategories along the lines of their properties and dimensions.

(Strauss and Corbin, 1998: 124)

Again, this is a clear indication that subcategories are involved, and its resemblance to Glaser's selective coding. The coding paradigm is further elaborated on and put forward as conditions (causal, intervening and contextual), actions/interactions (strategies are now put under this heading) and consequences (immediate, cumulative, reversible, foreseen and unseen).

What is interesting is that, in Corbin and Strauss' 2008 book, the coding paradigm loses its prominence. Corbin says, 'the paradigm is only a tool and not a set of directives'(Corbin and Strauss 2008) This represents a considerable departure from the previous books and an important one, given the paradigm's role in the split between Glaser and Strauss. That said, the book

Table 2.3   The evolving nature of the Strauss and Corbin paradigm

Coding paradigm	Comment on evolving use of paradigm
Conditions, interactions amongst the actors, strategies and consequences (Strauss 1987)	In the 1987 book, it is clear that the coding paradigm is not an optional part of coding. Researchers are told to 'follow the coding paradigm' (1987: 81).
Causal conditions, context, intervening conditions, action/ interaction, strategies and consequences (Strauss and Corbin 1990)	In the 1990 book, the paradigm is modified to include different types of conditions, plus actions.
Conditions (causal, intervening, and contextual), actions/interactions (strategic or routine tactics), consequences (immediate, cumulative, reversible, foreseen or unseen) (Strauss and Corbin 1998)	In the 1998 book, conditions are clustered together, strategies are clustered under actions and consequences elaborated on.
Conditions, interactions and emotions, consequences (Corbin and Strauss 2008)	In the 2008 book, the paradigm loses its prominence and is presented as an optional analytic tool for novice researchers. That said, the conditional/consequence matrix, used in previous editions to think about relationships between micro and macro conditions, now has a more central place in coding.

places a great deal of emphasis on the 'conditional/consequential matrix', to consider larger issues of context and macro conditions. In both cases, Corbin suggests that their use should be confined to novice as opposed to experienced researchers.

Theoretical coding

Glaser (1978) describes *theoretical coding* as how substantive codes (the codes generated thus far pertaining to the area under investigation) are then related to each other. This makes complete sense if we understand that theories are constructs and relationships.

So, theoretical coding is when we relate the codes to each other and look at the nature of the relationships between those codes. This is what builds the theory. In my own research work, I found that theoretical memos were invaluable for helping the theorising process. A surprising (or perhaps not surprising) number of these theoretical memos ended up being cut and pasted into my PhD thesis as, of course, I was explaining the evolving theory to myself.

Glaser's coding paradigms give ample food for thought as to how the categories might relate – some examples are given in Table 2.4.

Of course, you can – and, I think, should be able to – generate your own coding paradigms. Grounded theory, in my view, is, above all, about being faithful to what your analysis of the data suggests rather than shoehorning the data into some preconceived analytical framework, so it would go against

Table 2.4   A selection of Glaser's (1978; 2005) coding families

Family	Comment
The 6Cs – causes, contexts, contingencies, consequences, covariances and conditions	This basic coding family, together with the Strategy family, was adapted by Strauss and Corbin (1990) as their coding paradigm of 'causal conditions, context, intervening conditions, action/ interaction strategies and consequences'.
Process – stages, staging, phases, phasing, progressions, passages, gradations, transitions, steps, ranks, careers, ordering, trajectories, chains, sequencings, etc.	Glaser remarks that a process should have at least two stages. This family is similar to Spradley's 'a stage of'.
Dimension family – dimensions, elements, division, piece of, properties of, facet, slice, sector, portion, segment, part, aspect, section	As Glaser says, the more we learn about a category, the more we see of its dimensions. Of all theoretical codes, this is one that all researchers are likely to use. It is, of course, very similar to Spradley's 'is a part of'. It's also important to realise that, when theorising, we can privilege one dimension over another – it can become a full-blown category.
Type family – type, form, kinds, styles, classes, genre	Glaser says, while dimensions divide up the whole, types show variations *in* the whole. So, for instance, you might have a number of styles of introducing a problem in the conversation between a systems analyst and client in the example in Table 3.2.
Strategy family – strategies, tactics, mechanisms, managed, way, manipulation, manoeuvrings, dealing with, handling, techniques, ploys, means, goals, arrangements, dominating, positioning	As previously remarked, the Strauss and Corbin coding paradigm seems to be a mixture of this family and the first family.
Moment capture, when a quick intervention is critical to causing an optimal outcome, such as closing a deal	This is a new theoretical code introduced in Glaser's 2005 book.
Frames, which are excavated through discourse patterns and are sociocultural in nature	Also in the 2005 book. I used this idea in my own dissertation work in 1999.
Causal family – a relative of the 6Cs family, it includes several aspects: 1) bias random walk, 2) amplifying causal looping, 3) conjectural causation, 4) repetitive causal reproductions, 5) equifinality, 6) reciprocal causation, 7) triggers, 8) causal paths, 9) perpetual causal looping	Glaser (2005) gives some wonderful nuances of causation in this theoretical code family. 'Bias random walk' – all variables are in a flux, 'then on the introduction of a crucial variable ... then of a sudden all of the variables fall into organisation'. 'Amplifying causal looping' – 'consequences become causes, and one sees either worsening or improving progressions or escalating severity'. 'Conjectural causation' – it is not always easy to identify decisive causal combinations. 'Repetitive causal reproductions' – a repeated action keeps producing the same consequences. 'Equifinality' – no matter what the causes and paths, the same consequence will occur. 'Reciprocal causation' – there is a similar interaction of effects or amplified causal looping. 'Triggers' – sudden causes that set off a consequence or set of consequences. 'Causal paths' – used to intervene in changing or stopping a consequence. 'Perpetual causal looping' – a mathematical model, an ordered calculated growth of increased size based on a set temporal path.

the spirit of grounded theory to suggest that only Glaser's coding families should be used. Given that Glaser (Glaser 2005) himself introduced 23 more coding families, we can only assume that he, too, recognises the need to be very flexible about how categories relate. That said, I find the coding families very useful jumping off points to think about relationships in data and they are educational in themselves regarding theorising.

It's very important to understand what theories are and how they work, so you recognise that you are building a theory rather than just describing some interesting data analysis. Charmaz (2006) puts it well when she cautions us to not use theoretical codes to impose frameworks on the data and be aware of a possible aura of objectivity around those theoretical codes, as scholars would almost certainly disagree about which of those to apply. It's important to be reflective when doing theoretical coding.

Myths about GTM

Sometimes first-time users of GTM encounter certain myths about its use. There are many reasons for this, but we've already seen in the previous sections that it is a somewhat contested intellectual tradition with different interpretations. Hirschheim and Newman (1991), when talking about information systems development, use the following definition of myth:

> A dramatic narrative of imagined events, usually used to explain origins or transformations of something. Also, an unquestioned belief about the practical benefits of certain techniques and behaviors which is not supported by the demonstrated facts.
>
> (Trice and Beyer 1984: 655 in Hirschheim and Newman 1991: 34)

Roland Barthes (1972), in his book *Mythologies*, argued that (cultural) myths develop not as a result of lies or distortion but from a deceptive simplicity. So the myths I discuss here may indeed have a kernel of truth, but their very simplicity hides a more complex truth.

One sunny day in 2005, I was sitting with a colleague, Walter Fernández, in a Brisbane café. As GTM enthusiasts who have both undertaken successful postgraduate projects using it, we were bemoaning the fact that some of our colleagues clung most tenaciously to what Walter said were 'myths' of grounded theory, and discouraged postgraduate students from using it as a result. This phenomenon – of departments favouring particular methods of research and discouraging others – is, of course, not confined to grounded theory. GTM has spread far and wide from its home discipline of sociology and not all other disciplines are equally welcoming of qualitative methods.

There is also the fact that GTM is still not widely used in some disciplines, so there is sometimes a lack of knowledge and an unwillingness to supervise a student who would like to use GTM. So, Walter and I wrote a paper (Urquhart and Fernandez 2006) to help our postgraduates defend their use of GTM in an informed way. Below is a summary of the myths that we identified so that if you encounter them, you too can find ways to defend your particular use of GTM.

Myth 1: Researcher as blank slate

If there is one issue that most academics are aware of about GTM it is the idea that it is a controversial method, because it ignores the literature and is, thus, unacademic in some way. The idea that the GTM researcher is a 'blank slate' who launches into data collection without first looking at the literature is a particularly pervasive misconception (McCallin 2003; Andrew 2006). This despite the fact that, in a footnote in the original book, Glaser and Strauss (1967: 3) state that researchers do not approach reality as a *tabula rasa* (blank slate), but must have a perspective to then abstract significant categories from the data. Dey (1993), as mentioned earlier, speaks of the difference between an 'open mind and an empty head' (p.63).

According to Glaser (1992), the dictum in GTM is that there is no *need* to review the literature in the substantive area under study. As first suggested in Glaser and Strauss' book of 1967 (p.37) this idea, as later explained by Glaser 'is brought about by the concern that literature might stifle or contaminate or otherwise impede the researcher's effort to generate categories' (Glaser 1992: 31) In addition, Strauss (1987) says that the advice about delaying the scrutiny of related literature applies less to experienced researchers as they are more practised at subjecting theoretical statements to comparative analysis.

Like most myths, the idea of researchers as a blank slate has at its base a kernel of truth. However, it is more accurate to say that GTM research does not *start* with a theory to prove or disprove. It is also more helpful to think of the literature review as being simply *delayed* rather than not happening at all. In fact, the grounded theorist has an obligation, once the theory has emerged, to engage the emergent theory with the existing literature.

So, how might typical PhD students deal with the injunction to not examine the literature before coding? Such students may actually need to review the literature for many good reasons, including passing the research committee review. Thus, among many grounded theorists it is generally accepted that a pre-study literature review has to be conducted to find the research problem. However, this review should be done in such a way that the extant theories do not 'derail the emerging theory' (Nathaniel 2006: 40).

Martin (2006) suggests that appropriate use of the literature in GTM is a question of *phasing*. The first phase is *non-committal*, one in which researchers develop sensitivity and find their research problem. The second phase is *integrative*, in which they integrate the emergent theory with extant theories to render the new theory in the context of existing knowledge and, thus, make the theory more valuable.

In my experience, the tactic of a preliminary (non-committal) literature review works well when using GTM. It examines what theory exists in the area and how other people may have addressed aspects of a research problem, but does not then impose a framework on future data collection. Importantly, this preliminary literature review is conducted on the understanding it is the *generated* theory that will determine the relevance of the literature. The literature review is then revisited, and extended, once the theory has been generated from the data.

Myth 2: GTM is inflexible

The second myth follows on somewhat from the first. The dictum about the literature is erroneously seen as an inflexibility associated with GTM that makes it difficult to use. For instance, Allan (2003) talks of both the difficulty of putting aside preconceptions and coding at a micro level. Allan then concludes, however, that both these difficulties were satisfactorily resolved.

As GTM has developed, so have the procedures. Strauss (1987) and Strauss and Corbin (1990) do provide detailed guidelines for coding data. Some of these notions of inflexibility may have come from applying their guidelines (Strauss and Corbin 1990; 1998). For instance, Hansen and Kautz (2005), Melia (1996) and Kendall (1999) all report difficulties in using the Strauss and Corbin paradigm.

The notion that GTM is inflexible is not borne out when one considers its widespread use in many disciplines. It is also important to note that the procedures are commonly leveraged for the purposes of coding and building concepts as opposed to full-blown theory-building efforts. Disciplines such as health have reported that many researchers adopt GTM for a purpose other than developing theory – generally, data analysis (Benoliel 1996). A common use for GTM in the health field, for instance, is the generation of questionnaire constructs.

Myth 3: GTM produces low-level theories that don't do much

Like any myth, this has in it a kernel of truth. Because GTM is grounded in the data and the coding process starts at the word or sentence level, the theory produced tends to be rich and detailed. Also, Layder (1993), a prominent sociologist, has repeatedly said that GTM needs to break away from focusing on micro-phenomena as this prevents researchers from enriching the research with macro structures. This has tended to reinforce the myth that GTM is about low-level theories. Thus, the general impression of GTM is that it produces low-level theories that are difficult to 'scale up' (Urquhart 2001).

However, just because a low-level theory is produced does not mean that theory *cannot* be scaled up and, indeed, GTM places an obligation on researchers to do so. In fact, Glaser and Strauss (1967) acknowledged from the beginning that substantive theory development can and should shade into formal theories and devoted a whole chapter in their original book to this issue. They never saw GTM as only about micro theory and both worked at organisational levels. Strauss' interest in social arenas and social worlds led him beyond the micro level to the 'meso' level (Charmaz 2006) – he talks about the obligation, having produced a substantive theory, to wrestle with other theories (Strauss 1987). Glaser (1978), too, suggests several routes to extending and scaling up the theory, including considering similar theories and data in similar substantive areas and how the substantive theory relates to formal models and processes.

In practical terms, it is useful to 'scale up' substantive theories by considering whether or not the core categories that are generated can be grouped into further concepts or themes. The important point here is that generating a theory using GTM does not exclude researchers from the obligation of engaging their theories with the current theories in the field and doing so is, in fact, an important element of the method.

Myth 4: GTM is positivist/interpretivist

In 2002, I had a most enjoyable debate with Antony Bryant about whether or not GTM carries with it philosophical baggage in the shape of interpretivism or positivism inherent in the method (Bryant 2002; Urquhart 2002). The concern here is that if a myth exists about the inherent philosophical position of GTM, it may prevent its use if researchers happen to come from the (supposedly) opposing paradigm. This myth is not supported by the demonstrated facts.

A qualitative method, depending on its underlying epistemology, can be seen as positivist, interpretivist or critical (Klein and Myers 1999). Therefore, GTM 'in use' can be influenced by different underlying epistemologies. The fathers of GTM made no claim about the *correct* epistemology. Thus, we suggest in our paper (Urquhart and Fernandez 2006) that GTM as a research method is orthogonal not only to the type of data used but also can be appropriated by researchers with different assumptions about knowledge and how it can be obtained. This property of the method allows researchers with dissimilar epistemological stances to succeed in using it.

In fact, GTM has been characterised as both positivist *and* interpretivist by various commentators. Annells points to statements by Glaser (1992) about GTM focusing on 'concepts of reality' (1996: 14) and searching for 'true meaning' (p. 55) as evidence of a critical realist position and inherently positivist. Madill et al. (2000) argue convincingly that the philosophical position adopted when using grounded theory depends on the extent to which the findings are considered to be discovered within the data or the result of construction of intersubjective meanings. They locate the former view as Glaser's (1992) position and the latter as Strauss and Corbin's (1998).

Charmaz's (2006) view is that GTM, in many ways, is neutral and can be seen as a container into which any content can be poured. This would seem to be the most helpful position – simply to concentrate on GTM's undoubted strengths for coding and theory building rather than seek an inherent philo-sophical bias that may or may not be present in the method.

Myth 5: GTM takes a long time

This myth is perhaps less pervasive, but new PhD students will still come across it. It has its root in the idea that qualitative research takes longer than quantitative research because of the nature of data collected. I have even come across PhD students who have been advised to do a statistical PhD because it is quicker and save their qualitative yearnings for later, once they have their PhD!

So, is there any truth in the myth that a grounded theory PhD might take a long time to do? Certainly Walter Fernández and I have had students who have done grounded theory PhDs and it seems to have taken no longer than other PhDs. In fact, one advantage of doing a grounded theory PhD, we have observed, is that there is a wealth of material in it that can be used in subse-quent publications – it provides a rich platform for a future academic career.

Perhaps it is not a question of time, given that all the students I have supervised doing grounded theory have finished on time. I would hazard a guess that, even if the *analysis* phase takes longer than other methods, the level of engagement and associated theorising means that the *write-up* is quicker.

The likely explanation for the origin of this myth is that there is a per-ceived level of difficulty with qualitative analysis in general. One student of mine (now an esteemed colleague) described the process as difficult, a lot of hard work, but ultimately worthwhile. So, while grounded theory takes no longer than other methods of analysis, it is perhaps more challenging – and, I would add, more rewarding!

Summary

- This chapter discussed the discovery of grounded theory in 1967, how it all started and what the key characteristics of GTM are.
- I then spent some time talking about the fact that GTM has evolved into two major strands – the Glaserian and Straussian – due to a split between the founders in 1990. It is important to understand that split – I would go so far to

say, if you understand the dispute and its ramifications, you understand what grounded theory is about.

- I also traced the key publications in the history of grounded theory. While not wanting to be prescriptive about what people should read, it does seem to me that the grounded theory canon needs to be engaged with properly. It has such an extensive intellectual tradition that just reading one book by the founders is not sufficient.
- The chapter then went on to explore the different coding stages in GTM, depending on which strand is followed – Glaserian or Straussian. Now the use of the coding paradigm that caused the split is advisory rather than mandatory (Corbin and Strauss 2008), the Straussian strand has returned to some flexibility, and perhaps the strands can be seen as more equivalent.
- Finally, I concluded by discussing some myths about GTM that first-time users can encounter. These myths are not necessarily malevolent in character, but can prevent people from using what I think is an incredibly useful method. The major barrier to GTM use from a postgraduate perspective is the positioning of a literature review, when grounded theory suggests that this be delayed. Undertaking a non-committal literature review can help such students square the circle in this situation.
- As GTM is a living tradition, many adaptations and further debates are both possible and inevitable. The aim of this chapter has been to give you a good understanding of the foundations of GTM.

EXERCISES

1   Do a literature search in your own discipline to find out how GTM has been used to date. Can you identify which strand is being used and which intellectual traditions are being referred to? Have there been any debates in your discipline about the use of GTM? What do those debates tell you?

2   If you are working in a group, set up a role-play where one of you plays a sceptical senior colleague who talks about the barriers to using GTM and the other a new researcher who wants to use GTM for a piece of PhD research. What issues might come up? Can you think of any more myths about GTM you might encounter?

WEB RESOURCES

www.groundedtheory.com This is Dr Barney Glaser's official site. The emphasis here is on what he calls 'classic grounded theory'. As Glaser is still writing and working on GTM, there is a very real sense that this website represents a living and evolving method.

FURTHER READING

Melia, K. M. (1996) 'Rediscovering Glaser', *Qualitative Health Research*, 6(3): 368–73. This article, by Kath Melia, Professor of Nursing Studies at Edinburgh University and one of the early pioneers of grounded theory in nursing, is the best I have ever read about the split between the founders.

Walker, D. and Myrick, F. (2006) 'Grounded theory: An exploration of process and procedure', *Qualitative Health Research*, 16(4): 547–59. Discusses the differences between coding procedures in the Glaserian and Straussian strands in detail.

FREQUENTLY ASKED QUESTIONS

Does ignoring the literature not carry the risk of reinventing the wheel? If we investigate an area where there is a lot of literature, is there a danger that we will just come up with a similar theory and find nothing new?

This is an excellent question, which I will choose to answer in several ways. First, while the GTM dictum is to leave the literature review until later, there is, indeed, as mentioned earlier, a big difference between an open mind and an empty head! I would suggest it is unlikely, in an established discipline, that you would not already have some idea of prevailing theories and issues. Second, if you do choose to do a non-committal literature review, you provide yourself with a safety net in this instance. Finally – and this is perhaps the most important point – I have never come across an application of GTM that does not either contribute theory or extend existing theory in some way. I think this is because GTM, by dint of its systematic coding process, necessitates a very close look at the data and, because of this, something new is invariably discovered.

Which strand of GTM is best to use – the Straussian or Glaserian?

My own preference is for the Glaserian because I see it as more flexible and closer to the original ideas of grounded theory, as advanced in the 1967 book. That said, I have seen successful applications of the Straussian version and it's also important to remember that Corbin and Strauss' (2008) book is much more flexible about procedures. If you are a postgraduate student, you'll also have to consider which strand is more popular in your discipline and any previous work done by your supervisor using GTM.

3

Getting started with coding

This chapter:

- helps first-timers get started with the process of coding
- explains the crucial difference between analysis and description when generating codes
- explains how coding builds theory
- explains the differences between various coding approaches and GTM
- introduces the coding procedures of GTM.

Introduction

This chapter helps first-timers to get started with the process of coding. As a newcomer to GTM, you'll be confronted with endless references to codes and coding. This chapter aims to demystify the process and explains how codes build theory. This chapter also aims to place the coding process of GTM in the larger context of other coding approaches in qualitative research.

What is coding? *Coding* is the term used for attaching conceptual labels to data. When we attach a particular label to a particular chunk of data, we start to analyse that data. If we start to link together these codes in relationships, we can start to theorise about the data.

Coding, as a qualitative analysis technique, is not confined to GTM, but procedures for doing it are at the heart of the method. In this chapter we will spend some time considering different approaches to coding and where GTM fits within those approaches. This is an important distinction: *GTM uses coding, but not all coding is GTM*. This chapter gives examples of both general ways to approach coding and the GTM way of doing things.

In my view, it's very important to understand *how* to do coding, so this chapter contains examples and some exercises. There is no substitute for actually doing the analysis. I find that often my students only really understand the process of grounded theory when they try it. All the books and articles in the world cannot give you the skills in qualitative analysis, only examples. The first experience of detailed coding can be daunting, but one that quickly turns into a delight when you realise the insights it is possible to glean from the data.

We then need to understand the role of coding in theory building. Simply put, a theory is a relationship between constructs. So, if coding helps us build those constructs, then it is also vital to consider the relationships between those constructs.

I then give a brief introduction to grounded theory's stages of coding. We will go into these stages much more deeply in Chapters 5 and 6.

Coding – a first example

One of the hardest things to do when you first code a piece of data is to not simply *describe* the data but also go beyond that initial description and *analyse* it. So, ideally, you do not want a descriptive code, you want an analytical one. By coding I mean the act of attaching a concept to a piece of data, which is the heart of GTM and how we analyse the data. Schwandt (1997: 16) says that coding is 'a procedure that disaggregates the data, breaks it down into manageable segments, and identifies or names those segments'.

So, let us consider the coding of some lines of data from an interview, to help us understand the difference between a descriptive code and an analytical one and how coding might proceed. Figure 3.1 is an extract from a transcript of an interview between a systems analyst and his client, for whom he is endeavouring to solve a computer-related problem. This is their second meeting.

Analyst: What I've done, Jane, I've drawn up a couple of points from when we talked last …

Client: Yes.

Analyst: … when you gave me an overview of the system …

Client: Yes.

Analyst: … umm and basically what I've got down here is the database is about keeping statistics of approved and non-approved applicants or students for a Student Assistance Scheme.

Figure 3.1   Transcript excerpt for coding

The first thing to do is to read the whole excerpt, to try and get the feel of the exchange. The second thing to do is to describe it to yourself, then see if you can get behind the lines, as it were, to find out what is really happening – this is the analysis. As a whole, we can see that the analyst is recounting what happened at the last meeting. We can also see that the client is not saying much – perhaps if we had more than this small excerpt, we could speculate on reasons for this.

Let's examine the first line:

> What I've done, Jane, I've draw up a couple of points from when we talked last.

At a superficial level, we could simply label this an 'historical reference'. This is how I started out coding it. This would, of course, be a *descriptive* code. It does summarise neatly the words 'from when we talked last', but it does not add understanding at this point.

I also coded the analyst's use of the client's name as 'use of name'. Again, this is a pretty *descriptive* code, but I felt it was significant, and so it proved to be. I subsequently coded this use of her name as 'rapport building' – this can be seen as an *analytical* code. Once we reach this sort of analytical code, we can ask larger questions about his intentions. Why is he saying what he is saying? We can try to look behind the words. He is recounting what happened last time, attempting to build rapport and stating what he thinks the problem is, based on their last conversation.

Ultimately, I coded this whole excerpt as 'agenda setting'. This is an *analytic* code and goes beyond simply summarising what he is doing – instead, it is a code that helps us to start to theorise what might be happening and what strategies the analyst might be using. How problems are framed is a key part of professional activity (Schön 1983).

I realised with this excerpt that who defines the problem at the outset controls the conversation and, possibly, the outcome. One key thing to note here is that I may not have realised this was his strategy unless I had first coded his reference to the past (by asking, 'Why was it important?') and his use of her name (asking 'Why was he doing that?'). So often, a *descriptive* code is a necessary first stage of an *analytic* code which then helps us to theorise.

Different approaches to coding – what is and isn't GTM?

It's important to realise how coding is done outside GTM, too, so let's take a moment to consider different approaches to coding in general and how GTM fits within those approaches. This is all the more important when you consider that other coding approaches are frequently mislabelled as GTM, which can be very confusing to first-time users.

There are two key issues to be resolved when embarking on coding and what you decide regarding these will let you know pretty quickly if what you are proposing is, indeed, GTM or not. The first is whether or not you will use concepts from the literature – if you will, this is clearly *not* GTM. The second is, at what level should the coding be applied? What size should your data chunk be that you apply your code to? If you will not be applying your coding at a detailed level, then, again, you will probably not be using GTM, in the accepted sense.

So, let's look at the possible ways of doing coding, of which GTM is only one. There are four ways of thinking about how people apply coding in general to qualitative data.

Bottom-up coding (GTM)

Bottom-up coding is when codes are suggested by the *data*, not by the literature. GTM is a good example of this approach.

The importance of an open mind, as opposed to an empty head (Dey 1993) cannot be over–emphasised. GTM requires that researchers very consciously put their knowledge of the literature aside, so preconceptions are not imposed on the data.

Typically, coding occurs at the word and sentence level, which is said to be a strength of GTM. Holton (2007) says that line-by-line coding minimises the chance of missing an important category, among other things. I would go much further and say that coding at this level invariably gives new insights, which is one of the reasons I think GTM is so rewarding.

In our first example of coding earlier in this chapter – which is the bottom-up kind and GTM – I simply would not have arrived at the code of agenda setting without closely examining the use of language by the analyst and seeing how the original problem as coded was subtly changed during the course of the conversation. Similarly, I realised, after coding several interviews, that analysts were overwhelmingly data-focused and clients process-focused. Clients wanted to tell the story of their processes and problems; analysts wanted to structure the data in their clients' systems into a solution. Again, these kinds of insights would not have been possible without bottom-up coding.

Top-down coding

This is where codes from the literature are applied to the data. Generally, therefore, a coding scheme is generated from that literature. An example might be applying codes about conversation. In our first coding example above, instead of bottom-up coding, we could apply the codes used by Guinan (1988) in her study of systems analysts and their clients. She based her codes on the literature about 'framing' and 'reframing'. Reframing is described as:

> To reframe, then, means to change the conceptual and or emotional setting or viewpoint in relation to which a situation is experienced and place it in another frame which fits the facts of the same concrete situation equally well or better. What turns out to be changed as a result of reframing is the meaning attributed to the situation and its consequences, but not its concrete facts.

(Watzlawick et al. 1974: 94)

The idea of reframing is significant in analyst–client interactions because of the potential for mutual understanding that might occur as a result. The codes used by Guinan (1988) include 'as-if frames', 'outcome frames' and 'back track frames', where the analyst would variously discuss the problem as if it had been solved, possible outcomes of that solution and revisit the problem.

It is also not uncommon, however, to see researchers use top-down coding and add some bottom-up categories, too – those suggested by the data. Sometimes incidences of codes are counted and this is known as 'content analysis'.

Middle-range coding

Dey (1993) suggests that coding can also be in the middle range. In this approach, some distinctions are made in the data around commonsense categories.

Dey says that the analysis can either proceed to more detailed categories or the commonsense ones can be linked together to form larger categories. Categories can come from both the data *and* the literature.

Clearly this approach is a mixture of the previous two as whether codes come from the data or the literature is flexible. If the categories become quite large, they become themes, which we shall discuss in the next section.

Thematic coding

Often you will hear people say that they are doing thematic analysis, but, with the exception of Braun and Clarke (2006) little is written about how to do this type of analysis. It helps, in coding terms, to think of a theme as a large category applied to a larger chunk of data than in top-down or bottom-up coding approaches. It can be quite 'quick and dirty', if someone has simply picked out themes from, say, a set of interviews based on the questions asked, or it can be much more systematic and underpinned by smaller categories.

There are two options for thematic coding. These echo bottom-up and top-down approaches to coding, but are at a higher level of analysis:

- You can build a thematic framework from themes suggested by the data. If following this option, you can underpin these themes with smaller codes, as suggested by Braun and Clarke (2006). For instance, if you consider the coding example we looked at earlier, it could, in fact, be the basis for a thematic analysis. That particular excerpt comes from one of six detailed case studies of a key interaction between a systems analyst and their client. Based on the initial coding we did, it would be possible to examine each interaction and search for themes related to systems analysts' strategies (we found one based on the coding 'agenda settting'). It could be argued that this is similar to GTM because, in GTM, the aim is also to have just a few large categories underpinned by smaller ones, but there is a key difference here – thematic frameworks built in this manner rarely, if ever, attempt to relate those themes and build a theory as the aim is to find patterns in the data, not build a theory.
- A thematic framework can be built from relevant literature and applied to the data. Obviously, this echoes top-down coding, but is at a higher level. Of course, a thematic framework can be built from both the literature and themes found in the data itself. It's quite common, incidentally, to see this sort of theory building, using thematic frameworks, in dissertations. A thematic framework is constructed from the literature, applied to a phenomenon, then presented – often with some revisions after its application – as a theory-building contribution. Sometimes relationships are suggested between the themes, especially if they come from the literature. I supervised a Masters thesis in which the student built a framework of social media use by small businesses using knowledge management literature and marketing literature about social media. The framework was then elaborated on after interviews, where the ideas of knowledge management were refined with regard to content management. Again, this is different from GTM, which would: use theoretical sampling to build the theory; code at a very detailed level; and not use constructs from the literature as a starting point.

Figure 3.2 summarises the possible variations in coding approaches we've discussed so far. As previously mentioned, there are two key decisions to

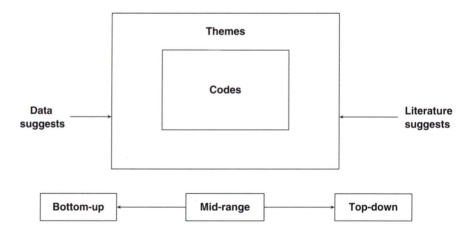

Figure 3.2   Approaches to coding

make – whether the codes come from the data or literature and what level of detail the data is coded at. If the codes are large and apply to large chunks of data, they become themes.

Coding as theory building – not just concepts but relationships, too

We have established that coding is the act of attaching a conceptual label to a piece of data and examined different ways in which it might be approached. So far so good, but *why* do we code?

We code to build concepts or find concepts. Those concepts, however, are of little use if they are not *related* to each other. That is because, then, all we are doing is labelling a phenomena, not building a theory. We are indulging in what Glaser (1992) calls 'conceptual description'.

What is very obvious is that sometimes people using GTM do the coding (attaching labels) but then fail to link them, using relationships, for the purpose of theory building. In my own discipline, the term 'grounded theory' itself has almost become a blanket term for a way of coding data. It's as if people want to give some authority to their coding and attaching it to a respected method such as grounded theory enables them to 'borrow' its reputation. Scholars in other fields have highlighted exactly the same issue – of GTM being viewed primarily as a way of coding data rather than a method for generating theory (Jones and Noble 2007). So, it's important to be clear how the method is being used in your research. While I don't have a problem with people leveraging the very well set out procedures of GTM, I think it's important to take that one step further and link the concepts you have to build some theory.

Let's use an example inspired by Dey (1993), who uses personal ads to illustrate coding issues, to show a way of linking categories. Supposing we analyse the profiles on dating websites, where single people advertise for prospective partners. Such profiles generally contain what individuals see as their personal qualities and interests. They also state if they are looking for a casual relationship or marriage.

During coding, we might identify a category for men who are over 40, have never married and are not interested in marriage now. We might call this category of men 'lifelong bachelor'. We might then turn to the way they describe themselves and note that some use phrases such as 'fun-loving' or 'fond of travelling'. We might call this category 'Novelty orientated' (remember, this is just an example!). We might 'saturate' these two categories – that is, find many instances in the data of these two categories. We might then

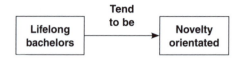

Figure 3.3   Relating categories to build a theory

speculate on the nature of the relationship between these two categories and develop some propositions around it. Are men who are novelty orientated more likely to be lifelong bachelors? How might they differ from men who describe themselves in the same way but say they are interested in marriage? What other qualities might come into play?

As shown in Figure 3.3, the relationship between these two categories could be 'tend to be', but it could be something else. What if the relationship tends the other way? Could it be that lifelong bachelors tend to end up as such because they are so novelty orientated they never have the chance to form steady relationships that lead to marriage? How would we investigate this? Perhaps we could look at what they say about the jobs they have performed. Perhaps we could interview them on this very subject. If we did, we would be using 'theoretical sampling', which is used in GTM – *deciding on analytic grounds where to sample from next*.

Once we have built our theory a little more, we could engage it with other theories, which is what GTM does. For instance, it may be that our lifelong bachelors didn't start out that way – it's just that lack of opportunities to form relationships in earlier years have led them to espouse a commitment-free lifestyle. We might want to look at psychological theories of post hoc rationalisation or any number of formal theories about individuals and how they narrate their social identities, to themselves and others. Strauss (1987) talks about the absolute obligation on grounded theorists' part to wrestle with other theories in this way.

I like the way Dey (1993: 52) talks about building walls in the analysis rather than palaces. This fits well with the GTM approach of literally building a theory from the ground up. When I think of building a 'wall' of theory, I like to think of the concepts as bricks and the connections between them as the mortar (see Figure 3.4). Without those connections, the wall could be kicked down quite easily!

We've already established that coding can take many different forms besides GTM. It should come as no surprise that, outside GTM, there is also advice on how to link categories. Spradley (1979), in his book on ethnographic analysis, suggests that domains – roughly equivalent to a core category in grounded theory – can contain 'folk' terms, used by members of a social setting (these are called 'in vivo' codes in grounded theory), and analytic terms, generated by the researcher and the literature (so a mixture of bottom-up and top-down

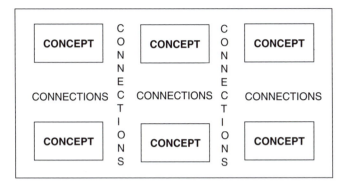

Figure 3.4 The 'wall of theory'

coding). Importantly, he also suggests nine *relationships* that can exist between domains (see Figure 3.5). These nine semantic relationships vary from strong causal relationships to those that specify characteristics.

The relationships are quite comprehensive and have the added benefit of simplicity. It is almost certain you will find categories that are, in fact, characteristics of others. The relationships 'Is a kind of' and 'Is a characteristic of' enable researchers to decide which of their codes are, in fact, aspects of others. The other relationships in the figure help us theorise and progress from quite weak to quite strong – 'Is a way to' to 'Is a result/cause of'. Personally, I shy away from identifying causal relationships because, in the social world that most of us are applying GTM to, it is very difficult to be certain about causes. That said, you may have a 'saturated' (many many instances) category linked to another saturated category, in which case you might feel it is a causal relationship.

From the body of GTM literature, as we saw in Chapter 2, there is extensive discussion and advice on how to relate categories through the discussion of theoretical coding and the Strauss and Corbin paradigm. This is part of the

- Is a kind of
- Is a part of/a place in
- Is a way to
- Is used for
- Is a reason for, is a stage of
- Is a result/cause of, is a place for
- Is a characteristic of

Figure 3.5 Spradley's (1979) semantic relationships

beauty of a qualitative method that has lasted many decades and GTM does give many more suggestions for relating categories – at the last count, Glaser (1978, 2005) had proposed a total of 38 coding 'families' that give many suggestions for relating categories (we saw some of these in the previous chapter).

To conclude this section, let's review the general coding approaches and their key characteristics (see Table 3.1) and compare them to GTM.

Table 3.1   Different coding approaches in the context of GTM

Coding approach	Level	Role of literature	Relationships between categories	Comment
Bottom up (GTM)	Detailed, line-by-line coding	**None** – the concepts come from the data.	Unlikely to be causal. Could use Spradley's semantic relationships for ideas on how categories relate. If doing GTM, then coding families and other tools are available to help decide on relationships.	GTM is **bottom-up** coding. However, some people use this approach and do not go on to build a theory.
Top down	Detailed, line-by-line coding	Extensive. A coding scheme is applied that comes from the literature.	Likely to use existing ideas from theories to help relate categories. May also use quantitative measures of codes to assess causal relationships between categories.	This type of coding can be used to subsequently build theory. Options include building statistical models of relationships between categories.
Mid-range	A catch-all description for making initial distinctions in the data, then either using codes from the literature, or the data or both.	The use of literature depends on whether codes are taken from the literature or generated from the data.	All options for relationships can be considered.	This coding description really illustrates how varied coding approaches can be and that they can be mixed in both categorisation and sizes of data chunks.
Thematic coding	A high-level categorisation of data. Essentially, themes can be seen as large categories. They can come from the literature or the data itself.	Often, thematic frameworks do come from the literature. Sometimes they come from the data.	Most thematic coding concentrates on patterns as opposed to finding relationships. That said, thematic frameworks from the literature can and do include relationships.	The one or two core categories for a theory, suggested by GTM, can also be seen as themes – they are, after all, large categories. However, core categories arise inductively from following a particular theoretical storyline in the data and are well grounded in coding. They are also related to each other. In a thematic framework, there may not be relationships and they are only sometimes grounded by smaller codes.

Having now looked at the main coding procedures and established where GTM fits in, let us now look more closely at GTM coding procedures.

Coding procedures used in GTM

The next sections give a brief introduction to GTM coding procedures. Chapters 5 and 6 go into these in much more detail and give fully worked examples, but the purpose of these sections is to give an overview of how GTM coding may be used. As noted in the previous chapter, the Glaserian version of GTM has three stages – *open coding*, *selective coding* and *theoretical coding*. The Straussian strand also has three – *open coding*, *axial coding* and *selective coding*. What makes it interesting (and confusing) is that the selective coding stage in each version is substantially different. For now, though, let's just get the essence of the steps involved in using GTM, following the simpler Glaser steps.

Open coding

Both versions of GTM start with *open coding*. Open coding, you will recall, is the process of assigning codes to a piece of data, line by line, sometimes word by word.

Let's revisit the excerpt of the transcript shown earlier in Figure 3.1 (reproduced as Figure 3.6 below, with the addition of line numbers) when we were discussing the difference between analysis and description. This study, described in Urquhart (1999), examined how systems analysts interacted with their clients when talking to them about problems in the clients' information systems. I observed analysts and clients talking together about those problems.

In Figure 3.7, I show how this excerpt was originally open coded. The open codes in boxes are the first descriptive open codes, which then morphed, on reflection, into other more analytical codes. By illustrating multiple open codes, I hope to be able to demonstrate that analysis is an iterative process

---

1 *Analyst:* What I've done, Jane, I've drawn up a couple of points from when we talked last

     ...

2 *Client:* Yes.

3 *Analyst:* ... when you gave me an overview of the system ...

4 *Client:* Yes.

5 *Analyst:* ... umm and basically what I've got down here is the database is about keeping statistics of approved and non-approved applicants or students for a Student Assistance Scheme.

Figure 3.6 Lines of a transcript for open coding

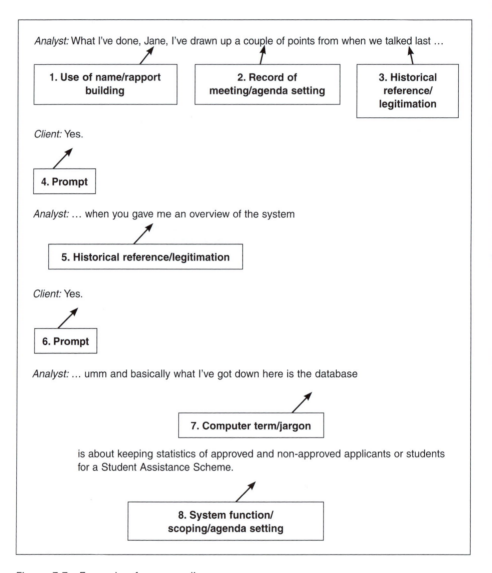

Figure 3.7   Example of open coding

and that the open coding phase acts as a foundation for larger codes as analysts decide what is important and move from initial descriptions to analytical priorities.

Also, this is just a fragment of the transcript. As I finished coding the whole transcript, I was able to see some of my initially descriptive codes in a more analytical way, when I reviewed the whole interview.

So, how did the coding proceed? I shall now share my thinking on the coding of each line.

Line 1: Initially, I noticed the analyst's use of the name of the client and coded this as **'use of name'**, which is a descriptive code and a good place to start. Then I asked myself, 'Why is the analyst using the client's name?' It seemed to me that he was trying to build rapport, so then my open code became **'rapport building'**. I first coded the rest of what the analyst said, about drawing up a 'couple of points', as **'record of meeting'**. As I read through the transcript and my interest in how the boundaries of the problem were defined, however, this became the much more analytical code of **'agenda setting'**. As is illustrated in Table 3.2, in the following section, that code became a selective code that then became a subcategory of the **'conversational strategies'** category. The reference to the previous meeting ('when we talked last'), I coded as an **'historical reference'**. On further reflection, and after considering line 3, it seemed to me that he was legitimating his actions by saying that the points were based on their meeting last week (or his perception of the same), so I coded it as **'legitimation'**.

Line 2: The client merely says 'Yes' at this point. When I looked at the video of the interview, it seemed to me that the client was, with her facial expressions accompanying the 'Yes', encouraging the analyst to go on, so I coded it as a **'prompt'**.

Line 3: The reference, once again, to the previous meeting ('when you gave me an overview') I simply coded as **'historical reference'**, as before. Given the subject was the same event as that in line 1, I eventually coded it as **'legitimation'**, too.

Line 4: The client says 'Yes' again at this point. Although she was starting to look somewhat sceptical in the video, she still seemed to be encouraging the analyst to continue, so I coded it as a **'prompt'** once again.

Line 5: What I noticed here was that the analyst used the term 'database', which I coded as **'computer term'**. This was later changed to **'jargon'**, as I realised that many analysts tend to use computer terms that baffle their clients.

I also initially coded this line **'system function'**, as the analyst is describing what he saw the function of the system to be. As I grew more familiar with how analysts go about their interviews, however, I realised that, in fact, he was also **'scoping'**. You can see this selective code, which ended up as a subcategory in the 'systems analysis strategies' category, in Table 3.2, in the next section. I also coded it as **'agenda setting'**, as it represents a conversational strategy, too.

The above example shows, I hope, that open coding is both an iterative and reflective process. You will notice that, again, we are moving from descriptive to analytic codes, as discussed earlier in the chapter. Sometimes it is necessary to categorise something descriptively – for instance, the use of the

Table 3.2   Example of selective coding

Category	Subcategory	Open codes
Conversational strategies	Negotiation	posits, future action, forward reframe, problem identification
	Agenda setting	conversation topic, issues
	Rapport building	'we', joint ownership, personal disclosures
Systems analysis strategies	Key searching	posits
	Information identification	information type, exemplification
	Process identification	posits, process rule, process exception, problem identification
	Scoping	posits, information typing
	Imagining	metaphors, vivid description, dialoguing, exemplification
	Reframing	metaphors, forward reframe

client's name – and then reflect on why it might be happening. As we code, analytical possibilities arise. This is what Dey (1993) means when he says that dimensions of the research problem emerge from coding.

The idea of coding line by line seems to be a major stumbling block for some students. Frankly, some of my students are appalled at this point in the process, and ask how long such an open coding exercise might take. This concern is particularly relevant I think for PhD students, who are often under pressure to finish their dissertation within a given time-frame.

There are various answers to this question of 'how long?' First, I draw on my own experience. I know, for instance, that it took me 60 hours to open code my very first transcript for my PhD work. I was also able to use that transcript as the basis for a coding scheme for subsequent transcripts, however.

Second, I point out that a detailed grounded theory analysis for a PhD thesis provides a foundation for a future research career in the form of many papers coming out of the PhD work.

Third, I point out that, in my experience, the amount of time it takes to do grounded theory analysis tends to be exaggerated by some academics, who may, for reasons of ignorance or malice, wish to show grounded theory in a bad light. The real truth, I think, is that the analysis stage does take a little longer than other methods, but the write-up stage of the work is much quicker, because the analysis is so extensive.

Also, the advice about line-by-line coding, like most advice in GTM, can be modified according to circumstances. For instance, if you have a very large dataset – one student of mine had all the documents relating to information technology in an organisation over ten years – it's impossible to code *all* of these sources. That said, that student did code sections of certain key documents line by line. Otherwise, certain insights and concepts would not have been possible.

Selective coding

What happens in selective coding is that the open codes are organised into selective codes that will eventually contribute to the core categories of your theory. Strictly speaking, in the Glaserian version of grounded theory (Glaser 1978), the selective coding stage is also where you are looking to code around a 'core variable'. Strauss (1987) also recommends having one or two core categories of a theory.

Put simply, selective coding is a process of scaling up your codes into those categories that are important for your research problem. In practice, while some key concepts emerge, most researchers find that, because of the bottom-up nature of the coding, there is quite a lot of grouping to do at this stage. I use subcategories to help me with this grouping process. What you will find is that some open codes, or variants of them, become larger categories and other open codes become properties or dimensions of these larger codes.

For instance, in my own work on conversations between systems analysts and clients, open codes of 'we', 'joint ownership' and 'personal disclosures' ended up as dimensions of a subcategory called 'rapport building' (see Table 3.2). 'Rapport building' had in fact been an open code, but I recognised it as a strategy that a systems analyst might use with a client and ploys such as 'joint ownership' as being dimensions of that strategy.

You should be able to see from this example that how you organise your selective codes is very much related to your research problem. What should be happening at this stage is that specific themes are emerging and, indeed, a core category or two that will comprise the eventual theory.

Ideally, you will start out with a general research problem. Glaser (1978) advises that you should stay within the confines of your discipline area when coding, which is excellent advice – there is no point in being charmed by what might be interesting dimensions of your data but take you outside your discipline area and away from your research problem! I know how tempting this is as, in my PhD work, I started out with a general research problem, about how system analysts and their clients approach the discussion of what is needed in a new information system. I noticed during my study, for instance, that there were clear gender politics at work in the interaction between some analysts and their clients, but considering these issues would have been beyond the disciplinary scope of my PhD. I ended up with the research question, 'What strategies and tactics do analysts and clients employ during the process of early requirements gathering?' as this is clearly related to the categories in Table 3.2.

As previously remarked, coding allows us to discover dimensions of the research problem (Dey 1993), so the selective phase is when more specific research questions can suggest themselves. It is also when you should break off from coding to write *theoretical memos* to help you theorise about categories (see Chapter 6 for more on this most important topic). Theoretical memos, you will recall, help you think about the relationships between categories and what might be an important and novel finding. You can think of theoretical memos as a way to allow you to muse on important ideas that occur to you during coding. They are a vital part of the coding process, in my view. Sometimes these ideas can even start to emerge as early on as the open coding phase.

With any luck, you should be able to organise the codes into what Glaser (1978) calls 'core variables'. In my own PhD work, as shown in Table 3.2, I was able to organise the open codes into two categories – conversational strategies and systems analysis strategies (which I subsequently organised into a core category of strategies in early requirements gathering).

Charmaz (2006) calls this stage *focused coding* and defines it as when, once some strong analytic directions have been defined, decisions need to be taken about which open codes make the most analytic sense in terms of categorising your data completely.

Theoretical coding

Theoretical coding is the stage when codes are related to each other. This is when the theory starts to be filled out, given that any theory consists of constructs (categories in grounded theory terms) and relationships. Glaser (1978) puts it well when he says, 'theoretical coding, in establishing new connections that make ideas (however recognisable) relevant, is so often the "new" and "original" about theory'. It is an incredibly important stage in theory building, but, surprisingly, is often neglected by those who use GTM. It as is if all the new concepts generated by the open coding and selective coding stages are thought to be enough – they are not! If we do not relate the categories, then we do not have a theory.

There are three possible sources of connections between categories:

- other categories
- ideas about relationships from literature such as Spradley (1979)
- and *theoretical codes*, as introduced by Glaser (1978).

The first of these – other categories – can often represent relationships. When examining our categories in the selective coding stage, it can sometimes become obvious that a category stands as a relationship between two other categories. For instance, in the previous example of selective codes given in

Table 3.2, it could be said that 'rapport building' is, in fact, the mechanism that relates conversational strategies with systems analysis strategies. We could theorise that, without rapport building, the systems analysis strategies are not effectively enabled. We would then need to make sure that this relationship was backed up by many different instances in the data, and examine those instances to further define the relationship.

Second, we can also get ideas for relationships from the literature. We might be inspired by something we have read in another literature stream. Glaser (1978) talks about the concept of 'theoretical sensitivity', meaning that researchers are sensitive to theories and have read widely. This wide reading, often not in our own domain, helps us understand how theorising works, and gives us the opportunity to think about different relationships in our data. The relationships advanced by Spradley (1979), discussed earlier in the chapter – such as, 'Is a way to', 'Is a part of' and so on – are good examples of this. In theoretical coding, we could connect the two categories in our previous example of 'conversational strategies' and 'systems analysis strategies' using a relationship such as 'conversational strategies *are used for* systems analysis strategies'. Again, to theorise about such a relationship would require plenty of instantiation from the data and, perhaps, could be argued against, in that some conversational strategies used by systems analysts could possibly *impede* systems analysis strategies!

Finally, Glaser's (1978) theoretical codes (as discussed in Chapter 2 and shown in Table 2.4) are extremely useful when thinking about relationships between categories. The *strategy* coding family (strategies, tactics, mechanisms, managed, way, manipulation, manoeuvrings, dealing with, handling, techniques, ploys, means, goals, arrangements, dominating, positioning) certainly provided me with a clear way of understanding the phenomenon I was dealing with in the research we have been looking at. When the systems analysts talked to their clients, they were, in fact, using an array of strategies and tactics. One option here would be to reorganise the selective codes using the strategy as the relationship – for example, 'imagining *is a strategy to* ...', 'information identification *is a tactic to* ...' and so on. We will explore the issue of theoretical coding much more in Chapter 6, but I hope the brief example above gives you an idea of how to go about relating categories in order to build a grounded theory.

Summary

- This chapter had two aims. First, to place GTM coding procedures in the larger context of coding approaches in qualitative research, and second, to give an introduction to GTM coding procedures.

- The chapter first gave an example of coding. From my point of view, it's important to start coding, and practising coding, as soon as possible – there is simply no substitute for doing it yourself! The example gave insight into the critical difference between description and analysis when coding and the necessity for both descriptive and analytic codes.
- The next part of the chapter described four types of coding approaches for qualitative data – bottom-up (which is GTM), top-down, mid-range and thematic coding. The key distinction of GTM is that it does not use codes from the literature and it proceeds bottom up using line-by-line coding. Themes tend to be very large categories and are often presented in frameworks.
- We then went on to discuss the importance of relationships and connecting categories in coding, so theory building can proceed. Using an example of online dating, this section described how we might build a relationship between two categories and, subsequently, how that emergent theory might be engaged with larger theories.
- The chapter then summarised the key differences between the four coding approaches and how they approach relationships for the purposes of theory building.
- The chapter concluded with a worked example of GTM coding. The three phases of Glaserian coding – open, selective and theoretical – were introduced and discussed.

EXERCISES

1 Take a paragraph from a news story in a newspaper or magazine. Try open coding it. Have a look at your codes. Can you tell which are descriptive and which are analytical?

2 Discuss your analysis with someone else and see what you learn from discussing it together.

3 Examine some journal articles that say they are engaging in qualitative analysis. Can you tell if they are doing top-down, mid-range or bottom-up coding? Are they applying a thematic framework? If so, does that framework come from the literature or the data?

4 Take some personal ads from a newspaper or some profiles from an online dating site. Apply the stages of open, selective and theoretical coding to them. Start with a general research problem. Draw some diagrams and make a few theoretical notes. Generate some research questions based on your theoretical coding phase. Can you come up with a theory about dating?

WEB RESOURCES

http://onlineqda.hud.ac.uk/Intro_QDA/how_what_to_code.php Most online resources about coding qualitative data give a huge range of approaches, which can be confusing to begin with. Huddersfield University's site, instead, simply gives some good advice and you should be able to identify coding approaches that are similar to the ones outlined in this chapter.

FURTHER READING

Miles, M.B. and Huberman, A.M. (1994) *Qualitative Data Analysis: An expanded sourcebook.* **Newbury Park, CA: Sage.** This book is an enduring classic. It is a great compendium of dozens of options for analysing qualitative data and is quite positivist in tone – probably a reflection of the time when it was written. It is still a good resource for general qualitative data analysis.

Saldaña, J. (2009) *The Coding Manual for Qualitative Researchers* **(2nd edn). London: Sage.** This book has received very good reviews and gives 32 different coding approaches, plus advice on analytic memos and writing up. A second edition will be available in 2013.

FREQUENTLY ASKED QUESTIONS

When I am coding, can I use concepts from the literature? Can I mix these concepts from the literature with some concepts I find in the data?

Of course. As long as you know that this is not GTM, but top-down coding (if you are using concepts from the literature) or a mid-range approach (if you are mixing these concepts with those that come from the data). It would even be possible to build a theory or model using this approach, if you looked at the relationships linking concepts. That said, in my opinion, you would not be doing the detailed analysis that comes with the GTM approach and, as a result, missing out on the systematic theory building of GTM.

Is it really possible to code in a bottom-up fashion without referencing the literature?

Yes! No one is asking you to *forget* what you have read, simply put it on one side while you code the data. You'll see many more possibilities and patterns if you examine the data step by step rather than rush to impose ideas on it. While the process seems strange to newcomers to GTM, it's worth pointing out that countless researchers have followed the method with very rewarding results.

How can I be sure that the codes I generate are correct? Would anyone agree with my codes?

Many students new to coding worry about this. Whether or not you should worry about this depends largely on whether you are doing positivist or interpretivist research. If you take an objectivist view, then, yes, you will need to organise a way of checking and debating your codes with another colleague, at the minimum, because you could be challenged on issues of validity. If you are more subjective in approach and not worried about validity issues, I would still recommend trying out your codes with colleagues, supervisors and friends. Debating the codes will help refine their meaning and your analysis.

4

Research design using GTM

This chapter:

- discusses some key first questions about GTM in research design
- discusses how the research philosophy, methodology and method might be considered when designing a grounded theory study
- explains how GTM might fit into various research designs
- discusses how theoretical sampling might be built into the research design
- discusses types of data collection, ethics, reflexivity, and the use of theoretical memos
- discusses the 'breadth v. depth' issue with regard to data collection.

Introduction

A good research design for a study is essential, as it will determine the success or failure of that piece of research. During my work as a journal editor, I've noticed that the one thing that makes work unpublishable is a flawed research design. Almost everything else is retrievable – deficiencies in the literature or analysis can be remedied – but if the design itself is flawed, it can be very difficult to remedy.

The problem of research design is more marked in PhD dissertation work where candidates are (of necessity) inexperienced, and the size of the study confers complexity. So, how might you approach research design when using GTM? What are the major issues grounded theorists encounter when seeking to design a GTM study?

The first decision to make is what *role* you would like GTM to take in your research. Are you building a theory, or planning to use the procedures for analysis only? GTM is good in areas where no previous theory exists and, in this fast-changing world, new domains crop up more often than you might think. It is also good for studying processes (Orlikowski 1993).

Essentially, then, there is a decision to be made about whether the study is focused on building theory or just uses GTM as a systematic way of analysing qualitative data. This decision then needs to be considered in the light of what is normal for your particular discipline. Is there an emphasis on qualitative theory building work in your discipline, or will your work be seen as unusual? This question is relevant because all academic disciplines use peer review and the eventual acceptance of your dissertation or published article depends on the norms of that discipline. One question I like to ask of PhD candidates quite early on in the process, therefore, is 'Who do you think might be your prospective examiners?' In the USA, this is already known, because of the existence of advisory committees. In other parts of the world, this decision about examiners is made much later. If the *type* of examiner can be anticipated, if not the *actual* examiner, this tells us a lot about the audience for the research. The research community that the research addresses itself to will have certain norms around its view of GTM. While it's possible to challenge those norms by doing excellent research, it's really important to know what they are, in order to couch your positioning of the theory-building process appropriately.

The discussion above shows how many disciplinary norms might intrude when considering a research design using GTM. In some disciplines, GTM is often leveraged to build concepts for questionnaires, as part of a theory-testing design. Personally, I think this is entirely reasonable – the coding procedures of grounded theory work well, in their own right, for building concepts. Because GTM has such a well-respected intellectual history, it also confers respectability on the research design in which it is used – that is, by referencing such a well-known method that uses such systematic procedures, researchers can demonstrate rigour.

What 'rigour' might mean in a particular discipline can vary, but it connects us to a most important point – what is the philosophy of the research? Again, from a peer review perspective, it's very important that the research method chosen, and how that method is used, is consistent with the philosophy of the research. So, in the next section, we'll discuss how your view of reality – in the form of your philosophical position on the research – influences how GTM is used in the research design.

Philosophical position

As we have seen, one key issue with any research design is the philosophical position of the research. Most of us are familiar with positivism and the scientific

Table 4.1 Epistemology and ontology (adapted from Crotty 1998 and Orlikowski and Baroudi 1991)

	Epistemology	Ontology
Crotty 1988	Objectivism, constructivism, subjectivism	
Orlikowski and Baroudi 1991	Criteria for constructing and evaluating knowledge	Whether social and physical worlds are objective and exist independently of humans or subjective and exist only through human action

method, but there are other views of the nature of research and knowledge and, given that most pieces of research are peer reviewed, it's important that the philosophical position is consistent with the method chosen.

New researchers embarking on their first piece of major research come in with ideas generally based on popular notions of science. They tend to assume that proper, rigorous research needs to have numbers in it and that validity is very important. In one philosophical position – positivism – this perception is correct, but there are other views and philosophies of research. I have also noted that, with dissertation students, the more they read and discover about the philosophy of research, the more likely it is that their position will change. This has important ramifications for the research design as, depending on the philosophy, different steps will need to be taken. While there can be flexibility in research design and data collection, it is important that the design and philosophy are consistent.

Depending on the academic discipline you come from, the terms used and their meanings will vary widely with regard to research philosophy – things may well be called something entirely different. The bottom line is that your *perception of reality* (how the world is constructed) and how *knowledge is constructed* in your discipline will hugely influence your research design. Orlikowski and Baroudi (1991) define the first as *ontology* and the second as *epistemology*. Some definitions are given in Table 4.1. In my experience, research students struggle with these terms, but at issue here is how reality itself is perceived.

Burrell and Morgan (1979) introduced a significant way of seeing the different ways research philosophies underpin our research investigations. They posited that there are four key debates around the nature of research in sociology.

- What is the nature of reality – was it a given or a product of the mind?
- Is it necessary to experience something in order to understand it?
- Do humans have free will or is their behaviour determined by their environment?
- Is understanding best gained directly or through the scientific method?

Their matrix (see Figure 4.1), which expresses these debates through two axes – subjective to objective and radical change to regulation – is, I think, quite helpful for understanding how research can be carried out from a range of positions.

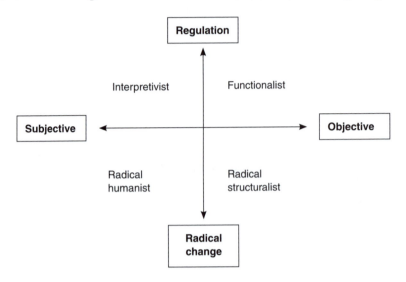

Figure 4.1   Paradigms of social theory (Burrell and Morgan 1979)

What is also interesting about this matrix is the claim that these views are diametrically opposed. It does, though, explain the extent of the debate that has raged in previous decades about research philosophy because it all depends on your point of view. It is obvious that someone who has a subjective point of view of reality (the idea that reality is itself a social construction) will not agree with someone who believes all reality is apprehendable. Similarly, someone who believes that society needs to be radically critiqued will not necessarily agree with someone who does not. While, in fact, the debates about research philosophy are often considerably more nuanced than this, Burrell and Morgan's (1979) matrix serves to remind us that some views are incommensurable, such as beliefs about the nature of reality.

In many academic disciplines in the 1980s and 1990s, discussions of ontology and epistemology marked a fight for the acceptance of qualitative research and more subjective approaches to research. In each discipline, this dispute has taken a different form. In many academic departments around the world, various research methods are preferred to others and, generally, this preference has its root in a particular view of phenomena, as well as the diametrically opposed nature of the paradigms put forward by Burrell and Morgan (1979).

If the previous few paragraphs have left you somewhat confused, help is at hand. While it is important to understand the philosophical debates around research, there are three basic categories based on underlying epistemology identified by Orlikowski and Baroudi (1991):

- positivist
- interpretive
- critical.

The definitions they put forward are given in Table 4.2.

Depending on your discipline, you will find other variations of these positions in writings about research methods. It is also important to note that qualitative research is not necessarily interpretive research, though sometimes the term can be used as a lazy shorthand for it. Qualitative research focuses on qualitative data; but it can be carried out within interpretive, positivist and critical philosophies.

For the purposes of our discussion about GTM in research design, though, I will concentrate on just positivist and interpretivist philosophy and the consequences of adopting each for use in GTM. It is important to note at this point, too, that GTM itself does not have an identifiable inherent philosophy, though people have debated this very point (Annells 1996; Madill et al. 2000; Bryant 2002) and come up with different conclusions. Because it is a method, it does not carry much philosophical baggage. This means, as Charmaz (2006)

Table 4.2 Positivist, interpretivist and critical research philosophies (Orlikowski and Baroudi 1991)

Research philosophy	Ontology	Epistemology
Positivism	Researchers assume an objective and social world that exists independently of humans, can be apprehended, characterised and measured.	Positivist researchers work in a deductive way to discover unilateral, causal relationships. There is a concern with the empirical testability of theories. Hypotheses, based on theory, are tested in the research for verification or falsification.
Interpretivism	Researchers have a presumption of social constructivism – that reality is a social construct and cannot be understood independent of the actors who make that reality.	Interpretive researchers study phenomena within their social settings. Constructs are generally derived from the field by in-depth examination of that field. Researchers aim to construct interpretations of practices and meanings.
Critical	Researchers have the view that social reality is historically constituted and people have the ability to change their social and material circumstances. That said, their capacity to change is constrained by systems of social domination. Social reality is produced by humans, but also possesses objective realities that dominate human experience.	With respect to knowledge, the epistemological belief of the critical perspective is that knowledge is grounded in social and historical practices. There can be no theory-independent collection and interpretation of evidence to conclusively prove or disprove a theory. Because of the commitment to a processual view of phenomena, critical studies tend to be longitudinal.

states, that it can be used safely in either a positivist or interpretivist paradigm. That said, how it is used in each paradigm will differ. These considerations need to be built into the research design.

Using GTM in a positivist paradigm

If using GTM in a positivist paradigm, where an objective social world is assumed to exist independently, then, obviously, issues of validity around coding will arise. The debate I had with Antony Bryant in 2002 (Bryant 2002; Urquhart 2002) was, in part, about if 'emergence', as put forward by Glaser (1992), implies that there is some objective truth waiting to be discovered in the data. This, of course, depends on your point of view.

Madill et al. (2000) do a great job in contrasting realist (that is, positivist) contextualist and radical constructivist epistemologies when coding using grounded theory. An interesting finding of theirs is that, regardless of the epistemology of the coder and whether or not extra coders are used, the major categories which emerge are very similar. I think it could be legitimately argued that coding using GTM will indeed uncover some basic structures in the data. This sits well with Bhaskar's (1998) idea that mechanisms are important, and human agency is made possible by certain social structures which themselves require certain actions and conditions.

From a research design point of view, then, anyone reading the research results of a study conducted within a positivist paradigm will want to know how it has been ensured that the interpretations made while coding are not purely subjective and the view of one person. One common solution here is to consider using more than one coder, to achieve inter-coder reliability. It helps in the write-up of the research if this process is properly described. For instance, the coding of a transcript could be done initially by one coder then cross-checked by others or the same transcript could be coded by more than one person. It's also possible to apply semantic space modelling techniques, such as hyperspace analogue to language (HAL), to coding (Burgess et al. 1998). Then frequently occurring word pairs from the analysis can be used to verify the coding, or at least supply another means of triangulation.

Triangulation is a well-known idea in research. Put simply, it is the idea that you use more than one research method to collect data on a particular phenomenon (Jick 1979). In the positivist paradigm, this makes sense – either findings can be verified by two or more having the same views on a phenomenon or differences can be explored. Another way of triangulating is to use more than one researcher in a single study, as suggested by Myers (2008).

Another issue that might come up when building a grounded theory in the positivist paradigm is the extent of the generalisability of that theory. One phrase that comes to mind here – oft repeated to my students – is that, in qualitative research, 'we generalise to a *theory*, not a *population*'. This is the view of Yin (2009), in the seminal book on case study research – that it is much better to generalise to theory using cases. Generally, the theory produced is of a substantive area and applies only to that area.

Even though the aim is to generalise to a theory, not a population, if you are following the positivist path, you will need to make sure that your initial sample is carefully selected to be representative of the substantive area. While *purposive* sampling is sometimes thought to be just what comes to hand, it is a lot more than that. The real meaning of purposive sampling is *sampling for a purpose* and you will have to explain your rationale for that purpose. For instance, you could choose a case or set of cases on the basis that those cases represent a cross-section of an industry or you might choose to concentrate on 'typical' or 'unique' cases (Schwandt 1997).

Theoretical sampling, which will be discussed later in this chapter, gives the option of sampling other substantive areas, to increase the scope of the theory. The substantive theory produced by the study can also be integrated with other, larger, more formal theories. Working within a positivist paradigm, it's important to make the point in the write-up that further theory building and testing would usually be required.

Using GTM in an interpretivist paradigm

Generally, using GTM in an interpretivist paradigm, where researchers construct interpretations of social practices, is easier because there is more commensurability between the notion of coding (generally subjective) and the idea of constructing interpretations. So, generally, verification of the coding is not required, but it is still useful to show how the coding proceeded and the steps taken, as this is part of a chain of evidence which can illustrate that this is an excellent piece of research. We will discuss the writing up of a grounded theory study further in Chapter 8, but one of the strengths of GTM is that it provides a chain of irrefutable evidence – for every concept produced, researchers can point to many instances of it.

While there is less onus on researchers to explain their selection of a particular case or cases within the interpretive paradigm, it's still important, I think, to explain your rationale for selecting a particular case. In interpretive research, the 'revelatory' case study is common – that is, when one case study is selected precisely because it is anticipated that it will be interesting and tell us a lot about the phenomenon.

In an interpretive design, the extent to which triangulation is used is a moot point. As Orlikowski and Baroudi (1991) point out, for the 'strong' constructivist, no triangulation is possible because this view of the world cannot accommodate positivistic beliefs and researchers are presumed to 'enact' the phenomena they are studying; there is no point of reality on which to triangulate. That said, Orlikowski and Baroudi (1991) also talk about the notion of 'weak' constructivism, when researchers try, through various data-collection techniques, to understand existing meaning systems shared by actors. The idea is that 'weak constructivism' complements positivist research by suggesting hypotheses for further investigation. From this perspective, triangulation is logical.

Myers (2008) sounds a cautionary note about triangulation that interpretive researchers would do well to heed. If different methods for data collection are to be used, they need to be commensurable. If the methods are substantially different – for instance, qualitative methods combined with quantitative methods (Myers 2008) – it can be challenging because the underlying philosophies of those methods are different.

My own view of triangulation is that, for interpretive researchers, it needs to be replaced with a gentler and kinder, but equally important, word – corroboration. The idea that more than one method can be used to collect data on a phenomenon is too useful to be skewered on arguments about the nature of reality. Most of the time, if more data, using different methods, is collected about a phenomenon, this will contribute to the credibility of the research. For instance, in my own PhD research about systems analysts and their clients, I collected data about a central interaction between analyst and client from several perspectives. The design was as follows. The analyst and the client were both interviewed about the upcoming interaction with each other. The analyst and client were then videoed talking to each other about the problem, then subsequently interviewed about the interaction. They were also asked to rate the interaction on a scale between 1 and 5. So, there were multiple viewpoints on the central interaction.

Methodology

Once the philosophical position has been settled, considering the methodology becomes easier. As previously mentioned, I find that PhD students may shift their philosophical positions as they think more deeply about them. The methodology, and methods, should be consistent with the philosophical position. I have come across dissertations where a particular position, such as interpretivism, is espoused, then quantitative methods have been applied to check the veracity of the GTM coding. Checking the validity of the coding is entirely legitimate, but how it is done should be consistent with the espoused philosophy. So, the aim is commensurability, regardless of whether the philosophical position shifts during the research or not.

Myers (2008) identifies three major methodologies for qualitative research, in addition to 'pure' grounded theory studies themselves:

- ethnographic
- case study
- action.

It is possible to use grounded theory within all these research methodologies, but answering this question is key:

Is GTM being used to build theory in the study?

As previously remarked, generally GTM is used in one of two ways in research:

- to build a theory
- as a coding technique.

When used as a coding technique, the concepts that emerge can be used for various purposes, such as building questionnaires or question items. This implies that there are two basic research designs available. The first is what I would call a *theory-building design*, the second is a *general design* leveraging GTM.

Next, we will consider theory-building designs, along with the issue of theoretical sampling. Theoretical sampling is a critical element of GTM and something that needs to be considered for a theory-building design. We then briefly discuss the implications of theoretical sampling for theory-building research designs using pure GTM, ethnography, case study and action research methodologies.

Theory-building designs

If you have made a decision to build a theory, then certain implications flow from that decision. Probably the most important is if you are going to follow a key tenet of GTM, which is *theoretical sampling* – that is, deciding on analytic grounds where to sample from next. It's useful to remember, too, that the use of theoretical sampling also enables *constant comparison* – another key tenet of GTM. As previously mentioned in Chapter 2, constant comparison is the process of comparing instances of data labelled in one category with other instances – a powerful but effective rule of thumb that really helps the analysis. Constant comparison can and should, of course, also be used independently of theoretical sampling, but, when it is used with theoretical sampling, it really helps to 'densify' particular categories because you are following a particular analytical path. The purpose of theoretical sampling is to end up with a better theory and, by following this strategy, you can extend the scope of your theory by sampling more slices of data.

Theoretical sampling implies *overlapping* data collection and analysis, which has implications for time spent in the field. Let us first look at what the options for theoretical sampling might be.

Theoretical sampling

Theoretical sampling is a key strategy for building a grounded theory and, indeed, there is a whole chapter on it in the classic foundational GTM text by Glaser and Strauss (1967). They describe the process as driven by two major questions.

- What groups or subgroups does one turn to next in data collection?
- For what theoretical purpose?

They point out that the simplest type of theoretical sampling is simply sampling groups of the same type – for instance, accounting departments in government organisations. This would then result in a substantive theory about these types of groups. A more general substantive theory would be achieved by comparing different departments in one government organisation (Glaser and Strauss 1967). The theory could then be built out further by comparing different types of departments in different government organisations, in subgroups. Finally, the generality of the theory could be increased by considering regional groups or, indeed, different nations (Glaser and Strauss 1967). Glaser and Strauss point out that the scope of a substantive theory can be controlled quite systematically by conscious sampling of groups (1967) and they outline four major strategies for theoretical sampling: maximising or minimising the differences between either groups or concepts in the data. They provide a useful table to show the effects of the different strategies, shown here, slightly adapted, in Table 4.3.

The important thing to note here is that differences can occur at the group level *and* the conceptual level. So, when theoretically sampling a similar group, this enables the filling out of categories if the data are similar. It also helps with understanding of category variation and possible hypotheses if the data are dissimilar. If theoretically sampling dissimilar groups, where the data are similar, this enables the theory to be built on key uniformities. If, however, the data are very diverse, this helps to establish the limits of the theory.

What if we don't have the luxury of overlapping analysis and data collection? It is true to say that, sometimes, for reasons of access and expense, researchers only get one shot at collecting data in the field and will not be able to analyse it while they are in the field. What *is* possible, in this situation, is to review data that have been collected and do a preliminary analysis

Table 4.3 Options for theoretical sampling (adapted from Glaser and Strauss 1967)

Group differences	Concepts in the data	
	Similar	**Diverse**
Minimised	Maximum similarity in data leads to: • verifying usefulness of category • generating basic properties • establishing a set of conditions for a degree of category. These can be used for prediction.	Identifying/developing fundamental differences under which category and hypotheses vary.
Maximised	Identifying/developing fundamental uniformities of greatest scope.	Maximum diversity in data quickly forces: • dense development of property of categories • integration of categories and properties • delimiting of scope of the theory.

of any emerging themes. Such analysis may give ideas for new interview questions and what to follow up in subsequent interviews. You might also decide to interview additional people suggested by the interviewee. Finally, if you have a two-phase research design, you can ensure that the concepts emerging from the first phase influence sampling in the second. While this 'light' form of theoretical sampling is nothing like the systematic theoretical sampling suggested by Glaser and Strauss (1967), it does show some sensitivity to emerging themes in the data.

Implications for methodology and theory-building research design

So, what might the need for theoretical sampling imply for the theory-building research design?

First, it implies that a sampling strategy needs to exist, and there is a field environment where 'slices' of data can be gained on the basis of categories as yet undeveloped. This might not fit too well into a dissertation proposal format where all details of data collection need to be specified. Charmaz (2006) gives some good practical advice here when she suggests that researchers seek approval for a second and possibly third phase of data collection and for the planned data collection to include observations as well as interviews. She also suggests that these successive phases can be constructed as 'member checking' and interviewees can be asked to elaborate on preliminary categories. Generally, when planning the research design, it does help to consider if the theory is going to be built out using successive cases and whether those subsequent cases will differ from the first case or not.

Second, the basis for theoretical sampling can be outlined in a systematic fashion, if necessary. For instance, in Lehmann's (2010) study of international information systems – which can be seen as an example of a classic grounded theory study – the decision on theoretical sampling was driven by the level of saturation of various categories. The second case was chosen on the basis of unsaturated categories, in order to maximise differences. Table 4.4, from Lehmann (2010), shows how his examination of unsaturated categories enabled him to arrive at requirements for the next case.

It's also worth noting here that Lehmann himself would say he used a case study methodology. This makes sense as, when planning to build a comprehensive theory, you need to sample from more than one case (or dataset). In this chapter, though, I am characterising it as a pure GTM study because of the extensive and systematic emphasis on theoretical sampling.

Myers (2008) defines the purpose of ethnographic research as gaining a deep understanding of people and their culture. The focus is *learning* from people rather than *studying* them, as you would in case study research. The data collected in the field will be supplemented by participant observation and, generally, there will be an extended amount of time spent in the field.

Table 4.4   Establishing theoretical sampling requirements for the next case (Lehmann 2010)

Unsaturated categories Business domain	Requirements of the next case
Nature of the business	The business should have a reasonably clear focus to allow an easy identification of any linkage between operations and the nature of the international information system.
Global business strategy	There is no specific preference for any particular global strategy, as long as the case's strategy is a clear one and can be readily compared within the Bartlett and Ghoshal framework.
Rejection of global information system	The case should be around an accepted international information system to allow ready investigation into what made the business accept it.
Analysis Business sameness Data/business Modelling Information system professional skills Information system conservatism Conceptual capability	The case should provide examples of the methods/ paradigms used, successfully, to develop and/or maintain the international information system.

In this research methodology, enacting theoretical sampling by overlapping data collection and analysis should be possible. You can start analysing the data as soon as the first interview or document. You can then sample future interviewees or documents. There is plenty of time to overlap the data collection and analysis and direct the data collection based on the emerging storyline of the analysis.

A thesis on ICTs in the rural Andes, written by my colleague Antonio Díaz Andrade (Díaz Andrade 2007), is a good example of using an ethnographic methodology with GTM. The thesis does a masterly job of conveying the rugged rural setting of the study, complete with photographs. It is clear that, by living with participants, Antonio gained a deep understanding of their world and their relationship with ICTs. In this case, because of field conditions, Antonio was unable to analyse data while in the field, but he was able to use his many fieldnotes to help him further develop interview questions and start thinking about the data.

Case study research, as outlined by Yin (2009) (in a positivist paradigm) and Walsham (1995) (in an interpretive paradigm), generally involves collecting data on phenomena within its context and is a very common methodology in qualitative research. Myers (2008) suggests that, in business at least, even in-depth case study research does not normally involve participant observation or fieldwork and the evidence in case studies normally comes from interviews and documents.

Eisenhardt (1989), in her seminal paper, talks specifically about the role of case studies in theory building. Her account of theoretical sampling is somewhat different, as her paper *draws* on GTM as opposed to following it exactly. She suggests that theoretical sampling can either replicate or extend the emerging theory and researchers can purposefully decide to select diverse cases. When using GTM, obviously the cases should be selected on the basis of emerging categories, wherever possible, as illustrated by Lehmann (2010). Eisenhardt's paper is based within a positivist framework, so gives helpful advice on the number of cases that might be required and so on for those working within a positivist framework.

I also have found it helpful to suggest to students (regardless of whether they are working in a positivist framework or not) that they discuss the research design in their dissertation under the headings suggested by Eisenhardt (1989). These headings are:

- Getting started
- Selecting cases
- Crafting instruments and protocols
- Entering the field
- Analysing the data
- Shaping hypotheses or theory
- Enfolding literature
- Reaching closure.

Considering each of these in turn leaves no methodological stone unturned! For the interpretive researcher, Walsham (1995) gives some excellent advice on the shape of an interpretive case study and the sorts of analytic generalisations that might be possible. He outlines these as:

1 development of concepts
2 generation of theory
3 drawing of specific implications (for particular domains of action, which may provide useful for other related contexts)
4 contribution to rich insight.

A grounded theory study, usually, would contribute in all of these areas.

To do an action research study using GTM is complex, but not impossible. My colleague Karen Day (Day 2007), at the University of Auckland, successfully used GTM to help her build a theory of change within a public healthcare organisation. As she points out, theoretical sampling in GTM assists with successive action research cycles. There is, in fact, a natural synergy between the idea of theoretical sampling and action research. That said, I would question if it is possible to do an action research study that builds a whole theory of the intervention, simply because, when combining methods, one method generally takes primacy. The scope of action research is generally quite wide, with many different data sources and various interventions/actions. The question then becomes whether or not all data sources are analysed in the quest for a grounded theory and if the primary objective of the study is, in fact, to study the interventions and their consequences rather than producing a theory. The Further reading section provides some examples of action research theses that also use GTM.

General designs using GTM

This section discusses research designs that leverage GTM for a purpose other than theory building.

The number of potential research designs using GTM is probably unlimited. What is more interesting is why researchers would choose to leverage the strengths of grounded theory to build concepts that are then used in some other way.

I can think of some reasons. First, the research design is directed at an emerging phenomenon, about which there is little in the way of existing theory. GTM is perfect for such situations. Researchers may wish to build concepts for a survey, which can also be combined with existing literature and that can then be tested in the field. So, in this way, grounded theory becomes a tool for (extended) theory testing.

Second, the coding procedures of GTM are well known and easily available. Thus, if a researcher is looking for a reliable method of coding data, then the *imprimatur* of grounded theory is quite attractive. Unfortunately, this does also lead to coding procedures being mislabelled as GTM when, in fact, they may not be purely inductive. For instance, researchers may have also used concepts from the data. This is legitimate, but the problem is that it is not GTM.

This leads to the third category, where GTM procedures are consciously and deliberately mixed and otherwise leveraged with other methods. For instance, researchers can decide to use open and axial coding, using the Strauss and Corbin paradigm, without proceeding to build a theory. They may also bring in other concepts from the literature. Examples of this are Lings and Lundell (2005) and Baskerville and Pries-Heje (1999), who mix GTM coding with action research cycles.

Data-collection methods

It is true to say that, once the basic methodology has been sorted out, then the methods themselves are straightforward. Myers (2008) identifies three broad categories – interviews, participant observation and fieldwork, plus documents. In GTM terms, data collection tends to focus on interviews and the idea of 'slices of data' that are many and varied.

As previously mentioned, key to data collection is the idea that theoretical sampling should direct where to sample from next. As well as interviews, GTM coding can be applied to documents, focus groups – pretty much any-thing that is a text can be coded. One problem, of course, is that a text – for instance, a transcribed interview – loses context once we cannot see the video or hear the tone of voice that the person used. So, as when coding, it is advisable to refer back to this context, as it influences the meaning of the data. This, then, has an implication for our methods. If we are interested in coding as much of the rich context as possible, then we need to consider video, recordings and photographs. Photographs are so important in conveying context, but it seems, in many academic disciplines, we still don't consider presenting them as part of the story.

Some interesting questions arise when we consider visual materials, such as, can they also be coded? I have colleagues who have coded photographic materials using GTM (Díaz Andrade and Arthanari 2009) and these have yielded interesting results. In the digital age, the importance of visual images, as opposed to text, cannot be denied. So, it is interesting to consider how GTM in particular and qualitative methods in general can be applied to vis-ual images occurring on websites, for instance. In my view, there is no rea-son for GTM to not be applied to visual images. There is, of course, a strong argument for supplying and analysing visual images in qualitative research because they supply much-needed context to the analysis. A picture is indeed worth a thousand words.

Ethics

Once the philosophy, methodology and data collection methods have been established, most researchers working in an institutional context, such as a university, will have to apply for ethics approval. Often, I suggest to post-graduate students that they work on an ethics application relatively early in the process, because the questions asked on the form mean that issues of philosophy, methodology and data collection are considered, as well as issues of access to the field of study.

The ethics approval process varies widely from one university to another. Myers (2008) quotes three ethical issues identified by Maylor and Blackmon (2005):

- maintaining privacy
- reporting and analysing your data honestly
- taking responsibility for the findings.

Qualitative research, by its very nature, often uncovers sensitive data. For instance, even an investigation into a failed information systems project may reveal sensitive information about interviewees' relationships with other colleagues. For this reason, informed consent should always be sought and participants given the right to withdraw their data at any time (sometimes an end date is given). If research participants are allowing us to enter their world, this is an act of trust on their part and we should honour that trust. This honouring should also include informing them as to how the data will be used and how it will be published.

It may be important, in some situations, to anonymise organisations and informants in the final write-up. I have found it very helpful to use a participant information sheet that summarises all these issues for participants, which they can keep as a record of their participation. A link to an example is included in the Web resources section at the end of this chapter.

Reflexivity

One important aspect to bear in mind, when conducting your research, is the issue of reflexivity. Put simply, reflexivity is the process of critical self-reflection on your biases, theoretical predispositions and so on (Schwandt 1997), as well as the entire research process.

In positivist research, this is particularly important, in order to establish validity for the accounts gathered from participants and possible biases on the part of researchers. Even in interpretive research, there are guidelines in existence to this effect. For instance, Klein and Myers (1999), in their seminal paper on principles for conducting interpretive case studies, give three principles that could be seen as reflexive:

- interaction between the researchers and the subjects – requiring critical reflection on the socially constructed nature of the findings as a consequence of the interaction between researchers and participants
- dialogical reasoning – requiring sensitivity to possible contradictions between the theoretical preconceptions guiding the research design and actual findings
- multiple interpretations – requiring sensitivity to differences in participants' interpretations of the same event.

Alvesson and Sköldberg (2009) take the idea of reflexivity beyond the handling of empirical material and towards a consideration of 'perceptual, cognitive, theoretical, linguistic, (inter) textual, political and cultural circumstances' that influence the interpretation of the material. This implies a much broader examination of findings and placing of them within the social and historical context. Interestingly, Clarke (2005) in her book *Situational Analysis: Grounded theory after the postmodern turn*, proposes the use of situational maps to 'pull' grounded theory round the postmodern turn. (This book makes for interesting reading, not least because it represents how the intellectual tradition of grounded theory continues to evolve in response to developments in research.)

Theoretical memos

Theoretical memos, you will recall from earlier, are a key tool for use in the field. They were first suggested by Glaser (1978) and the practice has spread to qualitative research in general. The idea is that, during coding, researchers can break off to write down their thoughts about the data in, to use Glaser's terminology, a theoretical memo.

Glaser describes such memoing as the 'bedrock of theory generation' (1978: 83) and I agree wholeheartedly. Theoretical memos allow researchers the freedom to muse creatively, on the page, about what might be going on in their data. I would suggest, therefore, regardless of whether you are engaging in a theory-building design or not, that you adopt this practice when coding your data. I think the brilliance of the theoretical memo comes from its non-linear timing. The very suggestion that you should break off and think differently (creatively) about the data, rather than just doing so when you've finished the coding, allows for that creative spark to be captured rather than lost.

We'll talk more about theoretical memos in Chapter 6, but, for now, I would urge you to plan for it to be part of your practice when analysing the data.

Breadth versus depth in research design

One common problem encountered with GTM studies is the issue of how much data to collect. Given that coding starts at the word and sentence level, a great deal of richness can be gained from only a few interviews. It is necessary, however, to reach theoretical saturation and, to do this, the sampling needs to be adequate.

If a theory is to be built, it needs to be at a sufficient level of abstraction. This has some implications. From a research point of view, what needs to be done is a balancing of the rich insights afforded by the detailed nature of GTM coding and the need to have sampled sufficiently across the substantive area of investigation. An example of this dilemma is a PhD study done by a student of mine, Mariyam Adam (2008), of the tourism sector in the Maldives. She felt that, in order to properly represent the sector, she needed to sample small, medium and large hotels and resorts, as well as interview people from government agencies. She ended up carrying out a total of 49 interviews, which meant a lot of coding. Was it a better study because the sampling was representative? Almost certainly. Was it more challenging to manage as a PhD project because of the volume of analysis required? Definitely. That said, the project was completed pretty much on time and, in my experience, dissertation studies using GTM take about the same time as other dissertations. The lesson to take from this example is to consciously consider the scale of the data collection part of your study and balance the time taken for analysis and the need to sample the substantive area appropriately.

Summary

- This chapter considered how GTM might be incorporated into a research design and covered the role of GTM in research design, the philosophical position, methodology, theoretical sampling, data collection methods, ethics of data collection, reflexivity, theoretical memos and breadth versus depth in research design.
- The first issue considered was the need to decide how precisely grounded theory is going to be used in the research – as a theory-building tool, as it was intended, or as an analysis method supporting other research objectives. Both uses are legitimate and common; they also vary by discipline.

- The second issue discussed was that of the research philosophy adopted (the worldview of the research) and how it influences our use of GTM. For the grounded theorist, subjectivity when coding has to be considered in the light of the chosen research philosophy. Issues of generalisability and how these play out in interpretive and positivist use of GTM were also discussed.
- The chapter then discussed two types of research designs. First, theory-building designs, then more general designs.
- Theory-building designs need to allow for theoretical sampling. How theoretical sampling might be carried out in theory-building designs was considered within four methodologies – a pure grounded theory study, ethnography, case study and action research. Reasons for general research designs to use grounded theory were then discussed.
- Data-collection methods were then discussed, particularly the types of data collection. GTM coding can be applied to pretty much any type of text, and the definition of 'text' can even be extended to visual materials, such as photographs. The importance of ethics in relation to data collection was also considered.
- The notion of reflexivity – the importance of critical reflection on your biases, theoretical predispositions and so on – was also suggested as a key consideration for researchers.
- The use of theoretical memos – an important tool for theorisation in the coding process – was also recommended, regardless of researchers' philosophical positions or their use of GTM.
- Finally, the chapter concluded with a discussion of the need to balance depth of data analysis with width of data collection. This is a particular issue with dissertation studies, estimating the amount of time needed to analyse the data and balancing that against issues of sampling the substantive area.

EXERCISES

1 Undertake a search of the top journals in your discipline area. Use the keywords 'Glaser and Strauss' or 'Strauss and Corbin' or 'grounded theory' or 'open coding'. See if you can then sort the research designs in those papers into theory-building and general designs. Are there any other categories of research designs? How is the use of GTM justified?

2 Look at the papers you have from the search in the previous exercise. How many different research philosophies are in evidence? Do the research designs seem consistent with the research philosophies?

3 In the set of papers you have, examine the methods used. Are they explained and justified? Is the coding procedure explained? How much context is evident in the data sources? Were transcripts used? How much was coded? In some papers, there will be little documentation of methods. Does this matter? Why? Why might there not be much documentation in some cases? How does the style of the journal impact on how grounded theory is represented?

4 Consider the following research problem. How do university students manage their social identities when using Facebook? Come up with two research designs to investigate this problem. The first, a theory-building research design that incorporates theoretical sampling. The second, a research design that uses grounded theory to build concepts to then combine with literature to create a survey instrument. Be sure, in both cases, to outline your philosophy, methodology and methods. Justify all of these.

WEB RESOURCES

www.auckland.ac.nz/uoa/re-uahpec This link gives extensive advice on ethics procedures at the University of Auckland. The applicants' manual, downloadable from here, gives some very good advice and applies very high ethical standards. While the approach is extensive and detailed, which is not necessary for all projects, it does allow researchers to ensure that all risks are more than catered for. The participant information sheet (PIS) contained in the manual is a very helpful pro forma for contacting participants and giving them a good level of information on the project.

http://ethos.bl.uk British Library repository of digitised theses, generally free to download. A great resource for all researchers.

FURTHER READING

Díaz Andrade, A. (2007) 'Interaction between existing social networks and information communication technology (ICT) tools: Evidence from rural Andes'. Unpublished PhD thesis, Information Systems and Operations Management, University of Auckland. Available online at: https://researchspace.auckland.ac.nz/handle/2292/2357 An interesting example of how a grounded theory might be generated using an ethnographic approach.

Eisenhardt, K. M. (1989) 'Building theories from case study research', *Academy of Management Review,* 14: 532–50. This seminal article discusses theory building within a case study. It is grounded theory inspired, in that the article talks about coding as a means of building theory from case studies.

Fern, E. (2008) 'The implications of how social workers conceptualise childhood, for developing child-directed practice: An action research study in Iceland'. Unpublished PhD thesis, University of Warwick. Available online at: http://wrap.warwick.ac.uk/2225 An interesting thesis that combines action research and grounded theory in a study of childhood as perceived by social workers in Iceland.

Fernández, W. and Lehmann, H. (2011) 'Case studies and grounded theory method in information systems research: Issues and use', *Journal of Information Technology Case and Application Research*, 13(1): 4–15. This is a fascinating paper by my colleagues Walter Fernández and Hans Lehmann. It's extremely helpful because it contains a comparison of Yin's criteria for case studies, and gives a grounded theory equivalent.

Klein, H. K. and Myers, M. D. (1999) 'A set of principles for conducting and evaluating interpretive field studies in information systems', *MIS Quarterly*, 23 (1): 167–94. This important article gives lots of guidance on interpretive case studies and how to conduct and evaluate those studies. While personally I don't think it is necessary to slavishly follow these guidelines, they do give an excellent insight into the characteristics of interpretive case studies and are very helpful to new researchers.

Lehmann, H. (2001) 'A grounded theory of international information systems'. Unpublished PhD thesis, University of Auckland. Available online at: https://researchspace.auckland.ac.nz/handle/2292/626 This thesis is an excellent example of a grounded theory study. In particular, his treatment of theoretical sampling – and the systematic way in which he assesses the saturation or otherwise of concepts – is extremely interesting.

Walsham, G. (1995) 'Interpretive case studies' in IS research: Nature and method', *European Journal of Information Systems*, 4(2): 74–81. This groundbreaking article gives helpful and actionable advice to researchers doing interpretive research case studies and holds for most disciplines, if not all. It is particularly helpful because it talks about the analytic generalisation possible from interpretive case studies.

FREQUENTLY ASKED QUESTIONS

I suggested using grounded theory to my supervisor, as I feel it is suitable for my research question, but they said it was a high-risk research strategy and no one from my department has the knowledge to supervise me. What should I do?

If GTM is perceived as a high-risk strategy in your department, it may be because qualitative research in general is perceived as high risk, or GTM in particular is perceived as high risk. The latter is easier to deal with than the former. If your department sees qualitative research as high risk, it is probably referring to the difficulty of getting such work accepted in your department or discipline. In some quarters, quantitative research is seen as 'easier' for students doing a PhD as the problem is more bounded. Given that doing a PhD is as much a social process of credentialling as it is a piece of research, it would pay to tread carefully at this point. If there is someone in your department who champions qualitative research, then it would be a good idea to talk to that person. If no such person exists, then it may not be the right place to do a PhD or you will have to reconcile yourself to doing quantitative research.

If it is the case that your supervisor is not familiar with GTM, but is familiar with qualitative research, then the answer is more straightforward. Remember that PhDs themselves are, of necessity, narrow. Supervisors will be expert in one method, the one they used in their own PhD. You can show your supervisor a number of papers and books on GTM and defend it as being suitable for your research problem. It will also help if you can point to other examples of people in your discipline who have used GTM. Finding people in your university as a whole who use GTM is also helpful. If appropriate, you can suggest to your supervisor a co-supervisor (or addition to your committee) who is expert on GTM.

> **While I was employed at my previous organisation, I collected a huge amount of data about the introduction of the new student enrolment system. I'm now at a different university and about to embark on my PhD, using the data I collected. I'd like to do a grounded theory study and employ theoretical sampling. Is this possible?**

If you have a large enough dataset, possibly covering a number of years and a number of different groups of people, it should be possible to employ theoretical sampling, by building a theory around one group/dataset, then extending your sampling to other groups, looking to saturate categories that are currently unsaturated. It would also be interesting, if possible, to return to the field and do a further round of interviews. These interviews would be based on the theory you have built and constitute further theoretical sampling.

> **My initial research design, agreed with my supervisor, was within the positivist paradigm. My problem is that now, after having done a lot of reading on the issue, I am more of an interpretivist. What do I do? My data collection is well advanced and has lots of positivist assumptions.**

This problem is commoner than you might think. It's not unusual for research students to change their views on more reading and reflection – it is generally a mark of a thoughtful and able student! The thing here is to remember that a PhD or Masters dissertation is essentially a *retrospective* write-up of your research; not every deviation in your journey can or should be reported. It should be possible to write up your research from an interpretive perspective.

More of a concern is whether or not your change of view will affect your relationship with your supervisor, and how interpretive research is assessed within your discipline. These questions need to be considered carefully.

Should I have a theoretical model?

Students are told that they need a literature review, often culminating in a theoretical model, for their thesis research. This is at direct odds with the GTM injunction that the literature should not influence the analysis process, but it is not at odds with

Glaser's (1978) notion of theoretical sensitivity. The idea here is that, in order to build theory, we need more than a passing acquaintance with what theory actually is like. The solution of a draft or non-committal literature review, when the relevance of the review is determined by the emergent theory, gets round this institutional requirement, as long as you remember that future coding needs to be done with 'an open mind not an empty head' (Dey 1993: 63).

The issue of a theoretical model is more vexed, however. A theoretical model that is open to interpretation, augmentation and possible abandonment is a possibility. One thing a theoretical model may do is encourage you as a student to look at larger, more formal theories that can be used as a lens through which to view the emergent findings. So, a theoretical model, which aids theoretical sensitivity and gives you a sense of formal theories in your discipline area, is no bad thing in my opinion. It can help you decide what formal theories are important to engage with. If you force your findings through that model, however, or impose concepts from the model on your findings, in no sense can your findings be called a grounded theory. So, there is a balance to be found here, with the quest being theoretical sensitivity and engaging your emergent theory, rather than determining the outcome of the study.

5

Coding and conceptualising

This chapter:

- gives an extended example of open and selective coding
- gives examples of 'elevating' open codes to selective codes
- shows how some codes end up as dimensions of other codes
- gives some exercises to try open and selective coding.

Introduction

This chapter provides extended examples of open and selective coding. One of the main stumbling blocks for any first-time user of GTM is a dearth of examples. This lack of examples makes sense when one considers that there is simply not the space in a journal article to include extensive findings *and* how those concepts were arrived at. One piece of advice I give to postgraduate students and colleagues who want to know how grounded theory works is to look at PhD dissertations because in them the authors are under an obligation to show how they arrived at their conclusions! That said, PhD theses vary tremendously and can be quite idiosyncratic, depending on what is being investigated.

This chapter gives two extended examples. The first is from Barack Obama's inaugural presidential address, and the second is from a Masters project. The reason for giving two extended examples is to demonstrate how versatile grounded theory is and also that, given the wide range of readership of this book, people may find one example more sympathetic to their background than the other!

Open coding: Example 1

As demonstrated in the previous example in Chapter 3, open coding is the vital first step of grounded theory. In many ways, open coding is the primary strength of GTM – from a detailed and 'open' analysis of the data, unique insights are possible. That is not to say there should not be some kind of overarching research problem. The key thing here is that the emerging analysis helps us develop the dimensions of the research problem.

How to begin open coding? I can well remember the terror I felt when faced with the challenge of coding my very first transcript using grounded theory and I observe the same kind of reaction in classes when I ask students to begin a practical coding exercise! In my experience, its best to first 'get' how to do the analysis by annotating the transcript in front of you in an old-fashioned pen and paper sort of way. Using software for analysis can come later. Students of mine have also used shading in different colours to indicate certain types of code (and there is nothing to stop you doing this in a word processing package, too, for instance).

The excerpt I've chosen (see Figure 5.1) for our first example is from Barack Obama's inaugural address in 2009. The election of the first black man to the Whitehouse was an historic event and Obama already had the reputation of being a fine orator. Let's see what this data excerpt can tell us.

For we know that our patchwork heritage is a strength, not a weakness. We are a nation of Christians and Muslims, Jews and Hindus, and non-believers. We are shaped by every language and culture, drawn from every end of this Earth; and because we have tasted the bitter swill of civil war and segregation, and emerged from that dark chapter stronger and more united, we cannot help but believe that the old hatreds shall someday pass; that the lines of tribe shall soon dissolve; that as the world grows smaller, our common humanity shall reveal itself; and that America must play its role in ushering in a new era of peace.

To the Muslim world, we seek a new way forward, based on mutual interest and mutual respect. To those leaders around the globe who seek to sow conflict, or blame their society's ills on the West, know that your people will judge you on what you can build, not what you destroy. *(Applause.)*

To those who cling to power through corruption and deceit and the silencing of dissent, know that you are on the wrong side of history, but that we will extend a hand if you are willing to unclench your fist. *(Applause.)*

To the people of poor nations, we pledge to work alongside you to make your farms flourish and let clean waters flow; to nourish starved bodies and feed hungry minds. And to those nations like ours that enjoy relative plenty, we say we can no longer afford indifference to the suffering outside our borders, nor can we consume the world's resources without regard to effect. For the world has changed, and we must change with it.

As we consider the role that unfolds before us, we remember with humble gratitude those brave Americans who at this very hour patrol far-off deserts and distant mountains. They have something to tell us, just as the fallen heroes who lie in Arlington whisper through the ages.

We honor them not only because they are the guardians of our liberty, but because they embody the spirit of service – a willingness to find meaning in something greater than themselves.

And yet at this moment, a moment that will define a generation, it is precisely this spirit that must inhabit us all. For as much as government can do, and must do, it is ultimately the faith and determination of the American people upon which this nation relies. It is the kindness to take in a stranger when the levees break, the selflessness of workers who would rather cut their hours than see a friend lose their job which sees us through our darkest hours. It is the firefighter's courage to storm a stairway filled with smoke, but also a parent's willingness to nurture a child that finally decides our fate.

Figure 5.1   Excerpt from President Obama's inauguration speech, 20th January 2009

We will start with a very open research problem: 'What are the major themes of the inaugural address and how are those themes put forward?' Now we can examine this excerpt paragraph by paragraph and code the sentences within. Let's look at the first chunk in detail (see Figure 5.2).

For we know that our patchwork heritage is a strength, not a weakness.

Diversity as strength
Diversity as history
Defence of diversity

We are a nation of Christians and Muslims, Jews and Hindus, and non-believers.

Nation of different religions
Non-believers
Inclusiveness

We are shaped by every language and culture, drawn from every end of this Earth;

Different languages
Different cultures
From every place
Inclusiveness

and because we have tasted the bitter swill of civil war and segregation,

History of civil war
Segregation

and emerged from that dark chapter stronger and more united,

Overcoming prejudice
Being united

we cannot help but believe that the old hatreds shall someday pass;

Hatred as a thing of the past

that the lines of tribe shall soon dissolve;

Tribalism as a thing of the past

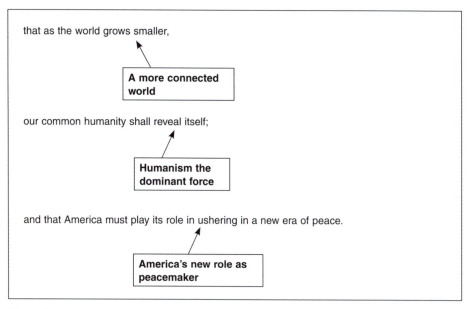

Figure 5.2   Open coding of first section of excerpt

In Chapter 3, I talked about the difference between a descriptive code and an analytic one. The aim is always to get to an analytic code – one that analyses the data rather than simply describes it. That said, I find that, with open coding, to break open the data to begin with, it often pays simply to summarise the data in a descriptive fashion. So, in the first code, 'patchwork' becomes diversity, so we have the code 'diversity as strength'. He also talks about heritage, however, so I put in the code 'diversity as history'. Finally – and this is as close as I can get to an analytic code to begin with – I put in 'defence of diversity' because my analysis, using the first two codes, leads me to think that this is what he may be attempting to do in that first sentence.

The second group of codes is somewhat similar, in that I summarise as 'nation of different religions' and 'non-believers', then add a more analytic code, 'inclusiveness'.

The third group of codes is also somewhat descriptive – 'different languages', 'different cultures' and 'from every place'. Again, I add the more analytic code, 'inclusiveness'.

The rest of the codes follow a similar pattern – generally summarising with the occasional analytic insight. I also make no claim for these codes being 'correct', because I come from an interpretivist perspective. Rather, the insight here is that, when actually doing open coding, it's helpful to follow a policy of summarising the data in an open code and more analytic codes will emerge.

Indeed, there are some very interesting themes emerging from this short excerpt, as well as some puzzles. Clearly, there is a theme of diversity coupled with inclusiveness. This theme is also anchored in history and hope for the

future. A 'smaller world' is possibly a shorthand reference to increased communication using technology, giving a more global outlook. This, though, is
only my interpretation – would it be interpreted this way by most people?

Let us look at the next chunk, in Figure 5.3.

In this chunk, a specific appeal is made to the Muslim world, coded as
'appeal to Muslim world'. This statement is swiftly followed by what I coded
as a 'balancing statement' where it is acknowledged that some of those leaders

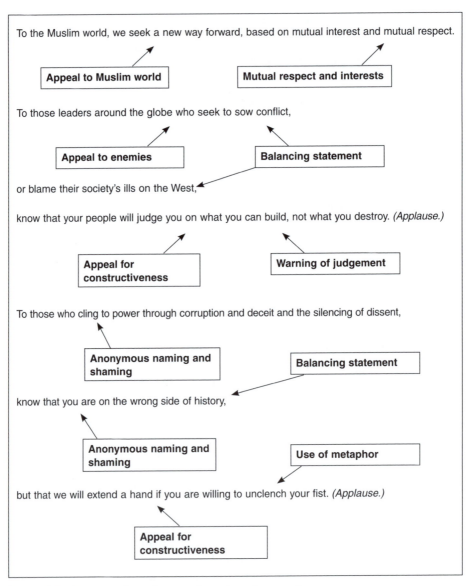

Figure 5.3   Open coding of second section of excerpt

may seek conflict. This is then followed by two more balancing statements that seem to say the USA is aware of despotic governments and under no illusion about the nature of some governments.

This chunk both begins and ends with appeals for constructiveness. A 'balancing statement' can be seen as an analytic code and raises the issue of whether or not multiple audiences are catered for in this speech – balancing statements are a device for doing just that. So, one possible emerging research question is: 'How does Obama cater for multiple audiences, both domestic and international?'

Another analytical code is 'use of metaphor'. Given Obama's reputation as an orator, another emerging research question might be: 'How does Obama uses metaphors to convince?'

Let's look now at the next chunk of this speech, addressed to poorer nations (see Figure 5.4).

This section of the speech is addressed to developing nations. The open code 'message to poorer nations' shows that this part is explicitly labelled as such. As we have seen in our analysis so far, the speech has sections in it addressed to different audiences. Sometimes those audiences are addressed separately, sometimes simultaneously (witness the 'balancing statements' found in the previous section).

In this part of the speech, Obama promises aid to developing countries, in terms of agriculture and clean water, and I have simply summarised this in the open code 'help with agriculture and clean water'. Again, there is a metaphor, which I have coded as 'use of metaphor', and there is another one shortly after (these instances are certainly mounting up). His reference to clean water shows that he understands development issues – an option would be to code this somehow, such as 'knowledge of development', but, because this is open coding and my overall research problem is not about his understanding of world issues, I chose not to.

Obama then puts out a clear message to developed nations that they can no longer afford to ignore developing nations and the differences in resources (hence the codes 'message to developed nations', 'developed nations need to give aid', 'developed nations need to consume fewer resources'). Again, most of my codes here are summarising. That said, there would be scope to introduce a more analytic code, which would be something like 'multiple audience', where he shifts, sometimes explicitly, from one audience to the other.

So, some interesting questions are emerging – is the speech constructed for multiple audiences and, if so, how? What is the role of metaphor, which seems to be quite a consistent element in the speech?

Let's look at the next section in Figure 5.5.

This section is fascinating. Obama makes reference to the role that America will take (coded as 'America's role unfolding'), then goes on to discuss the role of the military (coded as 'honouring soldiers in combat around the world'). In

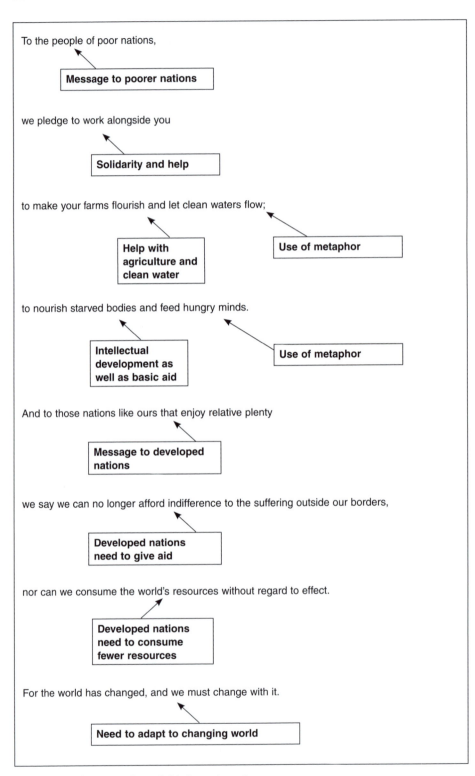

Figure 5.4   Open coding of third section of excerpt

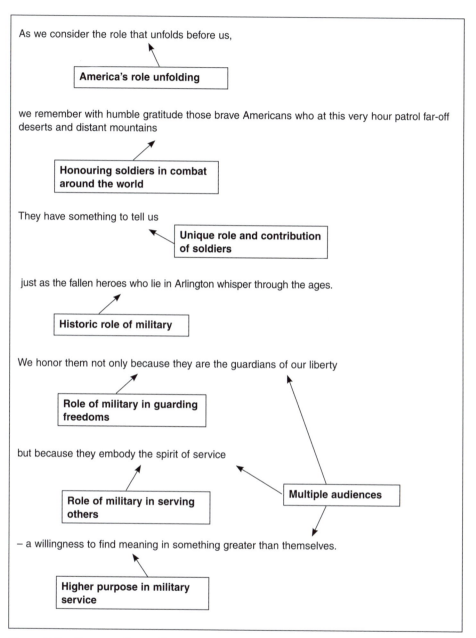

As we consider the role that unfolds before us,

> **America's role unfolding**

we remember with humble gratitude those brave Americans who at this very hour patrol far-off deserts and distant mountains

> **Honouring soldiers in combat around the world**

They have something to tell us

> **Unique role and contribution of soldiers**

just as the fallen heroes who lie in Arlington whisper through the ages.

> **Historic role of military**

We honor them not only because they are the guardians of our liberty

> **Role of military in guarding freedoms**

but because they embody the spirit of service

> **Role of military in serving others**

> **Multiple audiences**

– a willingness to find meaning in something greater than themselves.

> **Higher purpose in military service**

Figure 5.5   Open coding of fourth section of excerpt

talking about the role of the military (summarised in the code 'unique role and contribution of soldiers'), he again invokes history when talking about the military cemetery at Arlington (coded as 'historic role of military'). At the same time, he effectively redefines the role of the military, stressing their role in upholding of freedoms and serving others (coded as 'role of military in guarding freedoms' and 'role of military in serving others'). He also invokes a higher purpose in military service ('higher purpose in military service').

Coding the data at this detailed level helps us see the redefinition, but also the references to history and higher purpose (which could also be interpreted differently by religious and non-religious people).

So, who is the audience here? It seems that this section might be for multiple audiences – the global audience, for whom the role of the American military is often viewed in a less than positive light. I have, at this point, put in a more analytic code mentioned earlier – 'multiple audience' – especially as these shifts seem to be occurring quite frequently. This is a code that seems to have a number of instances and is an analytic code, so it could be significant later on.

Let us now look at the next part of the speech (see Figure 5.6).

One of the interesting things about the experience of coding this speech is that, sometimes, I found I created open codes that were larger and consisted of more words than the actual data chunk I was coding. I think that is because Obama is known to be an effective orator and manages to evoke meanings and certain emotions in just a few key phrases. In order to unpack them, sometimes the codes are longer than the text they are describing! As we have seen, there are layers of meaning in this speech, several different audiences are addressed and a number of rhetorical devices are used to make the speech more effective.

In this section, Obama talks of a defining moment, and I have coded it as such – 'a defining moment'. Again, he talks about a higher purpose, and here I have coded it as 'appeal for higher purpose'. We could also relate this back to the open code 'higher purpose in military service' in the previous section and consider whether or not we should just simply decide on an open code called 'higher purpose'. At this stage of open coding, though, I'd be interested in coding *all* aspects of higher purpose, *all* possible attributes, rather than narrowing the options down.

Obama goes on to talk about the role of the individual and the fact that government can only do so much (coded as 'government can only go so far' and 'nation also relies on individuals'). We could speculate about who this section of the speech is aimed at. The USA is well known for its individualistic culture, so maybe this is aimed at the home audience.

Obama also defines (or attempts to redefine) the role of individuality by giving examples of individuals – 'individuals who were kind during Katrina', 'individuals who cut hours to save jobs'. He talks about those people who we generally think of as heroes in society – firefighters – and also those we might not think of immediately in this way, such as parents ('unsung heroes in society – parents'). The choice of examples is interesting, so I also coded this as 'choice of examples'. For instance, he uses Hurricane Katrina, which hit an overwhelmingly black population in New Orleans in 2006 and was seen as a disaster for then-President Bush, in how it was handled. While he does not mention

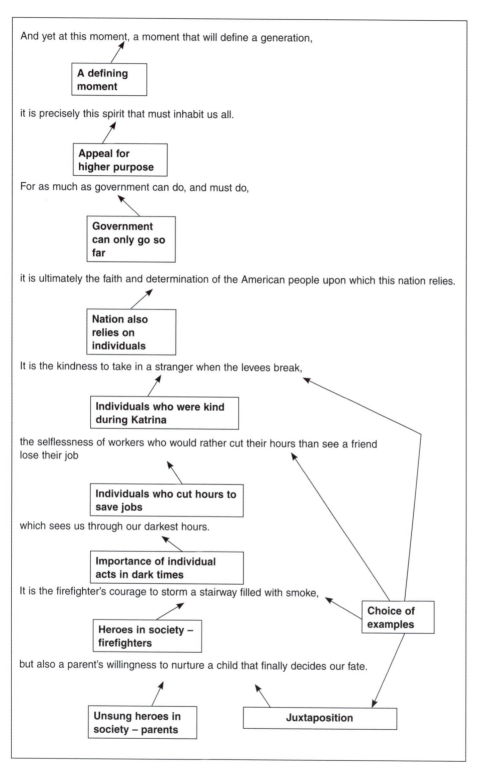

Figure 5.6   Open coding of fifth section of excerpt

the firefighters' role in 9/11 explicitly, I would suggest that they have become a metaphor in the USA for all that is brave and noble.

Again, then, there is a theme of inclusiveness in this section of the speech and a higher purpose that could also be read as spirituality or faith by some sections of his audience. He uses juxtaposition here, too, contrasting examples – I coded this as 'juxtaposition' because I was interested in whether or not he used this device generally in his speeches.

Now is the time to put all these open codes together, abstract a little and come up with some selective codes.

Selective coding: Example 1

Let us first remind ourselves of what selective coding sets out to do. As noted in Chapter 2, Glaser (1978) defines selective coding as the stage at which coding is limited to only those categories that relate to the core category. So, at this point, we are also looking for the major focus of our study and would expect our research problem to perhaps shift slightly and, certainly, deepen in the light of our analysis. As this happens, our selective codes should also point the way to future theoretical sampling, as a focus for the theory emerges.

The research question we started out with was, 'What are the major themes of the inaugural address and how are those themes put forward?' The process of coding raised some interesting issues. First, Obama's address is aimed at several audiences, including the worldwide audience and the domestic audience. Second, it is clear that he uses a number of techniques to balance those very different audiences. Given that coding enables us to identify dimensions of the research problem, we can see that our broader research question can be broken down into more specific research questions.

- What are the major themes of the speech?
- Who are the key audiences of the speech?
- What techniques does Obama use to reconcile different audiences?

If we look at the possible selective codes suggested in Table 5.1, one thing becomes clear: the selective codes provide us, through the open codes, with much richer dimensions of the research problem, which now are expressed in the research questions above.

The first thing we can ask ourselves about Table 5.1 is, do we have the right selective codes? Glaser (1978) and Charmaz (2006) recommend having one or two core categories for a theory. Table 5.1 gives us eight and we have only coded a fairly small segment of Obama's speech!

Table 5.1   Initial selective codes

Possible selective codes	Open codes
Diversity	Diversity as a strength, as history, different religions, non-believers, inclusiveness, from every place.
Historicity	Civil war, segregation, historic role of military, a defining moment.
Peacemaking	Hatred as a thing of the past, tribalism as a thing of the past, humanism the dominant force, appeal to enemies, appeal for constructiveness.
Higher purpose	Higher purpose in military service, appeal to higher purpose.
America's role	A more connected world, America's new role as peacemaker, mutual respect and interests, anonymous naming and shaming, need to adapt to a changing world, America's role unfolding.
Different audiences	Appeal to Muslim world, appeal for constructiveness, honouring soldiers in combat, unique role of soldiers, role of military in guarding freedoms, serving others.
Rhetorical devices	Use of metaphor, choice of examples, balancing statements.
American identity	Nation relies on individuals, individuals who were kind during Katrina, individuals who save others' jobs, importance of individuals, heroes and unsung heroes.

Here we come to what can sometimes be a major issue with grounded theory – the issue of abstraction. To be workable, and elegant, a theory needs to have only a few constructs or core categories, yet grounded theory throws up many codes because of the nature of the coding technique. The coding starts 'bottom up' and at a very detailed level, because of the injunction to grounded theorists to code line by line. This is the foundation of Layder's (1998) criticism of GTM – that it needs to break away from its examination of micro-phenomena.

Certainly, there does seem to be a view in some quarters that GTM produces very interesting, rich descriptions, but not much in the way of theory. This is a reflection, perhaps, of the fact that GTM has often been used more for the integrity of its coding procedures than for theory building per se.

So, what can the grounded theorist do when confronted with several selective codes? The first thing is to realise that coding is, of necessity, an iterative and reflective process. Part of theorising involves looking at codes and debating their meanings and relationships. You may choose to do a number of things during selective coding:

- group selective codes together
- consider if one selective code is an attribute of another
- consider if a selective code is, in fact, a relationship
- consider if any of the open codes in a selective code are a better name for that selective code
- consider if the name you have given to the selective code is truly representative.

So, let's apply some of these ideas to the selective codes in Table 5.1. An obvious merging could occur between 'Historicity' and 'American identity', with 'Historicity' being part of 'American identity'. Depending on the research question, this is then a grouping of the codes or a decision that 'Historicity' is slightly subordinate to 'American identity' and is an attribute of it. Either option would not prevent researchers from talking about how 'Historicity' is an aspect of 'American identity', nor from using the open codes to direct them to quotes illustrating that historicity.

When we look at the open codes for 'Historicity', however, we can see that we have 'a defining moment' – this is not about the past; this is about the future. Obama also talks about a new role for America and a more connected world in the selective category 'America's role'. What if we put these open codes into a selective code 'A changing world'?

We could also merge 'Higher purpose' with 'Peacemaking', especially as Obama specifically identifies a 'higher purpose in military service'. That said, if our research focus was on religious aspects of the American identity as exemplified by speeches by American presidents, this would be a selective code of its own.

It is hard to find selective codes that might be relationships in this table, but what if 'Higher purpose' was the connection Obama sees between 'America's role' and 'Peacemaking'? What if he is redefining the reasons for America's role in the world in a more spiritual way? We could develop this idea using a theoretical memo – Glaser (1978) and Strauss (1987) both give the very good advice that, if you have a thought like this about the data and the nature of the category, then you should break off and write a theoretical memo about it, as discussed in Chapter 4. Theoretical memos at this point might also show directions for future theoretical sampling (Glaser 1978). Chapter 6 elaborates on theoretical memos as part of the theoretical coding process.

While the names of the selective codes seem OK, I did wonder if one of the open codes – 'Balancing statement' – could be used as the name for 'Different audiences'. 'Balancing statements' is the device used to cater for different audiences and the open codes for the selective code of 'Different audiences' are effectively examples of balancing statements.

Again, such decisions are very linked to our research questions. We might decide that it is important to keep a selective code of 'Different audiences' as it answers a specific research question. So, we can see in this example how the coding interacts with the formation of the research questions and it helps us understand deeper aspects of the research problem.

Table 5.2 gives some revised selective codes. At this stage, though, they are still subject to change and not all the changes I suggested above have been included, as the theoretical coding process may reveal further issues. For now, I have added a new selective category – 'A changing world' – and merged 'American identity' with 'Historicity'.

Table 5.2 Second pass of selective coding

Possible selective codes	Open codes
Diversity	Diversity as a strength, as history, different religions, non-believers, inclusiveness, from every place.
A changing world	A defining moment, need to adapt to a changing world, a more connected world.
Peacemaking	Hatred as a thing of the past, tribalism as a thing of the past, humanism the dominant force, appeal to enemies, appeal for constructiveness.
Higher purpose	Higher purpose in military service, appeal to a higher purpose.
America's role	America's new role of peacemaker, mutual respect and interests, anonymous naming and shaming, America's role unfolding.
Different audiences	Appeal to Muslim world, appeal for constructiveness, honouring soldiers in combat, unique role of soldiers, role of military in guarding freedoms, serving others.
Rhetorical devices	Use of metaphor, choice of examples, balancing statements.
American identity	Nation relies on individuals, individuals who were kind during Katrina, individuals who save others' jobs, importance of individuals, heroes and unsung heroes, historicity, Civil war, segregation, historic role of military.

We will return to this example in Chapter 6 and look at the final stage of coding – theoretical coding – which is when relationships are considered and the theory is built.

Open coding: Example 2

The second example (see Figure 5.7) is an excerpt from an interview about the evaluation of training projects in developing countries. It comes from a Masters project I supervised at the University of Auckland. The overarching research problem for the study is: 'What are the major issues in IT skills training projects in developing countries?'

The person being interviewed is talking about IT skills and training projects and how they are evaluated. When faced with a block of data like this, it's a good idea to divide it into chunks for analysis, as we did in our first example. Often we can see these chunks as naturally occurring topics in the data. Indeed, these will often correspond to particular questions asked by the interviewer. If, however, if we simply stopped at topics (or themes) as some researchers do and put quotes under those headings in our findings, we would not be doing GTM.

OK let me tell you about three different kinds of ways of using IT skills training.

[…] There are organisations who provide generic IT skills.

[For example] learn to use Word, learn to browse the Internet, learn to use e-mail […]. Those are the easiest ones to measure because you can have them [the people] a test […] you can issue a certification based on that.

Now, we have also found that it is the one that has the least retention and maybe the least usefulness for people to actually solve their everyday problems. It's maybe is the easiest one to implement but not the most productive one.

Another type of training that takes place is within an industry. Industry-specific training in IT skills. […] the training is tailored to certain people and training them in the specific skills that are needed in that industry.

[…] that tends to work best especially when the intent is to help people get a job in that industry.

[…] one measure of success there is that people actually get jobs in that industry (Brad).

[…] the third area for training that we identified is when organisations are providing training that is helping people solve local problems in a way that is locally relevant. […] [Citizens] solving their own problems with the help of IT […] that is more in the area of community empowerment, of civic participation, of becoming more engaged citizens, of better networking with others […]

[The training] it needs to be very customised and locally relevant, it's not just taking people and teaching them how to use Excel, but understanding what their situation is and what their problems that they are facing and how IT skills can help them better solve their problems.

That kind of training is the most difficult but the most pervasive and the one that has the deepest impact of all the training in the community, but it is also the most difficult to measure in a standard way across the board.

[…] I have designed and set up an evaluation and monitoring system for […] and it covers programmes in one hundred countries around the world, since 2003.

[…] it's a combination of multiple approaches to evaluation. One of them is very quantitative […] One of them is very qualitative […]

They are not separate they compliment each other so they, so together they gave us a better picture than each one of them by themselves.

Figure 5.7 Excerpt from an interview about the evaluation of training projects in developing countries

So, let's see how the excerpt breaks down into data chunks (see Figure 5.8). Sometimes, when I find it hard to find my way into some data, I split it into chunks like this. It is an especially useful trick when looking at interviews because, generally, interviews have questions based on various themes, which can usefully be seen as data chunks.

So, let's take it chunk by chunk. The first chunk can be open coded, as shown in Figure 5.9.

Again, as in the previous example, you can see that my open coding consists, in the main, of summarising (what I would call a largely descriptive code). Examples of such codes are 'agencies providing generic skills'. It is interesting that the interviewee talks of some organisations that provide these generic skills – the implication being that some do, some don't. We don't have the available context in this paragraph, however, to decide whether or not it is significant that he says this. In a situation where we were viewing

OK let me tell you about three different kinds of ways of using IT skills training.

Generic IT skills

[...] There are organisations who provide generic IT skills.

[For example] learn to use Word, learn to browse the Internet, learn to use e-mail [...]. Those are the easiest ones to measure because you can have them [the people] a test [...] you can issue a certification based on that.

Now, we have also found that it is the one that has the least retention and maybe the least usefulness for people to actually solve their everyday problems. It maybe is the easiest one to implement but not the most productive one.

Industry-specific IT skills

Another type of training that takes place is within an industry. Industry-specific training in IT skills. [...] the training is tailored to certain people and training them in the specific skills that are needed in that industry.

[...] that tends to work best especially when the intent is to help people get a job in that industry.

[...] one measure of success there is that people actually get jobs in that industry.

Locally relevant IT skills

[...] the third area for training that we identified is when organisations are providing training that is helping people solve local problems in a way that is locally relevant. [...] [Citizens] solving their own problems with the help of IT [...] that is more in the area of community empowerment, of civic participation, of becoming more engaged citizens, of better networking with others [...]

[The training] it needs to be very customised and locally relevant, it's not just taking people and teaching them how to use Excel, but understanding what their situation is and what their problems that they are facing and how IT skills can help them better solve their problems.

That kind of training is the most difficult but the most pervasive and the one that has the deepest impact of all the training in the community, but it is also the most difficult to measure in a standard way across the board.

Evaluation and monitoring

[...] I have designed and set up an evaluation and monitoring system for [...] and it covers programmes in one hundred countries around the world, since 2003.

[...] it's a combination of multiple approaches to evaluation. One of them is very quantitative [...] One of them is very qualitative [...]

They are not separate they compliment each other so they, so together they gave us a better picture than each one of them by themselves.

Figure 5.8   Excerpt split into data chunks

the whole transcript, we would look back to see if it was. The point being that, in line-by-line coding, we should – initially, anyway – treat *everything* as being of significance, and use the principle of constant comparison to help us evaluate that significance.

The interviewee then goes on to outline what those generic skills are ('word-processing skill, Web-browsing skills, e-mail skills') and how they might be measured. He says that generic skills are easily measured by testing

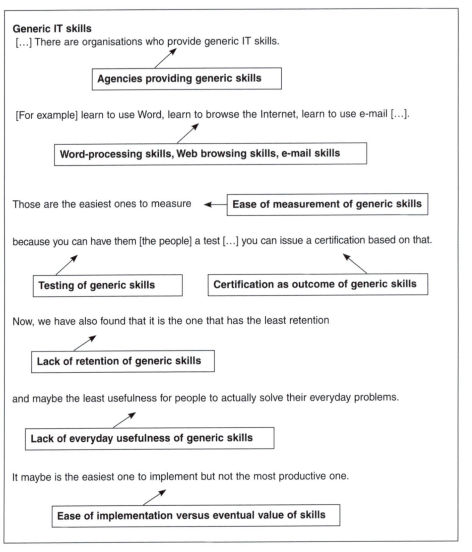

Figure 5.9   Open coding of first chunk of interview excerpt

('ease of measurement of generic skills') and certification of those skills can take place ('certification as outcome of generic skills'), leading to a qualification.

He then goes on to say that these skills are not easily retained ('lack of retention of generic skills') and are of limited use in helping with everyday problems ('lack of everyday usefulness of generic skills'). What are these everyday problems? Why do these generic skills not assist people with them? Surely certification would help an individual to get a job.

Perhaps the interviewer should have asked at the time. Certainly, in future interviews, the researcher could pick up on this issue. Grounded theory recommends overlapping data collection and analysis and here's a good example of why. The analysis here and the questions the coder is asking at this point provide the basis for theoretical sampling – that is, deciding on analytic grounds where to sample from next.

The interviewee also raises another issue – that of the usefulness of generic skills training. He then follows that up with a paradox – although generic skills are easy to teach, they may be the least useful. His overall reflection on ease of measurement versus eventual value of skills is easily the most the significant in the excerpt. It's an excellent example of why line-by-line coding works so well. Here, in this line, the interviewee, who is a highly skilled evaluator, is giving us his reflection on practice and it is a key insight – that the most easily measured skills are not the most valuable. He gives us what is probably an analytic code, and a possible way into a research question.

It is slightly difficult to code, but the fact that it is difficult to code should alert us to the fact that it may be important. The initial code I have put here is quite descriptive – 'Ease of implementation versus eventual value of skills'. Already his statement had me thinking about the concept of the difficulty of implementation or implementation trade-offs and other trade-offs that might exist in the arena of skills training in developing countries. So, it is a possibility that a future selective code might involve this notion of trade-offs.

Let us now examine the second chunk (see Figure 5.10).

Industry-specific IT skills
Another type of training that takes place is within an industry. Industry-specific training in IT skills. [...] the training is tailored to certain people and training them in the specific skills that are needed in that industry.

> **Industry-specific IT training**

[...] that tends to work best especially when the intent is to help people get a job in that industry.

> **Job-targeted IT training**

[...] one measure of success there is that people actually get jobs in that industry.

> **Job gain as success measure**

Figure 5.10   Open coding of second chunk of interview excerpt

In this chunk, we can see the open code of 'industry-specific training', together with 'job-targeted IT training'. Again, both these codes are pretty descriptive. 'Job gain as a success measure' is a more analytic code and leads us to think of what other success measures there may be.

In the third excerpt (see Figure 5.11), the interviewee discusses what he sees as locally relevant IT skills training. Here is an opportunity, immediately, to generate what Strauss (1987) calls an 'in vivo' code, which is when the naming of the code is suggested by the respondent. In vivo codes are very attractive from the researchers' perspective, for, in naming that code from the respondent's point of view, the point of view of that respondent is incorporated into the data interpretation. These codes can also give important analytic clues. Charmaz (2006) identifies three types of in vivo code.

- General terms that flag some significant meanings. She gives as an example the term 'battered woman', which, within a study, was not discovered to have the general meanings some might assume.
- Codes (and this primarily how I see them) that can be participants' innovative terms, capturing meanings or experience.
- Insider shorthand terms, such as those used in organisational settings. For instance, in some organisations there might be references to 'firefighting' as a daily part of work life.

The key thing with all these types of in vivo code, in my opinion, is that they deserve special attention precisely because they do come directly from the participants and may suggest something significant analytically. Certainly, in my experience, these codes *are* significant. For instance, in my research about systems analysts and their clients, I ended up with an in vivo code of 'imagining' after some instances of analysts saying that they were 'imagining' a particular process the clients were telling them about. This was an important analytic insight because, through the analysts' words, I realised that they did, literally, 'imagine' themselves in their clients' shoes and processes. At the time, there was very little literature about how analysts might successfully conceptualise their clients' needs.

Some researchers, such as myself, would argue that coding is a very subjective process, and that the selection of an in vivo code is similarly subjective. That said, it provides some corroboration for a particular view of the data from the respondent themselves. For other researchers coming from the critical realist position, the use of an in vivo code strengthens the authenticity of data interpretation as it is seen to come from the data itself.

Figure 5.11 shows the open coding for the third chunk.

This excerpt is very rich in open codes, which should alert us to the possibility that there is something interesting about the data. After naming 'locally relevant IT training' as an open code, which is also an in vivo code, we hit a problem – what organisations is the interviewee talking about? Do they have

Locally relevant IT skills
[...] the third area for training that we identified is when organisations are providing training that is helping people solve local problems in a way that is locally relevant. [...]

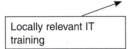

Locally relevant IT training

Local training by (local?) organisations

[Citizens] solving their own problems with the help of IT [...]

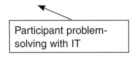

Participant problem-solving with IT

that is more in the area of community empowerment, of civic participation,

Community empowerment

of becoming more engaged citizens, of better networking with others [...]

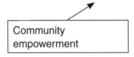

Benefits of local training

[The training] it needs to be very customised and locally relevant,

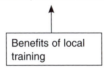

Need to customise

it's not just taking people and teaching them how to use Excel, but understanding what their situation is

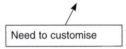

Need to understand local context

and what their problems that they are facing

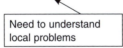

Need to understand local problems

and how IT skills can help them better solve their problems.

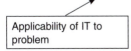

Applicability of IT to problem

(Continued)

Figure 5.11   (Continued)

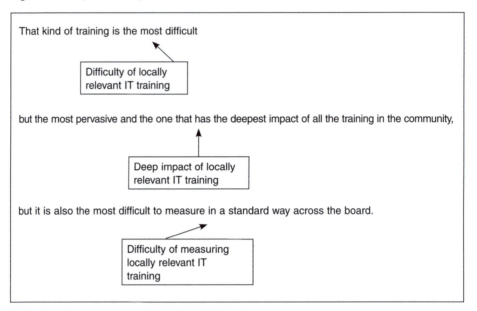

Figure 5.11   Open coding of third chunk of interview excerpt

to be local? Again, this is something that could have been followed up during the interview, but could also have been asked as a follow-up question. So, here is a compelling argument for overlapping data collection and analysis, enabling theoretical sampling – deciding on analytic grounds where to sample from next. In this case, we would have been able to find out more about the organisations in question. That said, theoretical sampling is not without its dangers – it very much depends on the framing of the research question. With a very open research question, the danger might be that you follow an analytical line of thought which later turns out to be unrewarding.

Moving on, we can see that the interviewee then mentions a key characteristic of locally relevant IT training – that it involves 'participant problem-solving with IT'. So, thinking ahead, we can wonder whether this open code is an attribute of a category of 'Locally relevant IT training' or it merely helps us to understand what may well be an interesting category. Similarly, we can see that 'community empowerment' as an open code could be a characteristic or attribute of 'Locally relevant IT training'.

The interviewee then goes on to outline a number of requirements that have to be fulfilled in order to do this type of training – the open codes 'need to customise', 'need to understand local context' and 'need to understand local problems'. He also talks about the applicability of IT to the problem, so this generates another open code. To my mind, the interviewee is pointing out that not only does the problem have to be understood but it also has to be amenable to being solved by IT.

As previously mentioned, theorising in the form of theoretical memos will generally occur during selective coding, but, as the example here shows, open coding and selective coding are not necessarily discrete stages – it is quite possible to be already anticipating selective coding while doing open coding and writing memos about key concepts.

The interviewee then talks about the difficulty of providing locally relevant IT training – this is quite an analytic code. He also talks about the 'deep impact' that such training can have. He then finishes by mentioning the difficulty of measuring such impacts (coded as 'difficulty of measuring locally relevant IT training').

From the point of view of selective coding, this is interesting. Should we couple the 'difficulty of providing locally relevant IT training' with the 'difficulty of measuring locally relevant IT training? Alternatively, is this simply that the more complex the training offering is, the more customised, the harder it is to measure? These sorts of thoughts about the data underline again, to my mind, the usefulness of carrying out overlapping collection and analysis. It would have been very useful to press the interviewee further on this issue of difficulty versus benefit.

In this example, many of the open codes seem quite descriptive and essentially summarise the data. I think this is a consequence of coding line by line, but we do have the beginnings of some analytic codes that will help us to decide what might be selective codes. In this excerpt, what is of most interest from an analytic standpoint is the issue of ease of measurement that the interviewee has raised.

Selective coding: Example 2

So, we have completed an initial open coding stage on the second excerpt. As we have attached the open codes, we have had some thoughts about the data and made efforts to not only have descriptive open codes but also, where possible, some codes that are more analytic. The number of questions raised about the data have demonstrated that, in this particular case, it might have been useful to have performed overlapping collection and analysis and asked the interviewee some further questions.

I have grouped the open codes in Table 5.3, with some tentative selective codes.

Note there are many, many decisions that can be made about this particular grouping of codes and those decisions are related to the research. For instance, we may decide that 'Locally relevant skills training' is the most interesting

Table 5.3   Possible selective codes for second example

Possible selective codes	Open codes
Generic skills training	Agencies providing generic skills, word-processing skills, Web browsing skills, e-mail skills, ease of measurement of generic skills, testing of generic skills, certification as outcome of generic skills, lack of retention of generic skills, lack of everyday usefulness of generic skills, ease of implementation versus eventual value of skills
Industry-specific IT skills training	Job-targeted IT training, job gain as success measure
Locally relevant skills training	Local training by (local?) organisations, participant problem-solving with IT, community empowerment, benefits of local training, need to customise, need to understand local context, need to understand local problem, applicability of IT to problem, difficulty of locally relevant IT training, deep impact of locally relevant IT training, difficulty of measuring locally relevant IT training

finding so far. If that is the case (and these early decisions are subject to much revision), we might think it worthy of a dedicated selective code – 'Locally relevant skills training'. Alternatively, we might decide that we want to group *all* the types of training into one selective code – 'Types of IT training'. If we did this, we could also put forward a selective code of 'Measurement of IT training'. This might suit our purposes better if our research interest was how different types of IT training might be measured. From the point of view of building a theory, though, 'Types of IT training' might be a better, larger code at a higher level of abstraction. This is why often, in my opinion, we need subcategories and more groupings than we might think, in order to get to the desired level of abstraction. This is particularly difficult for beginners, who tend to view their categories as pretty static rather than flexible. Grouping categories, then grouping them again, though, can be a useful device to help us see what the core issues and – eventually – the core categories might be.

How we group our categories also depends on our research problem. We can see here, for instance, that the issue of ease of implementation versus eventual impact is perhaps the most significant issue that the interviewee raised. The issue of measurement is also interesting. So, let's try another grouping that is less of a taxonomy of types of training, and more of a reflection on our thoughts about the benefits and measurement of types of training (see Table 5.4).

In this grouping, we can see that the focus is much more on the measurement and benefits of training rather than the individual types of training, which have been grouped into a further category of 'Types of skills training'.

Because I think it is an interesting issue, I have also created a category called the 'Context of training'. This comes from the open codes associated with 'locally relevant IT training'. One question I am asking myself at this

Table 5.4   Possible selective codes for second example – second pass

Possible selective codes	Open codes
Types of skills training	Industry-specific IT training, job-targeted IT training, agencies providing generic skills, word-processing skills, Web-browsing skills, e-mail skills, lack of everyday usefulness of generic skills, ease of implementation versus eventual value of skills, local training by (local?) organisations, participant problem-solving with IT, difficulty of locally relevant IT training
Benefits of skills training	Job gain as success measure, community empowerment, benefits of local training, certification as outcome of generic skills
Context of training	Need to understand local context, need to customise, need to understand local problem, applicability of IT to problem
Measurement of impact of skills training	Deep impact of locally relevant IT training, difficulty of measuring locally relevant IT training, ease of measurement of generic skills, testing of generic skills, lack of retention of generic skills

stage is whether or not the impact of training is related to how contextualised it is. This could be a fruitful subject for a theoretical memo. We could also ponder the relationship between 'Measurement of impact of skills training' and 'Benefits of skills training'.

When we start to ponder the relationships between selective codes in this way, we have effectively moved to the stage of theoretical coding. This example will be revisited in Chapter 6, along with the first example we looked at. We will start to think about relationships between selective codes and theorising about those relationships.

A word on software for data analysis

Once you have mastered the basics of coding, you can and should consider using a computer software package such as NVivo© or Atlas Ti© – but not before you have tried out coding *without* a package, for the reasons described below.

These packages are tremendously helpful from two perspectives. First, they help you manage all the data sources. Second, they allow you to retrieve quickly all instances of a given code. Note, though, that I think the advantages of software packages lie primarily in data *management*, rather than data *analysis* per se.

The reason for this point of view is that, after many years in IT, I have noticed that the difficulties of mastering any software package can get in the way of the basic concepts. There is, in effect, a double cognitive load – first, familiarisation with the software and, second, mastering analysis. Of the two, analysis, of course, is the most important. No software package is going to *do* the analysis for you. There is an old saying in IT – garbage in, garbage out (GIGO) – the point being that the software is only as good as the inputs you enter.

Another problem is that a software package may have embedded in it a particular view of how you should do that analysis, depending on the background of the authors of that software. So, I strongly advise that you familiarise yourself with the basic concepts of coding and try it by hand before using a software package. There are some resources regarding software packages at the end of this chapter, but do bear in mind that software packages are updated on a regular basis.

Summary

- This chapter examined, in detail, the process of open and selective coding through the use of two worked examples.
- If we look at Glaser and Strauss' original book (1967: 45) it states that the problem should 'emerge'. This does not necessarily work in practice, as it depends on the context of the research. A PhD student will not be able to say that the 'research problem will emerge' when faced with a demand for a 30-page research proposal. As discussed in Chapter 4, students will probably end up doing a 'non-committal' literature review. Also, in practice, most research, especially funded research, will already have a broad problem area in mind.
- What I hope this chapter has demonstrated is that the coding helps shape your research problem, and aspects of it do emerge when coding. Often this is hard for PhD students to accept – that detailed answers will emerge during coding, and the research problem will not remain static. To me this is also the continual delight of grounded theory, that there is always something to discover. It is very rare that something does *not* 'emerge'.
- However, if no research problem emerges, then you have to conclude that the research design is somehow flawed or the overarching research problem is ill founded. Even in that situation, the detailed coding procedures of grounded theory generally unmask some interesting aspects.
- This chapter has also attempted to give an honest insight into the coding process for first-time researchers embarking on GTM. In Figure 5.12, I give some tips for first-time coders.
- The other thing to note from this chapter is how permeable the boundaries are between selective and theoretical coding. Theoretical coding – relating selective categories to each other – is theory building. In the examples given in this chapter, we can see theory building beginning. Theoretical memos, which is when researchers break off from coding and write memos theorising about the concepts, have already been mentioned and can be used at the selective coding stage – they will also be further elaborated on in the next chapter.

1. Open coding is daunting to begin with, but, take heart and start by summarising the words in a descriptive open code. As you proceed you'll find yourself coming up with more analytic open codes, where you get at possible analytic interpretations of those words.

2. Proceed slowly, line by line. Sometimes this seems tedious and it is tempting to skip lines. Only skip lines if they are not relevant to your (hopefully very broad) research problem. There is real insight to be gained by this detailed examination – it is one of the strengths of GTM and not something to be rushed – it is here you will find the unique contributions to your research.

3. Start with pen and paper or at least a simple word-processing package, as opposed to qualitative analysis software. It's important to first concentrate on learning the process of coding, rather than be distracted by the cognitive load of learning what the software does. It's best to separate these processes and you can certainly use the software later. You can use coloured pens or highlight words on your screen.

4. Pay attention to 'in vivo' codes, which is when the naming of the code is suggested by the participant. These codes can be potentially important, for two reasons – first, they provide instant authenticity because the naming comes from the participant; and second, they can be the source of important analytic insights about the world of the participant.

5. Naming of categories, too, is all important. The name of a category gives meaning to the concept and so it should be chosen carefully. It is quite easy to pick a name for a category that is significant for you, the researcher, but has less meaning for the research audience at large. This is important because the naming will influence how people see and make sense of your emerging concepts and theory, so, it's worth checking how others perceive them and being flexible about naming.

6. As you code, ideas about selective coding – how to group categories and possible research questions – are bound to emerge. You can break off and write about your ideas in a 'theoretical memo' (discussed in more detail in the next chapter).

7. While coding, it is important to be comfortable with what seems like a lot of ambiguity and maintain a flexible mindset. Staying with the process and patiently coding line by line does bring its own rewards. During the analysis, try to stay as open-minded as possible about the data and your interpretation of it.

Figure 5.12   Tips for first-time coders

- We also saw how, in practice, researchers do start writing, thinking and theorising about the categories at the selective coding stage. As has previously been remarked, one problem that occurs in some applications of grounded theory is that the stage of theoretical coding is missed out altogether. While the richness and originality of the emergent categories is exciting, if we stop here without considering how the constructs relate, we are not building theory.

EXERCISES

1   Find an interview transcript to analyse and follow the steps suggested in this chapter. Try to start with a broad research problem. Analyse the first page or any part that seems interesting to you. If you don't have access to an interview transcript, try Masters and PhD dissertations as they often have excerpts that you can

analyse. Alternatively, try analysing a speech such as Obama's that we looked at in this chapter, or an interview in a newspaper.

2 Find a colleague to talk to about your codes – do they understand your codes and, in particular, the naming of those codes? Do they agree with how you have grouped the categories?

3 Reflect on the research problem you started with. Has it changed? Do you now have research questions that the coding process has suggested?

4 See if you can find examples of how other researchers have documented and described their coding procedures in journal papers and theses. Are the steps different? What adaptations have researchers made to these steps? Are you able to critique those procedures, based on what you have read in both Chapters 5 and 6?

WEB RESOURCES

www.qsrinternational.com/products_nvivo.aspx NVivo as per p.101 is an extremely well-known and established qualitative data analysis (QDA) software package. Visit the website for an overview. You will see that it contains key features for relating categories and managing the data.

www.atlasti.com Atlas Ti© is also a very well-known and established qualitative data analysis package. It has lots of flexibility and interesting ways of viewing the data.

http://onlineqda.hud.ac.uk/Which_software/which_package_comparison_ table.php This website gives a useful comparison of leading QDA packages. I am not sure that any package can be described as 'best' because people and their specific analysis needs vary. This website does not claim to be objective, but it does nevertheless give a very useful list of the strengths of various packages, which is very helpful.

FURTHER READING

Charmaz, K. (2006) *Constructing Grounded Theory: A practical guide through qualitative analysis.* **Thousand Oaks, CA: Sage.** This book gives very clear and helpful advice on coding. It describes the stages of initial (open), focused (selective), theoretical and axial coding (from Strauss and Corbin).

Glaser, B.G. (1978) *Theoretical Sensitivity: Advances in the methodology of grounded theory.* **Mill Valley, CA: The Sociology Press.** This book is a very significant in the GTM canon and, I think, a must if you are to understand the Glaserian approach. This book contains the very first advice given on open, selective and theoretical coding and it is an interesting and informative read.

FREQUENTLY ASKED QUESTIONS

How do I do open coding?

The answer is, do it! I can still remember how daunting it was to open code my first transcript. I'd advise doing it by hand to begin with, rather than experiencing the double cognitive burden of setting up qualitative software and thinking about how to analyse. Start with groups of words and proceed line by line. Give yourself plenty of time. You may find to begin with that your codes seem very descriptive, that you are simply labelling and/or summarising. With time, though, you'll be able to move from description to analysis and get behind the face value of the words to the meaning behind. It is also helpful to talk to your supervisor, friends or colleagues about the coding and have a session coding jointly – this gives you an idea of whether your analysis is intelligible to other people.

Should I open code all my data first before proceeding on to selective coding?

In my experience it's best to go through the first two stages – open, then selective coding – on one text, such as a transcript, to get an understanding of the coding process. When grouping the open codes together in selective codes, some analytical dimensions should emerge and even some questions about how those selective codes might relate to each other. Then you can proceed with coding the next set of texts, using the existing open codes, but also being open to new open codes suggested by the text. Having a tentative set of selective codes in the background helps sharpen the analysis.

I have conducted my interviews in another language – should I translate them all?

Many of my students have conducted fieldwork in their native language. So, what happens when there is the burden of translation on top of the coding process?

First things first. It's better to code in the language of the text, then translate the *codes* from the original language to English for the purposes of writing up. Why? The most pressing reason for doing it this way is that meanings are easier to appreciate in the native language than in a translation. You can debate the English labels for those codes with another person, to check that the English label actually coincides with the meaning you are trying to convey.

The second reason is simply that translating transcripts and documents takes time, so it makes sense to only translate the sections that are needed for the write-up of the findings. Of course, it is still important to try out the coding with your supervisor or a colleague, so you will need to do some translation early on in the process.

6

Building the theory

This chapter:

- gives two examples of theoretical coding, building on the examples in the previous chapter
- shows how relationships between categories at a lower level can be elevated
- shows how theoretical memos help us to theorise
- shows how diagrams help us understand relationships between categories.

Introduction

This chapter looks at *theoretical coding*, which, you will recall, is the process of relating categories. We do this in some detail, using the extended examples we have just seen in Chapter 5.

The previous chapter covered the first two stages of GTM – open and selective coding – and this is the third, most critical, stage: actually thinking about how the categories *relate* to each other. Without these statements of relationships, we are not theorising. If we go back to Chapter 1, where we discussed what a theory actually is, we can conclude that there are the following four components of a theory:

- **means of representation** – often in GTM this is a narrative framework, but it can also be in the form of propositions and/or an initial model
- **constructs** – in GTM, we hope to get to the stage of one or two core constructs or categories
- **statements of *relationship*** – the focus of this chapter
- **scope** – this pertains to the generalisability of the theory (in GTM, we can extend the theory through theoretical sampling, discussed in detail in Chapter 4).

Let us turn now to the point of this chapter – building the theory, using theoretical coding. We briefly discussed theoretical coding in Chapter 3, where a small example of grounded theory coding was given, and in Chapter 2, where we discussed the theoretical evolution of grounded theory. Here, I hope to show the process of theoretical coding in more detail.

As mentioned, theoretical coding is the process of relating categories and the process of theorising about those relationships. Interestingly, it is a stage quite often missed by researchers using GTM. I have lost count of the 'grounded theory' studies I have seen that, for some reason, produce fascinating categories and accounts of social worlds, with some fantastic insights, but do not culminate in a theory. They produce what Glaser called conceptual description, fully leveraging GTM's capacity to describe and build concepts without going on to the next stage. I am not sure why this is – perhaps the researchers feel that they have produced some compelling findings that stand on their own, but I also wonder if the aim has not been to produce a theory. That is not to say GTM cannot be useful when co-opted for purposes other than building theory – on the contrary, it has a long history of being a very useful qualitative analysis method. I can't help feeling, though, that sometimes the lack of moving to that next step, *relating* the categories, constitutes a missed opportunity, especially when so much care has already been taken with the first steps of the analysis.

This chapter, then, concentrates on the third step of GTM as described by Glaser (1978). This seminal book elaborated – quite brilliantly in my opinion – on the procedures outlined in the original book (Glaser and Strauss 1967). Reading this book is a revelation for the grounded theorist, simply because it contains some sympathetic and practical advice. Those who have read the books of Strauss and Corbin (Strauss and Corbin 1990; Strauss and Corbin 1998) will point out that this process of relating categories occurs in a different stage in the Straussian version – the axial coding stage – and is related to a particular coding paradigm, a particular way of relating categories. There is more information about the differences between the two strands in Chapters 2 and 3. It is altogether simpler to follow the Glaserian stages of open, selective and theoretical coding, in my opinion, as they have the virtue of being separate and easy to understand.

This chapter also discusses two key tools that really help us in this stage of theory building – theoretical memos and integrative diagrams. First, though, we need to ask the question, 'What is a theoretical code?'

What is a theoretical code?

Glaser (1978) puts it simply: there are two types of code to generate – substantive and theoretical codes. *Substantive* codes 'conceptualise the empirical substance of the area of research', while *theoretical* codes 'conceptualise how the substantive codes may relate to each other'.

Glaser points out that theoretical codes have to earn their way in the analysis, like any other code, as patterns start to emerge substantively. This narrows down the options for relating substantive codes. If you have read widely, you may already have some theoretical patterns in your heads, but Glaser warns us against 'forcing' a theoretical code on the data simply because they have 'grab' (Glaser 2005).

So, here's an interesting paradox about grounded theory. It is an inductive method that stresses emergence, but we could, potentially, derail that emergence by using a theoretical code which forces the theory down a particular route.

We have already seen coding families in Chapter 2 (Glaser 1978; Glaser 2005). Table 6.1 presents them again for your reference. What is fascinating about these codes is the options they offer. You can see echoes of many theories in them because what they do is abstract how elements of theories relate to each other.

So, these theoretical codes give many different options for relating categories and they are quite sophisticated – giving inspiration as to how we might build a theory. Yet, Glaser (2005) stresses that it is better to have no theoretical code than a forced one. It has to fit the data and assist in building the theory. It follows, of course, that the grounded theorist is not confined to Glaser's coding families. There are 18 coding families in the 1978 book and a further 23 in the 2005 book. I love the fact Glaser (2005) says the goal of a grounded theory researcher is 'to develop a repertoire of as many theoretical codes as possible' and that there could be hundreds! The point being that existing theoretical codes are there to inspire you while theorising, but, because theory-building is a creative endeavour, we can always develop our own.

You may remember that, in Chapter 3, I offered a very simple set of theoretical codes for relating categories (Spradley 1979). Spradley's book offered a coding scheme for analysing ethnographic data – he defined a 'domain' as an organising idea or concept, akin to a core category in grounded theory. The domains also contained 'folk' terms, used by the participants and equivalent to in vivo codes in grounded theory, and 'analytic terms' generated by researchers and relevant theories. Spradley's work is interesting because it illustrates that, however we approach the work of theory building, we need both concepts *and* relationships (his 'semantic relationships' are shown once more in Figure 6.1). So, I think it's quite possible to borrow ways of relating – from theories in your particular discipline and beyond, as well as from other qualitative analysis methodologies.

It's important to mention at this point, too, that an existing category can become a theoretical code. It may be that a category is, in fact, a relationship between two categories rather than a category in its own right. For instance, in my work on systems analysts and clients (Urquhart 1999) that we looked at in Chapter 3, I had a category 'Rapport building'. I could have considered this to be a relationship between the categories of 'Agenda setting' and 'Imagining' and theorised that, with appropriate rapport building by the systems

Table 6.1   A selection of open codes (Glaser 1978; 2005)

Family	Comment
The 6Cs – causes, contexts, contingencies, consequences, covariances and conditions	This basic coding family, together with the Strategy family, was adapted by Strauss and Corbin (1990) as their coding paradigm of 'causal conditions, context, intervening conditions, action/ interaction strategies and consequences'.
Process – stages, staging, phases, phasing, progresssions, passages, gradations, transititions, steps, ranks, careers, ordering, trajectories, chains, sequencings, etc.	Glaser remarks that a process should have at least two stages. This family is similar to Spradley's 'a stage of'.
Dimension family – dimensions, elements, division, piece of, properties of, facet, slice, sector, portion, segment, part, aspect, section	As Glaser says, the more we learn about a category, the more we see of its dimensions. Of all theoretical codes, this is one that all researchers are likely to use. It is, of course, very similar to Spradley's 'is a part of'. It's also important to realise that, when theorising, we can privilege one dimension over another – it can become a full-blown category.
Type family – type, form, kinds, styles, classes, genre	Glaser says, while dimensions divide up the whole, types show variations *in* the whole. So, for instance, you might have a number of styles of strategies, such as those in the conversation between a systems analyst and client in the example in Table 3.2.
Strategy family – strategies, tactics, mechanisms, managed, way, manipulation, manoeuvrings, dealing with, handling, techniques, ploys, means, goals, arrangements, dominating, positioning	As previously remarked, the Strauss and Corbin coding paradigm seems to be a mixture of this family and the first family.
Moment capture, when a quick intervention is critical to causing an optimal outcome, such as closing a deal	This is a new theoretical code introduced in Glaser's 2005 book.
Frames, which are excavated through discourse patterns and are sociocultural in nature	Also in the 2005 book. I used this idea in my own dissertation work in 1999.
Causal family – a relative of the 6Cs family, it includes several aspects: 1) bias random walk, 2) amplifying causal looping, 3) conjectural causation, 4) repetitive causal reproductions, 5) equifinality, 6) reciprocal causation, 7) triggers, 8) causal paths, 9) perpetual causal looping	Glaser (2005) gives some wonderful nuances of causation in this theoretical code family. 'Bias random walk' – all variables are in a flux, 'then on the introduction of a crucial variable … then of a sudden all of the variables fall into organisation'. 'Amplifying causal looping' – 'consequences become causes, and one sees either worsening or improving progressions or escalating severity'. 'Conjectural causation' – it is not always easy to identify decisive causal combinations. 'Repetitive causal reproductions' – a repeated action keeps producing the same consequences. 'Equifinality' – no matter what the causes and paths, the same consequence will occur. 'Reciprocal causation' – there is a similar interaction of effects or amplified causal looping. 'Triggers' – sudden causes that set off a consequence or set of consequences. 'Causal paths' – used to intervene in changing or stopping a consequence. 'Perpetual causal looping' – a mathematical model, an ordered calculated growth of increased size based on a set temporal path.

- Is a kind of
- Is a part of/a place in
- Is a way to
- Is used for
- Is a reason for, is a stage of
- Is a result/cause of, is a place for
- Is a characteristic of

Figure 6.1   Spradley's (1979) semantic relationships

analyst during agenda setting, more mutual 'imagining' of the system problem would occur.

So, to conclude this section, we can say that theoretical codes inspire us to think about different relationships between categories. These codes can be inspired by existing theories, as with some of Glaser's 'coding families', or other qualitative data analysis methods. Strauss and Corbin (Strauss 1987; Strauss and Corbin 1990) offer coding paradigms, which are also theoretical codes, but it is important to remember that we cannot force the data down a particular road and we can generate our *own* theoretical codes! Theoretical codes can also come from the process of theoretical memoing, which the next section looks at in detail.

Theoretical memos

As discussed in Chapter 4, theoretical memos are a vital tool for theorising. They allow researchers to break off during the coding process whenever good ideas occur to them and write them down in a theoretical memo. During my own PhD thesis writing, I found that a large percentage of the theoretical memoing I had done found its way into the findings and discussion sections of the thesis. This in itself should give you an idea of the benefits of memoing – that valuable and creative ideas about the findings and relationships between categories are written down during the process of analysis. They capture the 'lightbulb' moments we have about the data. Glaser (1978) gives some useful rules for generating memos, which are expressed in Figure 6.2.

My own experience of theoretical memoing has been a tremendously exciting and fruitful one and, to a large extent, I did follow the rules in Figure 6.2. Where possible, I 'grounded' my memos with examples from the data. It really did help, though, to have a process where I could step back from the data and abstract – let my mind run free through various possibilities. This

1. Keep memos and data separate – this helps the process of abstraction. You can, though, put individual examples of data instances in a memo if necessary.
2. Always interrupt coding for the writing of a memo, so the idea is not lost.
3. You can begin a memo by choosing to write about a code, but, if it is not flowing, don't force the process.
4. Don't be afraid to amend earlier memos.
5. Keep a list of emergent codes handy.
6. If too many memos on different codes are the same, think about whether or not those codes need to be merged or if you need to compare their dimensions for differences.
7. Follow through problematic digressions conceptually, but don't forget to 'ground' those digressions in data.
8. Keep on memoing for as long as resources allow.
9. When memoing, talk conceptually; do not talk about people.
10. If you have two burning ideas, write one up at a time, so you don't lose either of them.
11. Indicate in the memo if you think the category is now saturated.
12. Always be flexible with your memoing – if new ways of doing memos occur, follow them if they are worthwhile.

Figure 6.2   Rules for theoretical memos (adapted from Glaser 1978)

process helps with abstraction because we clearly distinguish the (sometimes mundane) process of coding from the creative process of theorising. In Figure 6.3, I give an example of a theoretical memo I wrote for my dissertation.

As I hope you can see from this example, my efforts to define 'Agenda setting' as a category led to some deep consideration of the consequences of analysts setting the agenda in conversations with their clients and how they might conceptualise the information systems problem. I was also interested in how this category might relate to existing bodies of literature, such as communications research. Subsequently, this category emerged as a major finding. If you look carefully at the theoretical memo in Figure 6.3, you can also see that I actively considered the notion of agenda setting as a relationship between codes – that is, a possible theoretical code.

I hope you can also see that, once the meaning of a category has been discussed in a theoretical memo like this, it is easy to literally 'cut and paste' some of these memos into the final write-up. I would go so far as to say that time spent writing theoretical memos is never wasted because it beats staring out of the window, wondering about your data and allows you to *productively* explore issues around your analysis.

It has often been said that writing is thinking. I encourage all my postgraduate students to start writing as soon as possible, especially during the analysis. The nature of theorising in grounded theory makes it very difficult to separate out the (sometimes mechanical, sometimes not) analysis process, from the theorising write-up. Therefore it's a disaster for postgraduate students using grounded theory to take the traditional attitude that they will first code the

Agenda setting as a key to both conceptualisation and tactics   ID 5297

The purpose of this memo is to try and clarify a few thoughts on *agenda setting*. Agenda setting has many elements, both conceptual and tactical. It could be defined as the process by which a participant (generally the analyst) sets out the topic for discussion, sometimes the process for managing that topic. Another way of viewing agenda setting is that it comprises a framework for conceptualisation and negotiation (which is a tactical element). Who actually sets the agenda for discussion gives some indicators as to the type of relationship between the analyst and client (cf Hirschiem's four models). There is evidence in negotiation literature that whoever sets up the framework for discussion is at a tactical advantage.

The way the topic is introduced gives many clues as to how the participant is conceptualising the problem. Therefore, by looking at how the analyst defines the problem, we can gain insight into the conceptual schema the analyst is using. What is also of interest is if this conceptual schema influences the solution proffered in the conversation. More broadly, the notion of a conceptual schema that the analyst employs can be seen to be important in the design of information systems. For instance, if the problem is narrowly defined by virtue of the conceptual schema, then the resultant design may be similarly narrow in scope. As the design of information systems rests purely on concepts, then the conceptual schema used becomes very important.

In addition, by examining how the client presents the problem, one can judge if differing schemas are bridged in a joint conceptualisation. If analysts recognise the schemas they are applying to an information system, then they can perhaps apply one or a number of schemas that are appropriate for the problem. It may be that bringing in a too rigid conceptual schema limits the solution and broader schemas are appropriate. It may also be that a tactic of information gathering, without bringing in a particular schema, might be more successful.

Agenda setting can be seen as a mediating process between tactics and concepts. As such, it could be construed as a relationship. It also provides a bridge between structure of the text and the social processes evidenced by the text, thus helping to resolve the structural/processual dichotomy encountered when analysing discourse. As agenda setting contains both conceptual and tactical elements, one can deduce from the text: the concepts that are informing tactics; how the problem is formulated influences tactics; how the tactics used by both participants influence joint conceptualisation.

Possibly, agenda setting is the core category of the study – that process of *how* analysts and clients reach agreement (which, after all, is the research question). Although the term agenda setting implies a starting point, communications research has put forward the notion of topic as a chain of subtopics – this also fits in neatly with the idea of evolving conceptualisation. The rest of this memo will give instances of agenda setting and its elements and will discuss how it might play a role in linking concepts and tactics.

Agenda setting and its elements

In both Cases 1 and 4, the analyst outlines the purpose of the discussion and this can be seen as setting the agenda for the subsequent discussion.

Case 1

1 'What I've done Jane I've drawn up a couple of points from when we talked last … when you gave me an overview of the system'

Apart from using a number of personal references as a tactic construed as joint ownership, this can be seen as putting forward a general *conversation topic* (a couple of points) using a *prop* (I've drawn up). This can be seen as a tactic.

5 'Basically what I've got down here is the database is about keeping statistics ... for a Student Assistance Scheme.'

The analyst refers to a *computer term* – 'the database' – almost immediately. One could deduce, then, that he sees the database as being of primary importance in solving the problem. Not surprising as presumably he is someone whose role it is to provide computer expertise. He then outlines the *system purpose* – a Student Assistance Scheme, and the *system function* – keeping statistics.

These codes can be seen as referring to conceptualisation.

Figure 6.3   Example of a theoretical memo (Urquhart 1999)

data, then write the findings up later. The overlapping processes of coding and theoretical memoing are what build the theory and have the added advantage of productivity, too. The findings are already, in a sense, being written up through the theoretical memos, even if not all are used in the final write-up.

Glaser (1978) talks about the importance of 'sorting' what can be termed a 'fund' of memos. Why is this? Well, memos are usually written in succession, over a long period of time, so are unlikely to occur in a perfectly analytic order. So, sorting the memos gives rise to new analytic insights as the memos are grouped together. Glaser (1978) also points out that a memo fund is the source of all writings from a grounded theory study. Certainly I found that to be so.

Charmaz (2006) offers the following possibilities for memos, outlined in Figure 6.4.

Note that Charmaz is expanding the possibilities for theoretical memos implied by Glaser's initial rules by suggesting that memos can be used to compare data with data and bring in raw data. The list in Figure 6.4 illustrates, too, how memos can be used to refine the coding process in quite a structured way and couples them with the coding process even more tightly than suggested by Glaser.

I would also add another possibility to this list – using a memo to not only develop the definition of a category but also explore what bodies of theory or literature might be relevant to that category. Again, this can lead to ideas for theoretical codes. I've also used memos to take stock of the analysis, and plan future theoretical sampling on the basis of that analysis.

In short, theoretical memos are a wonderful, flexible tool that can be used to support theorising in multiple ways. They could even contain diagrams, because diagrams can help us theorise, too. The next section looks at how they can support the theorising process.

- Defining each code or category by its analytic properties.
- Detailing processes subsumed by codes or categories.
- Making comparisons between data and data, data and codes, codes and codes, codes and categories, categories and categories.
- Bringing in raw data.
- Providing enough empirical evidence to support your claims about the category.
- Offering some conjectures to check in the field.
- Identifying gaps in the analysis.
- Interrogating a code or category by asking questions of it.

Figure 6.4   Possibilities for memos (Charmaz 2006)

Integrative diagrams

Something interesting happens when we put categories into a diagram. Strauss (1987) calls them *integrative diagrams* and I think that is a good term. He defines them as a visual device that furthers cumulative integration and gives rules of thumb for such diagrams (see Figure 6.5).

Many years ago, I can remember trying to make sense of my grounded theory categories when writing up my PhD thesis. Armed with a large glass of red wine (though this is not compulsory for analysis!) and piles of transcripts around me, I kept on drawing until I had integrated my categories into one final diagram. It goes without saying that the thinking behind such integration triggered a lot of writing, too.

Strauss (1987) makes an important point in his book that these diagrams build on each other. There may be many versions of those diagrams and they build on each other through a process of testing and questioning. Figure 6.6

1. An integrative diagram gives a clear picture of where you have come from after data collection, coding and memoing. It puts together in a larger (albeit provisional) form a lot of otherwise scattered materials.
2. An integrative diagram gives direction to the research. Just as with operational (ongoing) diagrams, black boxes will need to be opened up and relationships between them specified and clarified.
3. Integrative diagrams need to be related to the separate analytic clusters provided by ongoing diagrams and memo sorting.
4. There should not be *one* integrative diagram but a succession of them – each diagram incorporating the preceding one.
5. The number of such diagrams should not be numerous – it's important to not be obsessive about such diagrams at every point in the project. You are ready to draw another diagram if you look at it and it fails to incorporate what you now know.

Figure 6.5   Rules of thumb for integrative diagrams (adapted from Strauss 1987)

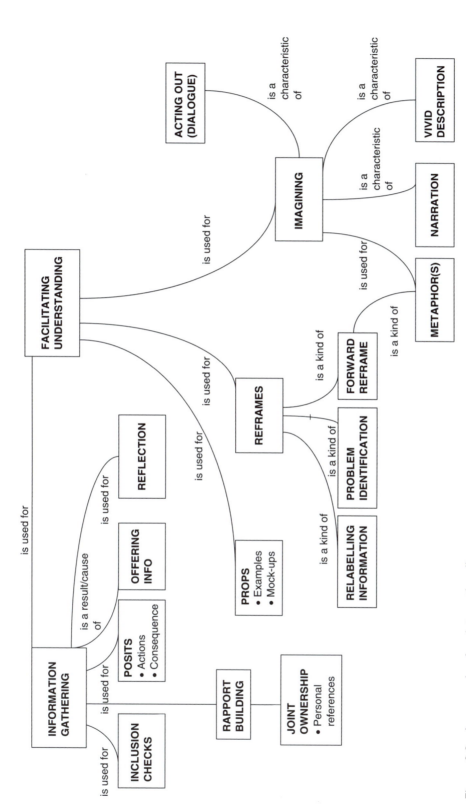

Figure 6.6   An example of an integrative diagram

is an example. It helped me see how my categories might relate and which might be subsidiary to others.

The key thing about such diagrams, if done carefully, is that they force us into thinking about the categories as not static textual concepts but conceptual objects that *relate* to each other. I cannot stress enough how important relating the categories is. Without thinking about relationships, we cannot claim to be building theory.

Often with grounded theory work, I come across diagrams of the categories that do not show relationships between them. Until we have related our categories, our thinking is not done. This is actually the most rewarding, and intellectually demanding, stage of grounded theory.

It is obvious, then, that the theoretical coding stage is as much about the relationships between categories as it is about the categories themselves. It is when we theorise about the data.

Let's now return to our extended examples of coding, started in Chapter 5, and apply the theoretical coding stage to them. In these extended examples you will see how both theoretical memos and diagrams are applied.

Theoretical coding: Example 1

We left off the example from Obama's inauguration speech with some unresolved questions about the relationships between the codes and three emerging possible questions.

> What are the major themes of the speech?
> Who are the key audiences of the speech?
> What techniques does Obama use to reconcile different audiences?

We also realised that some selective codes could be merged, so 'Historicity' was merged with 'American identity' to produce the selective codes shown in Table 6.2.

The emergent research questions give us a clue as to how we might organise our selective codes. For a parsimonious theory, where we trade off some explanatory power for the sake of simplicity, both Glaser (1978) and Strauss (1987) recommend having one or two core categories. Three also seems reasonable in this case. What if we were to have three major categories that correspond to the research issues that have emerged? Figure 6.7 shows these in an integrative diagram and groups the selective codes.

This, of course, is not the only potential grouping and this is both the delight and occasional curse of grounded theory. For instance, the selective code 'Higher purpose' is intriguing. It is possibly related to 'American identity',

Table 6.2 Selective codes for Example 1

Possible selective codes	Open codes
Diversity	Diversity as a strength, as history, different religions, non-believers, inclusiveness, from every place
A changing world	A defining moment, need to adapt to a changing world, a more connected world
Peacemaking	Hatred as a thing of the past, tribalism as a thing of the past, humanism the dominant force, appeal to enemies, appeal for constructiveness
Higher purpose	Higher purpose in military service, appeal to a higher purpose
America's role	America's new role of peacemaker, mutual respect and interests, anonymous naming and shaming, America's role unfolding
Different audiences	Appeal to Muslim world, appeal for constructiveness, honouring soldiers in combat, unique role of soldiers, role of military in guarding freedoms, serving others
Rhetorical devices	Use of metaphor, choice of examples, balancing statements
American identity	Nation relies on individuals, individuals who were kind during Katrina, individuals who save others' jobs, importance of individuals, heroes and unsung heroes, historicity, Civil war, segregation, historic role of military

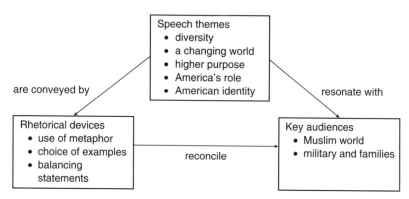

Figure 6.7 Potential selective codes for Example 1

in that religion plays a prominent role in the history of the country. For some researchers, this would be an emerging research question of interest. The stress on the individual – shown in the open codes in Table 6.2 as part of 'American identity' – would also stand out to those interested in American culture.

So, at the theoretical coding stage, it is very clear that there will be some toing and froing between this stage and the previous one of selective coding.

There can, and should be, reflexivity between the two stages. As the research questions, which are dimensions of the initial research problem, emerge, then there is bound to be some reflection on the selective codes. Aspects that can influence reorganisation of selective codes and the theoretical coding stage include:

- open codes that are in themselves so interesting they suggest a research question all by themselves – for instance, in this case, the role of the individual in the selective code 'American identity'
- open codes that suggest a relationship between selective codes – for instance, the open code of 'balancing statements' suggests the need to reconcile different audiences by use of same.

At this stage, it is important to consider the relationships in detail because, by doing so, we start to build theory. So, let's attempt to relate the three selective codes we have:

- We can come up with a relationship of 'reconcile' between the categories 'Rhetorical devices' and 'Key audiences', as it is clear that these are the devices used to help reach – and reconcile – different audiences.
- When considering the relationship between the categories 'Speech themes' and 'Key audiences', we can see that certain themes relate to certain audiences – for instance, the emphasis on diversity will resonate with the world audience – so, for this relationship, I chose 'resonate with'.
- When considering the relationship between the categories 'Speech themes' and 'Rhetorical devices', we can see that the devices are used 'to convey' those themes and we could speculate about which devices might be used to convey which themes.

These are my own, self-generated *theoretical codes* for relating these categories. Once we have arrived at such relationships or theoretical codes, it's also important to make sure we have instances of those theoretical codes. So, for instance, we could point to the statement in Obama's speech, 'To those who cling to power through corruption and deceit and the silencing of dissent, know that you are on the wrong side of history, but that we will extend a hand if you are willing to unclench your fist' as an instance of these relationships.

So, why use a coding family or the Strauss and Corbin coding paradigm instead of your own theoretical codes? Simply because they help us think about theory in general, and how theory might be constructed. Coding families can provide a useful jumping off point to consider the theory we are developing. For instance, let's consider a few coding families from Glaser (1978) that might be relevant to our example.

- Strategy family: strategies, tactics, mechanisms, managed, way, manipulation, manoeuvrings, dealing with, handling, techniques, ploys, means, goals, arrangements, dominating, positioning.

- Process: stages, staging, phases, phasing, progressions, passages, gradations, transitions, steps, ranks, careers, ordering, trajectories, chains, sequencings.

The first family is directly relevant to our research problem. It might be that we can identify further techniques and ploys in the speech and consider how Obama positions the themes.

The second family also gives pause for thought. Is there a sequence to the speech? Can particular stages be identified? Particular transitions in the speech, for instance, where Obama moves from one audience to another?

We could also take a simpler option for relating the categories, one mentioned in Chapter 3 – Spradley's (1979) relationships, mentioned in his book *The Ethnographic Interview*, shown once more for you in Figure 6.8. If you are finding it hard to relate categories, these relationships provide an easy way to start thinking about them.

At this point, you can start writing theoretical memos about the categories and their relationships, if you have not done so already.

As previously discussed in this chapter, theoretical memos are a method used within GTM (but not confined to it) that help us elaborate on ideas. They can be written at any stage in the coding, but are more commonly written in the selective and theoretical coding stages. You simply break off from coding at any point to write down ideas that occur. This is a wonderful aspect of GTM – one that allows for inspiration and creativity to be captured as it occurs. Usually, GTM theses can be relied on to produce some unique insights and, usually, researchers use theoretical memos to aid them in that process. Figure 6.9 shows an example of a fragment of a possible theoretical memo for Example 1.

This theoretical memo also helps us think about *theoretical sampling* – thinking about where to sample from next based on emerging concepts from the data. For instance, are the concepts emerging from Obama's speech unique and peculiar to his style of oratory or are they more general and do all great political speechmakers use these techniques? How might we expand and densify the theory by sampling other speeches?

- Is a kind of
- Is a part of/a place in
- Is a way to
- Is used for
- Is a reason for, is a stage of
- Is a result/cause of, is a place for
- Is a characteristic of

Figure 6.8   Spradley's (1979) semantic relationships

Rhetorical devices to reconcile

This theoretical memo has two purposes: first to think about rhetorical devices; second to think about how those devices might relate to key audiences.

The most obvious instance of a rhetorical device is the use of balancing statements. An example of such a statement in context is:

> To those who cling to power through corruption and deceit and the silencing of dissent, know that you are on the wrong side of history, but that we will extend a hand if you are willing to unclench your fist.

This statement faces both ways, in that the first part of it, about being on the wrong side of history, is directed at the domestic audience, while the second part is addressed at the international audience.

So what might be the relationship to key audiences? Clearly in this case, the balancing statement, 'we will extend a hand if you are willing to unclench your fist', is helping to *reconcile* the domestic and overseas audience. It is also using a metaphor. So, we can safely say that metaphors might be used in this way.

What if we look at the code choice of examples? Does that also reconcile audiences? He mentions individuals involved in Hurricane Katrina, individuals who cut hours to save jobs, firefighters, parents. It seems here he is reconciling different audiences within the USA, both white and black, both working-class and middle-class and so on. See the statement below.

> It is the kindness to take in a stranger when the levees break, the selflessness of workers who would rather cut their hours than see a friend lose their job which sees us through our darkest hours. It is the firefighter's courage to storm a stairway filled with smoke, but also a parent's willingness to nurture a child that finally decides our fate.

So, I think the theoretical code 'reconcile', so far, holds over different instances of rhetorical devices. It would be useful to look at the rest of the inaugural speech to see if there are more instances of this relationship.

This issue of different audiences has been picked up by political commentators such as Fever (2010) and it is pointed out that people from both home and abroad will be listening very carefully to what Obama says about Iraq and those audiences will interpret the same remarks very differently.

The speech also uses 'antithesis', when the audience is invited to contrast two different outcomes (Gorton 2010). It seems that, in this case, the speech uses the device of antithesis to help it make balancing statements. The speech also uses imagery in the form of metaphor to evoke an emotional response – apparently, a speech is much more memorable if it contains visual images.

Figure 6.9   Example of a fragment of a theoretical memo

In the next chapter, we'll return to this example, to consider the issue of how we deal with levels of theory. One of the major criticisms of grounded theory in the past has been that it tends to produce low-level theories. How can we best respond to this challenge? In Chapter 7, I'll discuss what the options might be when 'scaling up' your theory and relating it to the literature.

Theoretical coding: Example 2

Let's now turn to the second extended example. You will recall that, in Example 2 in Chapter 5, we suggested two different options for selective coding. The first simply selectively coded the different types of training. The second pass looked a bit deeper and tried to surface issues about the impact of the training and the measurement of that impact. Table 6.3 shows those selective codes again.

At this point, we should be aware that there is an interaction between our emerging analysis and the research questions. One of the most interesting aspects of the interview is the idea that the impact of the IT skills training is hard to measure and the locally relevant training has the most impact. So, one emerging research question might be:

* 'How can we measure the impact of IT skills training?'

Another might be:

* 'How important is the context of IT skills training?'

Figure 6.10 shows what happens if we put our selective codes into an integrative diagram and try to relate the codes. A number of things become clear when we examine the diagram.

Table 6.3 Selective codes for Example 2

Possible selective codes	Open codes
Types of skills training	Industry-specific IT training, job-targeted IT training, agencies providing generic skills, word-processing skills, Web-browsing skills, e-mail skills, lack of everyday usefulness of generic skills, ease of implementation versus eventual value of skills, local training by (local?) organisations, participant problem-solving with IT, difficulty of locally relevant IT training
Benefits of skills training	Job gain as success measure, community empowerment, benefits of local training, certification as outcome of generic skills
Context of training	Need to understand local context, need to customise, need to understand local problem, applicability of IT to problem
Measurement of impact of skills training	Deep impact of locally relevant IT training, difficulty of measuring locally relevant IT training, ease of measurement of generic skills, testing of generic skills, lack of retention of generic skills

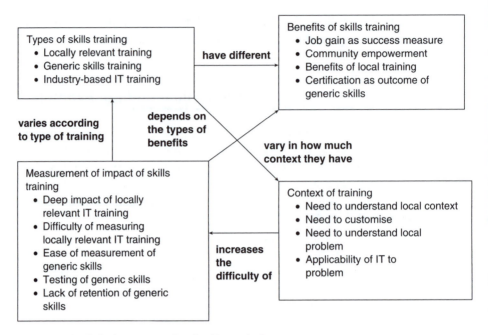

Figure 6.10   Relating categories for Example 2

We can re-examine the status of the 'Context of training' category. The open codes in that box are all associated with locally relevant IT training. Does this matter? Again, it is a question of emphasis and what research questions emerge. As a researcher working on this example, I decided that context *was* important and, possibly, a dimension of the research problem. Ideally, we could use this as a basis for theoretical sampling (deciding on analytic grounds where to sample from next), asking future interviewees what role they felt context or the environment might play in IT skills training. Having a selective code of context has allowed us to think about the relationship of context to all types of training, which may help us theorise about the role of context in *all* training.

Note, too, that the theoretical codes in this example, as in the previous one, are researcher-generated. We could also see if there are any *existing* theoretical codes to help us theorise – for instance, Glaser's (2005) 'Cross pressures' theoretical code (about when people are subject to diverse external pressures) could apply to the relationship between 'Measurement of impact on skills training' and 'Benefits of skills training'.

As soon as we think about relationships in this example, we are in interesting territory, which makes for some interesting theorising. For instance, it is clear that, the more intangible the benefit, the harder it is to measure the impact. Yet, the intangible benefits of such training may have more of an impact. Here is fertile ground for a theoretical memo. In Figure 6.11, I give an example of a theoretical memo about the measurement of impact and its relationship to the categories of 'Types of skills training' and 'Context of training'.

Measurement of impact and variation according to type and context of training

This memo looks at possibly the most interesting finding of the interview – that the IT skills training with the most impact (locally relevant IT skills training) was also the most difficult to measure. This discussion affects the category 'Measurement of impact of skills training' and the relationships (or theoretical codes) this category has with the category 'Types of skills training' and 'Context of training'. When talking about ease of measurement, the interviewee says:

> Those are the easiest ones to measure because you can have them [the people] a test […] you can issue a certification based on that. Now, we have also found that it is the one that has the least retention and maybe the least usefulness for people to actually solve their everyday problems.

What are we to make of this statement by the interviewee? It's certainly true to say that it is easier to measure certification or a job gained, as these are quantitative measures. So, the type of training determines the measurement. The interviewee is very insistent that locally relevant training has impact. How might we measure the impact of locally relevant training? Clearly, by what might be deemed as successful by the participants in that particular context. So, how would that be measured? The first thing that occurs is, this measurement would be qualitative and might include such things as people feeling that their lives had been improved by locally relevant IT training. A broader implication of this is that qualitative measures might not be taken that seriously by policymakers, despite this interviewee's view that this type of training has impact. One key thought here is that measurement of impact *varies according to* the type of training. So, this is one possible relationship or theoretical code we can posit between 'Measurement of impact of skills training' and 'Types of skills training'. It is also clearly related to the context of such training. Given the interviewee's insistence on the importance of context and the point made about the difficulty of measuring context-based training, we could say that the 'Context of training' *increases the difficulty of* 'Measurement of impact of skills training'.

Can we point to some data to ground this relationship of 'varies according to'? When talking about generic skills, we already know that the interviewee says it can be evaluated by certification.

When talking about industry-based training, he says:

> one measure of success there is that people actually get jobs in that industry.

When talking about locally relevant training he says:

> solving their own problems with the help of IT […] that is more in the area of community empowerment, of civic participation, of becoming more engaged citizens, of better networking with others […]

So, we can definitely say that the measurement would certainly vary according to the type of training.

What about the relationship 'increases the difficulty of' between 'Context of training' and 'Measurement of impact of skills training'? Can this also be grounded? The interviewee says of the measurement of locally relevant training:

> That kind of training is the most difficult but the most pervasive and the one that has the deepest impact of all the training in the community, but it is also the most difficult to measure

(Continued)

Figure 6.11   (Continued)

He also says:

> I have designed and set up an evaluation and monitoring system for [...] it's a combination
> of multiple approaches to evaluation. One of them is very quantitative [...] One of them is
> very qualitative [...]

One inference from this statement we could make is that qualitative measures are needed to
evaluate the impact of locally relevant training. Certainly, it would be hard to quantitatively
measure community empowerment. Possibly we can link this back also to the difficulty of
measuring the impact of locally relevant training.

What exactly is meant by impact? We assume that, from the interviewee's perspective, impact
is linked to development and this impact is also long-lasting. At this point, it's worth thinking
about how we might develop such measures of impact. For instance, the open codes tell us
that the problem with generic skills training is it is not easily retained. So, one dimension of
impact could be that the change lasts over a period of time and is deemed to have been
sustained. There are various literatures that we could look at this point. For instance,
evaluation theories. There are many ways to evaluate development projects, but, historically,
IT projects have been less well evaluated. Why? For complex reasons, such as the difficulties
with measurement that we are talking about now, but also possibly because IT projects have
an element of 'build it and they will come' – that is, almost magical properties are assigned to
IT (Ramiller 2001). If we look at development theories, why not evaluate an IT skills
programme using the five freedoms proposed by Sen (1999), which includes not only
economic aspects, but also social opportunities.

Figure 6.11   Example of a theoretical memo for Example 2

Another important point to raise here is the importance of discussing your
selective codes with a colleague. It is good to try out the codes, their meanings and relationships, with a 'critical friend', such as a colleague or dissertation supervisor. As you theorise, it's really important that people understand the components in your theory and what is meant by a particular
concept. If the emerging theory is not immediately understandable by a
colleague once you have given a careful explanation, then this points to
problems of conceptualisation or how you justify that conceptualisation. In
GTM, researchers can usually point to a saturated category as justification,
so the issue is much more likely to be how you have conceptualised that
particular category and what role it plays in your emerging theory. It may
also be around how you are using your theoretical codes to relate those categories.

If you are working within a positivist framework, this issue of inter-coder
reliability is important, and the process you follow needs to be carefully documented. Generally, it's useful to get other coders to code the same transcript
or, ideally, a broad sample of transcripts and agree on the selective codes.
For instance, in Levina and Vaast (2005), coding interpretations were actively

challenged by dint of each author writing up their analysis of the case. Interpretations were also checked with participants to ensure their rigour.

In the next chapter, we'll return to this extended example to consider the issue of how we deal with levels of theory. In Chapter 7, I'll discuss what the options might be when 'scaling up' your theory and relating it to the literature.

Summary

- This chapter examined the act of theoretical coding through two extended examples that we first looked at in Chapter 5. It also discussed the role of theoretical memos and integrative diagrams in supporting theoretical coding.
- What exactly a theoretical code might comprise of was discussed. A theoretical code is one that defines the relationship between two substantive codes.
- Different options for theoretical codes were discussed, such as Glaser's theoretical codes and ways of naming relationships. It was also pointed out that theoretical codes are very often researcher-generated rather than previously existing. To try and impose a theoretical code on your data would be tantamount to 'forcing' the theory down a certain path.
- Coding families, as suggested by Glaser (1978, 2005), and the coding paradigm, as suggested by Strauss (1987) and Strauss and Corbin (1990), can give ideas for relationships between codes. Spradley's (1979) nine semantic relationships ('is a way to', 'is a part of' and so on) can also provide a simple and helpful starting point for thinking about relationships.
- Theoretical memos are key tools at this stage and highly recommended. They can also be used during the selective coding stage. Theoretical memos help us capture key ideas about the data and often prove to contain creative insights regarding the emerging theory, so tend to find their way into the final write-up of the research. Theoretical memos also provide an opportunity to start relating the emergent theory to the extant literature – again, this is useful for the final write-up.
- Integrative diagrams help us think about relationships between categories and the grouping of categories. It is likely, too, that the first integrative diagram you draw will not be your last – they tend to build on each other, reflecting the theory-building process.
- The processes of selective coding and theoretical coding are reflexive rather than sequential. Although the phases are presented sequentially for the purposes of this book, the examples show how there is considerable overlap between the stages. What tends to happen is that aspects of the research problem emerge at this stage, which then prompts a reconsideration of the selective codes and, sometimes, also the open codes. For instance, during theoretical coding, an open code may be so interesting, on reflection, that it suggests a research question. This means that the open code needs to be elevated and the codes regrouped. Another possibility is that an open code suggests a relationship between selective codes.
- In Figure 6.12 overleaf I give some tips for the theoretical coding stage, based on this chapter.

1. Theoretical coding is an incredibly important point in coding – it builds theory and adds immeasurably to your findings. Without the theoretical coding stage, we are not doing grounded theory.

2. It's an exciting stage of grounded theory because this is where the theorising happens. Theoretical memos are a vital tool to help this theorising.

3. There is a balance to be found between the concept of theoretical sensitivity (Glaser 1978), where we find inspiration for theoretical codes from existing theories, and making sure we don't impose those theoretical codes on the data in our enthusiasm.

4. The stage of theoretical coding inevitably brings a reconsideration of categories, so be prepared to regroup and reconsider your categories.

5. This stage also brings into focus the research question and suggests new routes for theoretical sampling.

6. When you have come up with a relationship, revisit your data – does the relationship properly express what is in the data?

7. It is important to discuss the naming of categories and how they relate to each other with colleagues. This is because the meaning of the theory is expressed through that naming.

Figure 6.12   Tips on theoretical coding

EXERCISES

1   Continue to analyse the interview transcript you sourced when you did the first exercise in Chapter 5. Apply theoretical coding to your selective coding. Write a theoretical memo. Try applying a theoretical coding family or paradigm, as well as generating your own theoretical codes.

2   Consider how you would theoretically sample for more data, based on your emerging core categories. How would you further sample for your emerging relationships?

3   Reflect on your experience of theoretical coding. Did you regroup codes? Has the research problem changed? What difficulties did you encounter?

WEB RESOURCES

http://shadow.foreignpolicy.com/posts/2010/08/29/what_can_obama_say_about_iraq Peter Fever (2010) 'What can Obama say about Iraq?', *Foreign Policy Magazine*, 29 August.

www.suite101.com/content/language-techniques-of-effective-speech-making-a222379 Angela Gorton (2010) 'Language techniques of effective speech making', 7 April.

FURTHER READING

Glaser, B. J. (2005) *The Grounded Theory Perspective III: Theoretical coding.* Mill Valley, CA: The Sociology Press.* This book gives an inspired and honest account of the issues around theoretical coding.

Levina, N. and Vaast, E. (2005) 'The emergence of boundary spanning competence in practice: Implications for implementation and use of information systems', *MIS Quarterly, 29* (2): 335–63. This paper gives an interesting account of grounded theory generation from a positivist perspective. It is notable for two reasons: it is very clear that its aim is to generate a formal theory; it shows clearly through its explanation of its coding methodology how rigour was ensured.

FREQUENTLY ASKED QUESTIONS

I have too many core categories, what do I do?

I have lost count of how many times this issue comes up and it is almost bound to, given that the analysis starts with line-by-line coding.

The simple answer is to regroup the categories into larger ones. So, even if you feel you have gone through all three stages of open coding, selective coding and theoretical coding, reconsider those selective codes and see if you can group them again. Consider that the founders of GTM suggested having one or two core categories. If you can get to this level of abstraction, it is much, much, easier to engage your theory with higher-level ones. You can still report the richness of your findings via the lower-level categories, but the more abstracted your categories are, the more likely you are to be able to make a clear theoretical contribution.

I have lots of relationships between lower-level categories, but it's hard to think of relationships between my core categories – what do I do?

Consider carefully those relationships between the lower-level categories. It may be that you can elevate one of those relationships to become a major relationship. Given that there may be competing relationships among subcategories, it takes a lot of thinking and theorising to decide what might be the most important and, possibly, a reconsideration of the major category itself. Obviously it is helpful to write a theoretical memo about possible relationships.

Another possibility is to come up with an entirely *new* relationship, inspired by your own thinking, existing theoretical codes you know of and theories you have come across. Once you have a relationship, consider if it is justified by the data.

Surely, if I find a theoretical family and fit my data to it, this is forcing! I don't understand how we are encouraged to not let theories interfere with our coding, then there are all these theoretical codes, which look like, well, theories.

Letting the analytical storyline emerge in the open coding and selective stages is an important tenet of GTM. Examining the data closely and without preconceptions enables new discoveries. If we impose theories at this stage, we are going against the major strength of GTM, which is its ability to come up with something new.

If you look closely at the theoretical families suggested by Glaser, you can see that they are inspired *by* theories rather than being theories themselves. They focus on the different types of relationships that are possible in a theory rather than impose a theory. You can do this yourself, by looking at existing theories in your area and abstracting various relationships from them.

Glaser (2005) devotes a whole chapter to the issue of 'forcing' theoretical codes. He points out that sometimes forcing occurs because it is an excellent way of resolving personal confusion. I do agree with this – sometimes people find it hard to live with what might seem like an ambiguous analysis and they want resolution. Glaser's advice here is very helpful – better no theoretical code than a forced one! Remember that the number of theoretical codes is not limited to the suggestions in front of you. They can, and often do, come from your own creativity when coding the data.

7

Scaling up the theory

This chapter:

- discusses the need to scale up the theory
- discusses descriptive, substantive and formal levels of theory
- discusses how the generated theory can be related to the literature
- discusses how theoretical sampling can be used to extend the generalisability of the theory.

Introduction

One of the commonest criticisms of GTM is that it produces low-level theories around micro-phenomena (Layder 1993; 1998).

Like many criticisms that may seem unwarranted at first glance, it has a grain of truth in it. Because GTM starts off coding line by line and often word by word, codes are necessarily detailed to begin with. Sometimes this means that the grounded theorist can end up mired in low-level concepts simply because the starting point is richness.

How do grounded theorists deal with all this richness and make sure that a sufficiently abstract theory is produced? Also, how do we then relate that emerging theory to other theories in our discipline?

While there is advice on this issue in the GTM canon, starting with Glaser and Strauss (1967), it remains an issue that many users of GTM do not, at present, leverage the method to its full extent to produce substantive theories, let alone formal theories, as suggested by Glaser and Strauss. So, the purpose of this chapter is to examine how we might get our emergent theory to a greater level of abstraction that goes beyond micro-phenomena.

In this chapter, I explore a number of issues. First, why there might be a need to 'scale up' the theory produced by grounded theory procedures. Second, the nature of theory itself is worth discussing. Levels of theory exist and it is worth considering how grounded theory can shade into larger theories. Theoretical sampling can assist here, as we can use it to increase both the scope and the level of the theory. Third, we shall look at what the best way is to relate the emergent grounded theory to the literature. Fourth, the founding fathers of GTM had specific and actionable advice on how we might increase the generalisability of a theory, so we will apply this to the examples given in the previous chapters.

Why scale up the theory?

As discussed in the Introduction, it cannot be denied that the technique of grounded theory coding can result in a dense micro-theory because the starting point of the coding is often a line-by-line examination of the text. This approach means that rich concepts emerge and unique insights are gained. Sometimes these insights are so interesting and the story so unique that researchers forget to do a vital part of their job – the scholarly job of relating the concepts they discover to the literature. In order to do that scholarly job, the emergent theory has to be at a sufficient level of abstraction and it is here that the challenge lies. It's also important to remember, when the theory is emerging, the direction of that emergence will point to other literature researchers can use to enrich the theory. In my opinion, the job is not done until we have integrated our emerging theory with the existing ones in the field. We need to be able to say how our theory contradicts, confirms or extends existing theories.

In different disciplines there will be different norms about how important it is to scale up the theory. Whether scaling up is important or not often depends on the aim of the research and its philosophy. If you are doing an ethnographic study using grounded theory, the details of the participants' worlds will be important, and generating an abstract theory less so. If you are working in a positivist paradigm, it is likely there will be more emphasis on generating propositions that could be tested in future, so the need to abstract or scale up the theory somewhat may be greater.

In order to scale up the theory, the concepts produced by it usually need to be at a higher level than where they often start out. Often this can be achieved by simply grouping concepts into larger ones to make them more abstract. We saw this in Chapter 6, in Example 1, when eight selective codes were grouped into three larger categories.

Thinking about where our emergent theory might fit within the extant literature is not only an obligation of being a scholar but also takes considerable effort. As Strauss says, 'after your theory has begun to integrate and densify

to a considerable degree ... then supplementary or complementary or con-
flicting analyses should be grappled with' (1987: 282). To me, the word 'grapple' says everything! I would also maintain that it is difficult to do that
grappling unless your own emergent theory is at a sufficient level of
abstraction – otherwise the process of relating becomes difficult, as the scale
of the concepts to be related are too different.

In the next section, we talk about levels of theory, which should also help
with understanding the scaling up of theory.

Levels of theory

If grounded theories are low-level theories, what is a high-level theory?

The highest level of abstraction in grounded theory is called a *formal theory*. Formal theories focus on conceptual entities (Strauss 1987), such as
organisational knowledge, organisational learning or collaborative work.
Other examples of formal theories would be theories on social capital, actor
network theory and structuration theory.

One of the ironies of the grounded theory history thus far is that GTM is
still primarily known for its strengths in qualitative data analysis as opposed
to its capabilities in theory generation – this despite the fact that in Glaser and
Strauss' 1967 book, there is a chapter, early on in the book, entitled 'From
substantive to formal theory'. In that chapter, they make a compelling case for
grounded formal theory as closing the gap between abstract theories and
detailed sociological studies and point to the dangers of being guided by very
abstract formal theories in research.

In a paper that I wrote with my colleagues Hans Lehmann and Michael
Myers (Urquhart, Lehmann, and Myers 2010), we suggest that, first, grounded
theories exist at different levels of abstraction and second, those levels have a
relationship with the degree of conceptualisation that takes place.

We suggest that a grounded theory starts with a bounded context, where
we are looking at a few seed concepts. Seed concepts can be seen as hunches
and sources of ideas that do not come from the data. For instance, a researcher
might have a hunch, founded on her experience of work with homeless clients,
that the process of looking for paid employment is seen differently by those
clients. She might then gather data on that substantive phenomena, the phenomena of how paid employment is sought and perceived by homeless people.
Many grounded theories are at the level of substantive phenomena. The final
level is that of formal theories with formal concepts. Obviously, these levels
shade into one another as a theory becomes more and more abstracted (see
Figure 7.1).

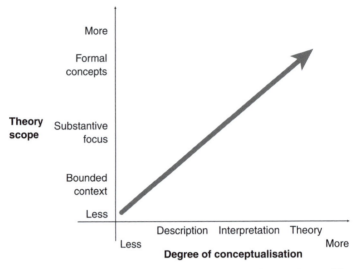

Figure 7.1   The scope and degree of conceptualisation of your theory (Urquhart et al. 2010)

We also suggest that the level of abstraction is related to the degree of conceptualisation that takes place. In the first instance, people might simply wish to describe what happens by attaching a descriptive label to the data. In the second instance, people move from description to analysis in their labelling of the data. This move was discussed in Chapter 3. Finally, theory is built by dint of relating categories, or, in general theory terms, constructs.

This framework came from our examination of grounded theories in the information systems discipline. We noticed that some theories were quite well conceptualised, but mainly at the substantive level, adding some credence to the claim that most grounded theories are low-level theories. We also observed that some uses of GTM at the substantive level did not relate categories, so did not fully conceptualise. Note, too, that this framework is grounded in many different instances, so comprises a substantive theory in of itself. In order to increase the scope of this framework, we would have to theoretically sample many more theories from different disciplines, but more of this in the next section.

So, we have now looked in detail at the levels of theory from a GTM perspective. It is also useful, at this stage, to consider more conventional formulations of what a theory might consist of and how that stacks up against the GTM way of building theory. Table 7.1 analyses Whetten's (1989) 'building blocks of theory' and how those ideas about the components of theory might apply to a grounded theory.

Table 7.1   Applying Whetten's (1989) building blocks of theory to grounded theory

Whetten's (1989) building blocks of theory	Application in grounded theory generation
What factors should be considered to be part of the explanation of the phenomena of interest? Comprehensiveness and parsimony are important.	While GTM starts with a general research problem, theoretical sampling ensures the comprehensive nature of the theory. Deciding on which categories are 'core' categories and selectively coding until saturation is reached also provides a comprehensive theory that is well-grounded in the data. Because each category needs to be 'saturated' – that is well-represented by many instances in the data – the theory generated is also parsimonious. Having only one or two core categories also contributes to parsimony.
How are the factors related? This introduces the relationships (often embracing causality) between the *what* objects. Objects and relationships form the 'domain' or 'subject' of the theory.	GTM provides a very versatile method of relating categories through theoretical coding. The relationships between categories can be of many different types, not just causal. Glaser's (1978) coding families give many options for theory building, including causal relationships and generation of hypotheses. Other options include considering limit, range, intensity, intent, aspects, types, dimensions, mutual interactions, ends and goals, clusters and agreements.
What and *why*. What justifies the selection of factors and the proposed (causal) relationships. What are the underlying psychological, economic or social dynamics? Why should colleagues give credence to this particular representation of the phenomena? *Why* are the factors behaving like they do? This aspect of a theory supplies the plausible, cogent explanation for 'why we should expect certain relationships in the *what* and *how* data' (Whetten 1989). Weick (1989) refers to this as *relevance* and Glaser (1978: 93) adds an element of urgency when he points out that theory should 'account for … which is relevant *and problematic* for those involved'.	The substantive research problem in a grounded theory study can be justified in ways similar to those in other studies. Because the theory is grounded in data, this provides automatic justification for factors and relationships – it is empirically justified. More interesting is the suggestion that the underlying dynamics in the wider field of investigation be identified. In grounded theory terms, this can be seen as relating and extending the substantive theory to formal theories. Thus, logic starts to accompany data as the basis for evaluation.
Who, where, when are the temporal and contextual factors that set the limit on the theory's range – that is, determine how generalisable it is. Bacharach (1989) adds 'values' (which he defines as the theorist's *assumptions,* especially those of a paradigmatic nature) as another set of *who* variables that bound a theory.	In grounded theory, the substantive scope (and generalisability) can be extended by additional theoretical sampling.

Let's look at Whetten's formulations for a moment, because they give us an important insight into how theory is seen in some disciplines. When, as academics and researchers, we present what we say is a theory, it is also important to remember that a common representation of a theory is as constructs and causal relationships tested by quantitative methods. Obviously this varies by discipline – for instance, in sociology, many 'meta' theories exist, such as structuration theory, which are not usually represented in quantitative terms.

If we start with the need for comprehensiveness and parsimony in a theory, we can see that GTM provides this in two ways. First, theoretical sampling, which is deciding where to sample data from next based on the emerging analytical dimensions, ensures that the theory will be comprehensive – that is, it will cover the most important aspects. Saturation, which is ensuring that categories are well represented by the data, will also contribute to parsimony because only the most important categories will be present. The aim of having just one to two core categories should also assist with the aim of parsimony. If we look at Lehmann's (2010) study of international information systems, we can see that all these elements are present. Theoretical sampling was carefully carried out, using as yet unsaturated categories, to ensure both differences between cases and the delimiting of the theory. Lehmann ended up with a sum total of 18 core categories, but did demonstrate parsimony by showing that the ratio between raw categories and core categories was in the region of ten to one.

When it comes to relating factors – which are what we would call categories in GTM – we have a rich range of relationships at our disposal and these are not always causal. Coding families, the coding paradigm, other sets of relationships such as Spradley's (1979) semantic relationships and finally and importantly, our own creativity, give rich options for relating categories. It is also important to say that GTM does give the option of being able to make propositions that could then be operationalised and tested quantitatively.

To return to Lehmann (2010) for a moment, this study made a number of propositions about the interactions between IT and businesspeople in the cases, a selection of which are shown in Table 7.2.

The 'why and what' challenges that Whetten raises are easily answered in a GTM study. The 'why' is often answered by the use of theoretical memos, when the grounded theorist ponders the relationships between categories and theorises. Figure 7.2 shows an example of a theoretical memo pondering the role of conflict in projects. It looks at the possible relationships and consequences of such conflicts (Fernández 2003).

The 'what' is easily answered – each category is justified by many instances in the data and only categories that are 'saturated' are included in the theory. So, there is always empirical justification for the 'what'. Depending on what paradigm the GTM study is being conducted within, counts can be made to demonstrate the extent of the saturation.

Table 7.2   Examples of propositions in a grounded theory study (Lehmann 2010: 188)

Theorem D	Business and IT people act as antagonists in dialectical interaction within a force field.
	The following theorems describe the relationships between the factors that influence the strength (neutral/indifferent to forceful) and nature (positive or negative) of these interactions.
Theorem E	Response depends on utility and the level of undue control.
Thesis El	Design with (net) utility leads to acceptance.
Thesis E2	Design without (net) utility leads to rejection.
Thesis E3	Utility and undue control interact with response in the following ways: • E3(a) utility adds to positive response – that is, acceptance. • E3(b) undue control subtracts from the utility towards negative response – that is, rejection. • E3(c) net utility is the sum of utility minus control.

Perception of conflict, 01/11/01, 09:36:38 a.m.

How conflict is perceived may affect the way project managers deal with team members, bringing conflict to their attention. Mark, for example, was annoyed by Maria coming up with issues with what it was perceived as a pedantic attitude. Mark also perceived this as a threat to his authority – that is, Maria taking the role of project manager (as mentioned by Mark during interview).

However, if conflict reporting is perceived as having a potentially constructive role – by this I mean the identification of conflict (real or potential) that leads to the understanding and resolution of the conflict – it is likely that the project manager would appreciate the input and thorough approach of the tech leader as a positive contribution to the project.

Conversely, as our data shows, the project manager may choose to ignore the advice (or even to get rid of the adviser) if the reported conflict is perceived as (a) unnecessarily adding to the substantial number of problems the project manager is dealing with and (b) a consequence of personal attitude regarding the vendor or simply being pedantic about minor details.

Figure 7.2   Example of a theoretical memo giving the 'why' of conflict in a project (Fernández 2003)

Who, where and when are the temporal and contextual factors that set the limit on the theory's range and relate to the theory's scope. A grounded theory starts with a few seed concepts, then extends to a substantive area. There are a number of recommendations made in Glaser and Strauss' original book (1967) that suggest how theoretical sampling can be used to extend the scope of the emergent theory. They stress that groups can be sampled and that these groups can not only come from the field but also these 'slices of data' can come from secondary data in the form of studies done by other researchers, too. We'll discuss how this might be done later in the chapter.

Relating the emergent theory to the literature

As discussed earlier in Chapter 4, GTM is generally used in two ways – either as a standalone method of qualitative data analysis, or as a way of building theory. In this section, we are concerned with how we might relate the theory we have built to existing literature. Our theory at this point has not been tested or proven, but we can improve what is known as its analytic generalisability by relating it to other theories in the literature.

Generally, other theories in the existing literature fall into two categories: ones at the same level or slightly higher than the one we are developing (hence the need to abstract a grounded theory, so we can relate it sufficiently) or meta theories.

By meta theories I mean the 'grand' or 'formal' theories that Glaser and Strauss (1967) referred to. These tend to have a very wide scope and apply to almost all aspects of organisational or social life. Good examples would be structuration theory or actor–network theory or theories of social capital. Meta theories can often form an interesting lens through which to view an emergent theory – for instance, Levina and Vaast (2005) use a practice lens from Bourdieu through which to view their theory on boundary-spanning individuals in organisations.

Having established that it is both necessary and desirable to relate an emergent theory to the literature, how might we go about it?

Most researchers will already have done a non-committal literature review (Urquhart and Fernández 2006), so the first thing to note is that the developing theory determines the *relevance* of that review. In practice, most people end up looking for some more literature once their theory has developed. Where this literature comes from depends largely on the discipline area relating to the work being done. Postgraduates doing dissertations probably need to keep one eye on examiners who also know the discipline area. More experienced researchers might want to look outside their discipline as well as within it. My experience is that, because GTM does often lead to new discoveries, researchers need to keep an open mind about what literature might be useful. I think this is also why Glaser stresses maintaining *theoretical sensitivity* – that is, the need to read widely and be sensitive to what theory actually is. This can be quite demanding, in that not only does the emergent theory need to be engaged with different sets of literature but also those different sets of literature need to be integrated, too.

As has been previously stated, it helps if the theory you have developed is of a sufficient level of abstraction as this helps in the process of theoretical integration. I find it helpful, too, to think of how the emergent theory relates to the literature in one of two ways.

- Does the emergent theory confirm the existing literature? Hopefully, that is not all the emergent theory does, and it also contributes by extending the existing literature. It helps, at this point, to make this explicit and explain exactly what new concepts are being contributed to the literature and how it extends the existing literature.
- Does the emergent theory contradict the existing literature? This can be exciting, interesting and suggest new avenues for future research.

In any case, how the emergent theory relates to the existing literature needs to be carefully explicated. This is necessary, I think, because, while GTM remains a minority pursuit in academia (however well done), it is necessary to explain that it is, well, about building theory. Also, it is much easier to demonstrate that it is making a scholarly contribution if the role of the new theory can be demonstrated in the context of existing theory.

Let's revisit our extended examples from Chapters 5 and 6 and see how we might proceed with integrating our findings with the literature.

Relating the emergent theory to the literature: Example 1

In Example 1, where we analysed President Obama's inauguration speech, we ended up with three emergent core categories – 'Speech themes', 'Rhetorical devices' and 'Key audiences', reproduced in Figure 7.3.

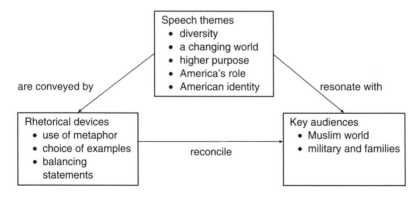

Figure 7.3   Emergent categories for Example 1

What might be the options here for relating these to theory? There are several areas of theory that we could choose. Rhetorical studies might be a fruitful avenue. Presidents' inaugural speeches have been studied quite extensively, as they provide a freely available cache of secondary data for communications scholars. This might also be helpful in terms of future theoretical sampling, if we wanted to extend our emergent theory to all inauguration speeches or all US presidents. There has been some work on how metaphors operate within political speeches and we can examine this literature to see if our findings show if Obama does something different with metaphors than other speechmakers. The literature on leadership may also have something to say. Some relevant literature is shown in Table 7.3.

It is interesting to note that, while the international audience is considered in Dudash (2007), the issue of how the messages to this audience are reconciled with the domestic audience are not, so our findings can be seen to be an extension of how international audiences are dealt with using 'balancing statements'.

There is also the question of how multiple domestic audiences might be reconciled in our category of 'Key audiences'. Rowland (2002) points to the issue of reassuring allies and warning enemies and it is possible that the 'balancing statements' identified in the emerging theory are key to this. Many of

Table 7.3   Relating the literature to Example 1 in Chapters 5 and 6

Category	Relevant literature
Rhetorical devices	**Mio et al. (2005)** Highly charismatic presidents use twice as many metaphors as non-charismatic presidents. Some use root metaphors that extend over the whole speech.
	Seyranian and Bligh (2008) They suggest that charismatic leaders use more inclusive language, more imagery and appeal more to higher values.
	Emrich et al. (2001) Suggest, too, that those US presidents who use imagery in their speeches are considered more charismatic, whereas those who use 'concept words', appealing to logic, are not.
Speech themes	**Dudash (2007)** Regarding inaugural speeches and international audiences, inaugural speeches generally contain themes of American ideals and American identity (Beasley 2001).
	Rowland (2002) Says the address needs to be formal, commit to values, place the nation in the context of history and be ceremonial.
	Coe and Reitzes (2010) They identify hope and change as major themes in Obama's early speeches. Also appeals to policy, thematic appeals, morality appeals and factious appeals. They also consider the context of those speeches.
	Frank (2009) Explicitly considers religious themes in Obama's 'More Perfect Union' speech of 2008.
Key audiences	**Rowland (2002)** Says that inaugural speeches 'reassure the allies and warn enemies'.

the 'balancing statements' identified were in the form of metaphors, so another possible contribution of the emergent theory is how metaphors might be used in this way. We could also link metaphors to the use of images (Emrich et al. 2001) and reconsider in our coding whether we wish to examine images further or not.

In the analysis we also have 'higher purpose' coded under 'Speech themes' and Frank (2009) has examined religious themes in Obama's speeches. Coe and Reitzes (2010) also identify that Obama's speeches have 'morality appeals', where key values, religion, patriotism and family are covered. So, one interesting future direction of this research might be how Obama explores morality and if his explorations in his speeches are different from those of other presidents.

The discussion in Dudash (2007) is also useful for theoretical sampling, when she discusses whether or not inaugural speeches constitute a unique group for study. The point that message dissemination – how the speech is conveyed – has changed over time is also interesting. We might find that the question of multiple audiences is even more important given the widespread accessibility of inaugural speeches in the internet age and this question of satisfying multiple audiences is a potential contribution of our emergent theory. The context of Obama's speech – and other inaugural speeches – may also need to be taken into account, depending on how our original research questions evolve.

We had three emerging research questions for Example 1 that we identified in Chapter 6:

- What are the major themes of the speech?
- Who are the key audiences of the speech?
- What techniques does Obama use to reconcile different audiences?

Of these three, we can see plenty of supporting evidence in the literature for the first and some supporting evidence for the second. It looks as if we may be able to extend the literature with our third research question and relate it to how metaphors and images are used to reconcile audiences.

Note, too, that the literature here comes from various disciplines. This may just reflect the fact that I am an information systems academic and so not rooted in communication studies, linguistics or related fields, but it also illustrates the brilliance of the idea of theoretical sensitivity – the principle that, by being sensitive to theories in general, in all fields, we can enrich our categories and emergent theory from many different sources.

Finally, we could think about the implications for theoretical sampling, to increase the scope and generalisability of the theory. We could sample all inaugural addresses or all speeches by Obama to extend the theory. We would need to consider the similarities and differences of these speeches and, to some extent, it would depend on how we wish to proceed – is this a theory about Obama or all presidents or inauguration speeches? Another option would be to look at other contemporary political speeches made by leaders in the Western world, thus tying the speeches together and to a particular historical context. The shifting context of such speeches is important and how Obama's speeches (and other presidential speeches) might need to respond to those shifting contexts might also be a potential contribution of the emergent theory, especially with reference to the rhetorical devices used.

Relating the emergent theory to the literature: Example 2

In the second example in Chapter 6, in our an analysis of an interview about IT skills training in developing countries, we ended up with four emergent categories, shown in Figure 7.4.

One clear finding here is that the evaluation of skills training will vary by type and also, possibly, the more difficult to measure skills might be the most relevant. So, what literature might be relevant here? Again, as in the previous example, the literature has been drawn from different fields. The sources come from development studies literature, the ICT for development literature (a niche area of information systems, with its own journals) and evaluation literature (see Table 7.4).

With regard to the types of IT skills training, Lockheed (2009) gives some very useful insights into the extent of customisation that might be possible on such courses, which indicates that the types of IT skills training might even be finer-grained. It also suggests that perhaps the research question could be refined to focus only on customised IT skills training, especially as Badshah

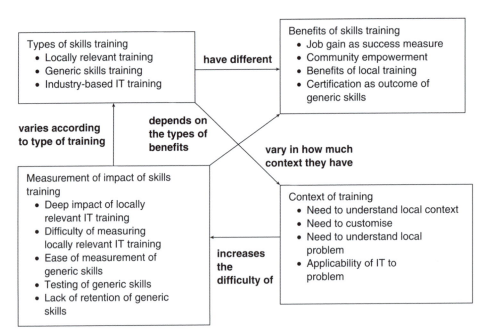

Figure 7.4   Emergent categories for Example 2

Table 7.4   Relating the literature to categories in Example 2

Category	Relevant literature
Types of skills training	**Lockheed (2009)** Suggests that adult learners need content relevant to issues facing the participants in their country, a pedagogical approach involving having participants develop 'action plans' specifying how participants will apply the skills and knowledge from the course, a longer course with fewer participants (but with diminishing returns) and a course that has been professionally designed. Course 'tailoring' to fit the participants is also associated with positive outcomes ('tailoring' including alignment of the course to the participants' job, homogeneity of participants in terms of occupation and responsibilities and specific country focus).
	Brunello (2010) Suggests that the majority of training and education using ICT has a mechanistic focus and the context of development projects on the ground, and donor requirements, mean that beneficiaries are sometimes ignored.
Benefits of skills training	**Badshah (2010)** Suggests that a focus on community empowerment, strong and effective intermediary organisations, local ownership and impacts and local leadership must be in place for IT skills programmes – IT alone does not confer the benefit.
Measurement of impact of skills training	**Heeks and Molla (2009)** Suggest that the impact of ICT4D projects consists of outputs, outcomes and development. These occur after the deliverables of a project and are connected with adoption and sustainability. Heeks and Molla also classify impact assessment frameworks as generic, discipline-based, issue-specific and application-specific.
	Jeffrey et al. (2005) Suggest a means of evaluating educational achievement using social capital theories (such as Bourdieu (1986 and White 2010), Discuss what impact means in development circles and suggest that evaluators and donors have different definitions. Evaluators see impact as what occurs after the project and its long-term effects, whereas funders see it as the difference between intervention and non-intervention.
	Ruth (2000) Suggests that ICT training in the developing world is typically only measured immediately after training and proposes a longer-term model, the Kirkpatrick model, which treats the training event as a first step in a process that ultimately changes attitudes, behaviours and even lifestyles.
	Lockheed (2009) Suggests that mixed methods evaluation is now more common, but it increases the cost of evaluation.
Context of training	**Badshah (2010)** Gives several examples from the field for which the context makes the difference between success and failure.
	Kuruvilla et al. (2002) They suggest that the Singapore model of skills training might be transferable to other developing countries – elements include training institutions, an alignment with the economic strategy and industry partners.

(2010) also talks about the context of training as being vital. Brunello (2010), in a view from the field, says that most types of IT skills training tends to be generic and mechanistic.

One striking thing about the search for relevant literature is that there was little available on the benefits of IT training – it is almost as if these are assumed. Yet, such an assumption is opposed by views such as Brunello's (2010) – he feels that the tangible nature of ICT tends to lead to a very mechanistic evaluation. That said, Badshah (2010) mounts a strong argument for there being benefits from such training, as long as it is implemented in a way that focuses on empowerment. Both views, interestingly, come from practitioners. Badshah (2010) is talking about the same skills development programme as the interviewee in the data excerpt, so the mutual emphasis on community empowerment is perhaps not surprising.

With regard to the measurement of the impact of such training, Heeks and Molla (2009) give a very useful taxonomy of available ways to evaluate the impact of an ICT4D project. What would be interesting here would be to consider the available options to see which might be most appropriate. For instance, we could consider whether our measurement could be discipline-based or application-based, that is, tailored to ICT skills training specifically. Because ICT skills training builds a person's capacity, perhaps a social capital theory approach to evaluation would be appropriate (Jeffrey et al. 2005). Certainly the lack of literature on ICT skills evaluation indicates that we would be extending the theory in this area.

Our brief exploration of the literature also indicates the importance of the context of the training and the discussion in Badshah (2010) gives examples of how varying contexts make a difference to the success of such training. Kuruvilla et al. (2002) take a broader view of IT skills training and pose the question as to whether or not a nationwide programme such as Singapore's is transferable to other contexts.

Our emergent research question is, 'How can we measure the impact of skills training' and, so far, there is some literature on the subject of impact and options for evaluation, as well as how that skills training might be characterised. Looking at the literature above, it might be that we could be more specific about the nature of the skills training we hope to measure the impact of, or at least opt for a more nuanced classification than we have at present, which implies more theoretical sampling along these lines.

Similarly, we can see that the context is important and this raises some important questions for the direction of the research – do we explore many different contexts or just one – say, a programme in one country or several countries? We could opt for the approach taken by Heeks and Molla (2009) and consider a taxonomy of approaches for evaluating IT training, depending on the type of context, benefits and type of training.

So what might be the implications of this for theoretical sampling, to increase the scope and generalisability of the theory? We could sample different programmes and different countries – this would increase the scope of the theory quite quickly. Alternatively, we might decide to stay with one programme (in this case, it was Microsoft's Unlimited Potential Program) and see how it plays out in different countries – this would give us much more insight into the relationship between benefits and context.

Increasing the scope and generalisability of the theory

As previously noted, Glaser and Strauss (1967) devoted a chapter in their book to the issue of moving from substantive to formal theory. The first suggestion is the *rewrite method*, which is when the theory is rewritten to omit specifics. So, for example, instead of talking about the strategies used by analysts when talking to their clients (first introduced in Chapter 3), we could talk about the strategies used by professionals when dealing with their clients. Still, though, this is abstracting a theory upwards, based on only one substantive area, so there is a second suggestion. Sample diverse substantive groups. In the previous example, it would make sense to sample other client–professional relationships, such as those between accountants and their clients or doctors and their patients.

Table 7.5 gives a few possibilities for extending the scope of the example discussed previously of the study of systems analysts and their clients. The table is adapted from Glaser and Strauss (1967), who give some guidance on theoretical sampling of groups.

Table 7.5 Using theoretical sampling to extend the scope of a theory (adapted from Glaser and Strauss 1967)

Group differences	Concepts in the data	
	Similar	Diverse
Minimised	Sampling more systems analysts and clients in public agencies in Tasmania. Sampling more systems analysts and clients in public agencies in Australia.	Sampling systems analysts and clients in the private sector in Tasmania. Sampling more systems analysts and clients in the private sector in Australia. Finding other published studies and datasets of systems analysts and their clients.
	Maximum similarity in data leads to: • verifying usefulness of category • generating basic properties • establishing a set of conditions for a degree of category – these can be used for prediction.	Identifying/developing fundamental differences under which category and hypotheses vary.

(Continued)

Table 7.5   (Continued)

Group differences	Concepts in the data	
	Similar	**Diverse**
Maximised	Sampling other professional relationships in public agencies in Tasmania – for instance, accountants and financial advisers and their internal clients.	Sampling other professional relationships in the private sector in Tasmania – for instance, accountants and financial advisers and their internal clients.
	Sampling other professional relationships in the public agencies in Australia.	Sampling other professional relationships in the private sector in Australia.
		Examining published studies and articles about all sorts of professional relationships where a client exists.
	Identifying/developing fundamental uniformities of greatest scope.	Maximum diversity in data quickly forces: <ul><li>dense developing of property of categories</li><li>integrating of categories and properties</li><li>delimiting scope of theory.</li></ul>

Table 7.5 illustrates a key strength of GTM, which to date still seems under-utilised – the ability to systematically extend the scope and generalisability of a theory by conscious selection of groups. The only puzzle is why this technique is not more visibly used in the literature and why GTM is criticised as producing low-level theories when the issue of scaling up was clearly important to its founders.

Summary

- The first point discussed was why there should be a need to scale up the theory at all. I think this is a big issue for grounded theorists, given that the critique of GTM as producing low-level theories has some evidence to back it up. So, in my view, the theory-building potential of GTM in many disciplines remains untapped.
- We then went on to discuss levels of theory. If a grounded theory starts as a low-level theory, we need to know what a higher-level theory looks like. This section looked at issues of the scope of a theory and degree of conceptualisation in grounded theory terms. We then looked at more conventional formulations of a theory, referring to Whetten (1989), and discussed how each component plays out in GTM.

- The actual business of relating the emergent theory to the literature was then discussed. While this might seem straightforward, it is important to consider two things. First, the emergent theory needs to be at a sufficient level of abstraction in order to be related to the extant literature. Second, how the emergent theory either confirms, contradicts or extends existing theories should also be considered.

- We then returned to the extended examples that we started to analyse in Chapter 5 to show how the emergent theory might be related to the relevant literature in each case. In both examples, the literature came from a wide range of disciplines. This illustrated an important point about theoretical sensitivity – by allowing the emergent theory to dictate what is relevant literature, we are more likely to enrich our categories by linking it with a number of different sources. I also discussed some possibilities for extending both emergent theories by dint of theoretical sampling.

- Finally, I discussed the options for extending the scope and generalisability of a theory using the original suggestions made by Glaser and Strauss (1967) and applying them to an example given originally in Chapter 3. These suggestions about comparison groups can be used to quite quickly increase the scope of a theory and densify it.

EXERCISES

1   Consider the theories used in your own academic discipline. Can you identify the main theories used? Do they come from inside your discipline or outside it? Can you identify seminal papers or books that set out these theories?

2   Once you have identified the seminal papers or books that advance key theories in your academic discipline, see if you can ascertain their level – are they formal or substantive theories? What phenomena do these theories cover?

3   Once you have investigated the previous two points, consider if you can say what the accepted ways of theory building in your discipline are. Does the bulk of theory building come from statistical models or qualitative research? What standards of generalisation hold in your discipline? How is new theory engaged with existing theory?

WEB RESOURCES

http://istheory.byu.edu/wiki/Main_Page This site examines all theories used in information systems research. There are many, which is a reflection of the applied nature of the IS discipline. This site gives useful links to many seminal works from many different theoretical traditions.

www.uiowa.edu/~commstud/resources/rhetorical.html A useful compendium of resources for rhetorical studies, should you wish to investigate Example 1 further.

http://knowgramming.com/metaphor_systems_in_speeches.htm (Casnig, J. D. (1997–2009) *A Language of Metaphors*. Kingston, Ontario, Canada: Know gramming.com) This site posits that metaphors in speeches can be seen as systems, with a premise and a conclusion. It was referred to in the discussion about Example 1.

FURTHER READING

Corley, K. and Gioia, D. (2011) 'Building theory about theory building: What constitutes a theoretical contribution?', *Academy of Management Review*, 36: 12–32. This paper updates Whetten (see below) and extends the idea of theoretical contribution into originality and utility. It comes from a special issue of the *Academy of Management Review* on building theory – the whole issue is worth a look, for a very useful current debate about how theory is built.

Whetten, D.A. (1989) 'What constitutes a theoretical contribution?', *Academy of Management Review*, 14(4): 490–5. This paper outlines very clearly the components of a theory and what might constitute a theoretical contribution. It has a positivist perspective and is a product of its time, but, nevertheless, maps out very clearly what a theory is and is a seminal reference about theory.

FREQUENTLY ASKED QUESTIONS

Why does theory matter? Can't I just do my research and enjoy it without worrying about all this theory stuff?

Sometimes theory does seem very abstract and not related to real-world concerns. Theory may not be the reason you got into doing research in the first place. That said, the beauty of grounded theory is that it *is* rooted in real-world concerns. Better than that, because it is so well-grounded in the data, it can be persuasive and help to change things in a given setting.

Theory, to me, is wedded to scholarship. Can we really claim to be academics if we are not contributing to our respective disciplines via theory development? Good scholars, as stated earlier, will engage their emergent GTM theory with other theories. GTM offers a perfect route to contribute via theories that are grounded not only in the original substantive areas but also in other areas, via theoretical sampling.

If I am interested in generating theory that could be scaled up, should I write that theory in the form of propositions?

I think this largely depends on what you want to do with it next. If, for instance, you've generated a substantive theory about teachers and their relationships with students, you might want to sample more of the same sort of teachers or teachers in many different subjects in different types of schools. If you want to abstract it much further, you might look at the relationships between students and other figures, such as youth workers and counsellors.

If, however, you want to move towards testing and verifying the theory, propositions are useful. A model of relationships between categories is possibly more useful. You may also want to consider using Glaser's more causal theoretical codes, too, such as the 'Causal family', a relative of 'The 6Cs' family includes several relationships – '1) Bias random walk, 2) Amplifying causal looping, 3) Conjectural causation, 4) Repetitive causal reproductions, 5) Equifinality, 6) Reciprocal causation, 7) Triggers, 8) Causal paths, 9) Perpetual causal looping' – that could potentially be modelled mathematically. If you have such causal relationships between categories, it makes for easier transition between qualitative and quantitative data. Going beyond simple propositions towards an initial model, which could then be the basis of a simulation model or statistical models, can further ground the theory in quantitative data.

8

Writing up a grounded theory study

This chapter:

- discusses the process of writing up
- discusses the presentation of GTM in a study write-up
- discusses the need to show how the analysis of the data was conducted
- discusses how the chain of evidence afforded by GTM might be presented
- considers how the theory-building aspect can be presented and how this might differ depending on whether the study is being written up for a journal paper or a thesis.

Introduction

Once you have completed a grounded theory study, there remains one more challenge – how to write up and present it. In fact, there are two challenges. The first is actually the issue of the writing process itself, which can often dog postgraduates and colleagues alike and, in my view, is given insufficient attention in research training. So, the first part of this chapter looks at this process.

Then there are the particular issues associated with writing up a grounded theory study. GTM gives a set of particular challenges when writing up the study. Some of these issues are not confined to grounded theory studies – any qualitative study will have rich findings and accompanying issues in terms of how the chain of evidence should be presented. That said, I think there are particular ways that these issues play out in grounded theory studies. This chapter showcases the many and varied ways in which my students and colleagues have responded to those issues, and I am very grateful to them for being able to share here what is a whole range of examples.

First of all, though, this chapter looks at the writing process – why is it sometimes difficult and how can it be made easier?

The writing up process

The process of writing up is not much discussed in typical research methods training, which is why I wish to discuss it here. Difficulties in writing up can plague all levels of academic researchers, from students to professors, and there are ways we can make our writing more efficient and productive.

First, I do not find the assumption that there will be a writing up 'phase' in people's dissertations is a terribly helpful one for candidates. If the writing process is delayed until later, rather than occurring concurrently with data collection and analysis, it forms an obstacle to completion that is harder to get past than people might think. It also means that students are less likely to publish academic papers during their dissertations, but this helps so much for those candidates who aspire to an academic career. Luckily, GTM encourages the use of theoretical memos, which should mean that students will be starting, effectively, to write up, given that so many theoretical memos do find their way into the write up. I always strongly advise my own students to think, from the very outset, in terms of the document that they have to produce and the size of the writing task. There is no reason for bits of theoretical memos, the research proposal, and early analyses of literature, to not be simply cut and pasted into a draft thesis document very early on in the research process. I find that this relatively easy mechanism really helps create a focus on what needs to be produced. If a student is doing the PhD by publication model, the same advice still applies – that the draft papers need to be planned early and targeted well should be obvious. It's important to note too that, with the PhD by publication model, an introduction and conclusion wrapping and linking the papers needs to be written, which can be a substantial piece of work in itself – up to about 30,000 words.

One issue that is problematic for students and academic staff alike is the issue of time. As someone who did my own PhD part-time and completed this book with no study leave, I feel that I know this issue intimately!

I've always been taken by the time management remark I read once that there is no point in complaining about lack of time, we have the same 10,080 minutes everyone else has. It's not an entirely true remark, as those with childcare or other responsibilities will attest, but it highlights a really important issue – how we use our time to write. I often meet people who say they will get on with whatever writing project it is – just as soon as they get a block of time to do it in. For hard-pressed academics, getting blocks of time to do anything becomes increasingly hard, faced as we are with competing demands of teaching and administration, which can seem so much more urgent than writing.

It seems to me that writing for publication comes into the 'important but not urgent' category of time management and we need to find ways to prioritise that writing. To paraphrase a colleague of mine, Lynne M. Markus, research isn't finished until it is published – and it's not going to be published until we finish writing it!

When writing up my own PhD during a busy teaching period, I used to spend 30 minutes in the morning on it before I did anything else. When I propose this method to colleagues and students, they sometimes say that they need at least a day to connect properly with what they are doing. My reply to this is, if they stayed connected with the work on a regular basis (say for that 30 minutes a day), they would not need this reimmersion time. Felder and Brent (2008) make a similar point in their brilliant short piece entitled 'How to write anything', about the importance of taking regular short periods of time to write. They also point out that when you *do* get that block of time, you'll be much more effective because you will be warmed up in the first place. It is astounding how much these regular short writing periods can add to the total word count. I've also found it very motivating – what can be better than working on your own goals every day, even if it is only for 30 minutes?

Felder and Brent (2008) also make the point that the writing process should be kept separate from the editing function. It's much easier for the process of writing to simply write, unimpeded by worries of spelling or headings – all this can be fixed later and should not be allowed to distract from the task of producing the manuscript or thesis in the first place.

When we do get the time to write – be it half an hour or a whole day – can we use it effectively? Felder and Brent (2008) say they do not claim the tactic is necessarily easy, and I agree with that. What happens if you get time and find yourself unable to write? The fact is that some blocks to our writing are emotional rather than practical. We may find ourselves unable to write because we are distracted by fears about the project or feelings about people in our environment that seem to in some way impede the writing project.

Some years ago, I ran a writing retreat for some PhD students, because they asked me to. I gave them the following exercise to do, which is based on Julia Cameron's 'unblocking' exercise in her seminal book on creativity, *The Artist's Way* (Cameron 2011). We tend to forget, I think, that research is an essentially creative process, so how we feel about writing is important.

Essentially, the exercise asks you to write down your fears and resentments about the project, then decide to concentrate on the quantity rather than the quality of the writing. The idea is that someone else (God, A Higher Power, a colleague, a supervisor, a friend) can help with quality issues. Obviously this goes back to the earlier advice, too – to just write regularly and not worry about editing issues. This exercise is reproduced in Figure 8.1.

Unblocking exercise

Often, the reasons we are blocked in our writing are not practical but emotional. We may, in fact, have enough time or be able to use our time effectively if we are feeling positive about our writing. Often, what is blocking us is not immediately apparent, but there may be buried resentment (anger) and resistance (fear) behind a block. These are often defences against what is perceived (rightly or wrongly) as a hostile environment. This unblocking exercise comes with a guarantee – try it!

List any resentments you have in connection with this writing project. It does not matter how petty, picky or irrational these resentments may appear.

Examples
I am fed up with having to do this research in my so-called spare time when my Head of Department gives me lots of extra work!
All my supervisor ever does is pick fault with my work.
I am fed up with being a poor PhD student.

List any and all fears you have about this project. These fears can be as dumb as any two-year-old's!

Examples
I'm afraid my work will be awful and I won't know it.
I'm afraid my work will be good and they won't know it.
I'm afraid my ideas are ahead of my time.
I'm afraid my ideas are outdated.
I'm afraid I'll never finish.

Ask yourself 'Is that all?' Have you left out any 'little' fears? Suppressed any 'stupid' anger? Get it all on the page.

Ask yourself what you stand to gain by not doing this piece of work.

Examples
If I don't write it, no one will hate it.
If I don't finish it, I get to complain about it.
I can criticise others, knowing that I can do better.

Make this deal with yourself. The deal is simple and has only two elements.

Leave it to others/the Universe/God/your supervisor to take care of the quality.

You take care of the quantity!!!

So get writing!

Figure 8.1   Unblocking exercise (based on Cameron 1995, 'Blasting through the blocks exercise')

I can vividly remember the first time I did this exercise with the group of students on the retreat. The rage, anger and fear in the room was palpable as they all set about writing down their fears and resentments about their PhDs. I wasn't surprised, because I had done the exercise myself and found my own resentments to be pretty palpable, too!

There is a human dimension to the process of creating a piece of writing and we don't often acknowledge the fears associated with that act of creation. The great thing about this exercise, though, is that it, first, encourages the person to recognise those fears and then identify what payback there might be in staying stuck. In my experience, there is always a payback to staying stuck, even if it is just simply the chance to complain to someone how you are being prevented from writing. The good news is that this exercise does work and many students of mine have testified to its efficacy. It's as if, having faced those fears, they are then free to write without worrying. It does achieve a remarkable mindset shift and, for this, myself and countless others are indebted to Julia Cameron's writing on creativity.

Having now 'unblocked', let us turn to the specific challenges for writing up grounded theory studies.

The challenges of writing up a grounded theory study

This section looks at the challenges of writing up a grounded theory study. As previously stated, some of these challenges apply to all qualitative studies. I would contend that they play out in particular ways in grounded theory studies because of the unique characteristics of GTM.

The challenges are outlined below.

- How much context of the study should be presented to the reader?
- How should the coding procedure be represented and to what level of detail?
- GTM gives an opportunity to present a chain of evidence – to what extent should that chain be presented?
- GTM gives rich findings – what is the best way to present those findings?
- GTM also gives a substantive theory – what is the best way to present a substantive theory?
- GTM also requires theoretical integration and a different approach to the literature review – how can this be presented in the format reviewers and readers expect?

The process of writing up the study involves balancing all these issues. How this is done depends very much on the audience of the study – fellow researchers, examiners, your home academic discipline – and how much space is allowed in the write-up, as a journal paper with a limit of 8000 words is very different from a dissertation. Let's examine each issue in turn.

How much context of the study should be presented?

The issue of the balance between the description of the context and the analysis is an important one in the research write-up. Too little description and the write-up becomes unanchored from its context and hard to understand. Too much description and we are left wondering if the research is nothing more than 'a nice story', to borrow the words of a North American academic who explained to me that this was his reason for completely discounting qualitative research. I was a PhD student at the time – I heartily disagreed, of course, but those words stayed with me. Many years later, I came to realise that he did indeed have a point. There are some qualitative research studies in which the researcher has become so bound up in the richness of the context that it is impossible to draw any analytic conclusions or see how the findings might relate to existing literature. This degree of richness may be appropriate for some research traditions, such as ethnography, of course, but it is important to note that a grounded theory study does give the opportunity to abstract and analyse in a systematic manner and go well beyond rich description.

So, the question is, how much rich description should there be in a grounded theory study?

The extent to which the context features in the write-up is influenced by a number of factors. The first is to do with the access agreements you may have made with the host research organisation or community. It may well be that you cannot provide too much detail of participants because mentioning details such as age or position in the organisation would lead to their identification. Similarly, you may have made an agreement with a company that some details are 'commercial in confidence' so need to be excluded from the write-up. All that said, I think it is important to provide *some* context, simply because readers are more likely to be convinced of your analysis if you share with them some of the background as well.

There are several ways of describing the context, such as tables giving company and interviewee characteristics, descriptions of company or country background, photographs and vignettes. An example of a vignette from my own PhD work about systems analysts and their clients is given in Figure 8.2.

You can see in the example that there is some analysis intertwined with the description, which occurs in many write-ups. My own opinion, though, is that providing such a descriptive context sets the scene and helps readers understand the analysis.

In Federal Agency B, the Accreditation Officer has arranged to meet with the Senior Systems Consultant about her suggestion that agenda details regarding accreditation of courses be automatically generated from the Access database where they are held, rather than being generated independently using Word. Both analyst and client are approximately the same age and have met only briefly prior to this meeting – the client is new to the organisation. Most of the time is spent discussing the processes from the client's perspective [processes associated with system] and the problem as raised by the client [problem identification]. The analyst, taking an organisational view, points out that some of the client's information is also relevant to another section in the same organisation (links in information). He also points out that there is no key to link course accreditation and registration (links in information) and is informed that a member of the client's section is already in the process of linking the two databases. There is also a great deal of discussion about where the client's processes fit in to organisational changes (organisational context), possibly because the client is new to the organisation and the analyst is unfamiliar with the work that the client's section undertakes. The interaction is quite wide-ranging, identifies a number of issues associated with the client's database (problem identification) and the analyst decides to pursue possible commonalities in information by discussing it with the relevant section head (links in information).

Figure 8.2   Example of a vignette

Representing the coding procedure

To what extent the coding procedure is presented in the write-up depends largely on the audience. In a dissertation, it will be crucial to describe how the data was coded. In a journal paper, there may not be space to say anything other than open coding, selective coding and theoretical coding were applied and, perhaps, give an example of each.

One of the very real problems that may occur in a dissertation situation is that, in fact, the coding has not proceeded in a textbook way. There may have been modifications to the procedure for good reasons or reasons simply of convenience. One obvious way to represent a coding procedure is to use a diagram. Figure 8.3 shows an example, courtesy of Karin Olesen (2006), a former PhD student of mine in New Zealand.

There are various other things that could be added to Figure 8.3 – for instance, theoretical sampling could be shown, even specific theoretical coding concepts that directed the next phase. Note, though, that this particular example shows a modified grounded theory procedure, and the theoretical coding stage – where selective codes are related to each other – has been omitted. In this case, the theory-building aspect is supplied with the technology-in-use and technology strategy aspects.

In a dissertation, giving an example of how the coding proceeded is possible *and* advisable, given that the main point of a dissertation is to persuade the examiner(s) that the author is a competent researcher. By giving an example, readers can actually see how the coding was applied, which makes it more

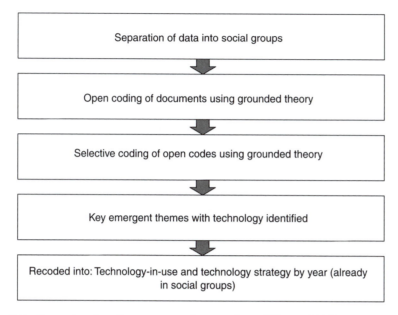

Figure 8.3   Example of coding process diagram from (Olesen 2006)

credible and convincing. Let's have a look at another PhD thesis, this time by Gillian Reid (2006), which looked at how chief executive officers (CEOs) perceived the role of a particular type of IT project – infrastructure projects.

First, Reid explains her open coding by means of a simple table giving some examples (Table 8.1).

After discussing how she applied the process of open coding, she then goes on to explain her selective codes, again by using an example. In Table 8.2, we can see how various open codes were grouped into selective codes. It might not be necessary, however, to put such codes into a table; it might be sufficient to simply explain the process. Tables are more popular in some disciplines than others and, in arts-based disciplines, may not be appropriate to a more flowing writing style. That said, tables and other displays can be

Table 8.1   Example of open coding (from Reid 2006)

'Nugget' from interview transcript	Initial open code
Technical jargon is a barrier to understanding what is happening.	Technology barriers
So much background we just don't have as non-ICT managers, which makes information and advice hard to understand/believe.	ICT background deficiencies
ICT people just focused on what can be done with the technology.	Technology focus
Technology developments make it possible to do things better, faster, more cost-effectively. Can't afford to stop.	Productivity benefits
ICT should build better communications links with end-users and management.	Comms expectations

Table 8.2 Example of selective codes (Reid 2006)

Jargon barriers	Business of ICT/I	Professional relationship issues	Technology organisation issues	Executive engagement issues	Strategic issues	ICT/I project skills issues	Implementation issues	ICT/I project success factors
Jargon issues	Technology/business balance	ICT/business expectations	ICT responsibilities	Change management issues	Business value of ICT/I	Business capabilities	PIR activities	ICT/I project strategies
Jargon interpretation	Management support	ICT/comms quality	Infrastructure challenges	Executive involvement	Organisational leadership and strategy	ICT project skills sourcing	ICT/I project delivery	ICT/I project scoping
Management's ICT understanding	ICT business understanding	ICT imperialism	Technology dependency	ICT/I expertise concerns	Project priority conflicts	ICT project skills dependencies	Project expectations	Organisational buy-in
	ICT reporting structure	ICT insularity	Technology seduction	Technology adoption	Technology key business driver		Project management	Risk management
	ICT/user interface	Management dissatisfaction			Technology opportunities		Project progress reporting	Training
		Cultural disconnects					Project scope change	

incredibly useful as a means of summarising and, given the scepticism about GTM that can occur in some disciplines, they can unequivocally demonstrate a strong chain of evidence, as shown in Table 8.2.

Once Reid (2006) has discussed the process of selective coding in depth, including how various categories were renamed, in what was an iterative process, she then goes on to provide Figure 8.4, showing the path of relationships between selective codes.

Figure 8.4 is useful because it does show how selective codes are connected. Again, an alternative option would be to discuss each connection or the process of each connection in the text.

Reid then concludes by giving an overview diagram of the entire coding process (see Figure 8.5). This is helpful because it gives a clear overview, with examples. Also notice the honesty of the diagram – it represents several successive groupings of categories.

By laying out the coding process like this, what is achieved? First, I think that this is good research because the researcher is laying out the methodology very clearly, which means it could be followed by fellow researchers. Second, it allows the researcher to reflect on the coding process. Often new researchers are hesitant to admit that the coding process was not perfect or the stages were not precisely followed, yet this is the reality of doing research. We learn from that process of reflection and so do others.

In a journal paper, it is unlikely that there will be space to represent the coding process in detail, yet I think it is important to convey a sense of how the analysis proceeded, rather than just saying that grounded theory procedures were applied. Personally, I think that our reflection on those procedures and the fact that they don't always go as we might expect is part of a scholarly duty we have to engage in. Journal papers are one of the primary ways in which an academic community communicates with

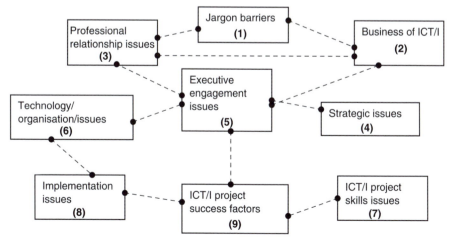

Figure 8.4   Diagram showing relationship paths between selective codes (Reid, 2006)

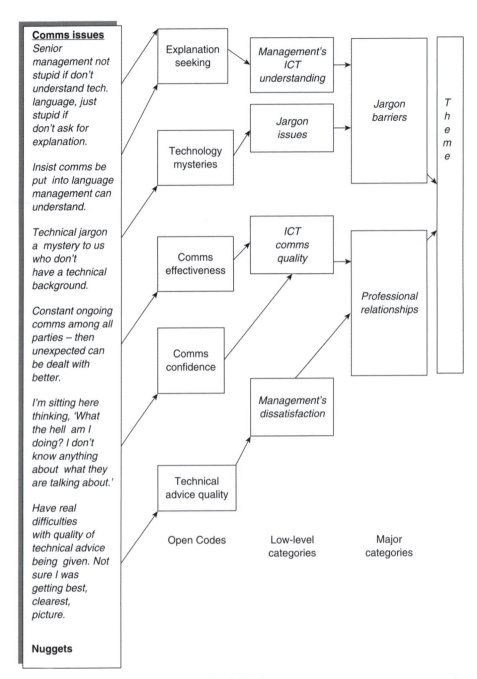

Figure 8.5 Overall coding process (Reid 2006)

each other. We learn from our colleagues' reflections. Of course, one thing that happens is that we can change our views, but the text we wrote remains out there in the discourse, speaking for us! It is important, then, to bear in mind that whatever we write is bound by the context of our experience at that time and our views can and should change as we discover more.

In the next section, we'll consider how we can present a chain of evidence in grounded theory.

Presenting a chain of evidence

One of the major strengths of grounded theory is that it results in a chain of evidence. For every concept that comes from the data, there are dozens of instances, thanks to the practices of constant comparison and theoretical saturation. This means that grounded theory studies can avoid the charges that are sometimes levelled at qualitative research – namely, that qualitative researchers are selective about the data they use to back up certain findings. Because of the emphasis on theoretical saturation, the researcher can be sure that the findings are representative – that is, not just detected once or twice in the data. In some research paradigms, this can be important.

How far you go in demonstrating your chain of evidence will depend on your philosophical position. If you are a 'weak constructivist' (Orlikowski and Baroudi 1991), you might merely want to show that the codes occurred sufficiently in the data analysed. If you come from a critical realist position, you might want to actually count the occurrences of codes. I have also seen analyses of the most frequently occurring words in a transcript used in conjunction with grounded theory analysis.

Here's one idea I used in my own thesis – to show how the codes occurred in an interview. I had divided my transcripts into topic chunks for ease of analysis. In my research, I was focusing on how systems analysts interacted with their clients when designing information systems and did six detailed case studies of such interactions. Table 8.3 shows a chain of evidence for one transcript in one case study.

If you use this type of documentation, you rapidly build up a chain of evidence that is unassailable. In this particular example, I then went on to demonstrate the occurrence of themes (high-level categories based on grouping selective codes) in all of the data sources in all the case studies (shown in Table 8.4).

There are probably many other ways to demonstrate a chain of evidence, but the key point here is that GTM does offer the opportunity to do so. In a dissertation, there is the space to show a chain of evidence and it strengthens the thesis to do this. In a journal article, there may be no space to show a chain of evidence, but it can always be provided if asked for by reviewers and put in an appendix.

Table 8.3   Example of a chain of evidence of codes (Urquhart 1999)

Number	Topic	Dominant grounded theory codes
1	Issues to be discussed	agenda setting, conversation topic, key searching, forward reframe
2	Numbering of subdivision	key searching, information identification, forward reframe, problem identification, reflection, exemplification, information justification
3	Capacity of proposed numbering	information identification, key searching
4	Prefix for proposed numbering	information identification, key searching, prop, exemplification
5	Need for date received field	information identification
6	Reporting requirements	problem identification, organisational context, process identification
7	Recording of closing dates	information identification, process identification, process justification, imagining, exemplification
8	Using closing dates for enquiries	process identification, exemplification, process justification, imagining, forward reframe, information identification, imagining
9	Process of recording objections	process identification, information identification, exemplification, imagining, dialoguing, organisational context, problem identification, forward reframe, process justification
10	Time period for objections	posit, forward reframe, problem identification, process identification, information identification, exemplification, imagining, forward reframe
11	Process for objections in new system	process identification, key searching, organisational context, future solution, imagining, dialoguing, negotiation
12	Implementing new process	reflection, negotiation, future action, process identification
13	Stop and start dates	problem identification, information identification, process identification, exemplification
14	Reporting stop and start dates	process identification, imagining, dialoguing, information identification
15	Overriding stop dates	problem identification, process identification, future action, imagining, prop
16	Procedure for override	problem identification, process identification, negotiation, future action
17	Referral information	problem identification, information identification
18	Process of referrals	posit, exemplification, dialoguing, imagining, process justification
19	Implementing recording of referrals	future solution, prop, forward reframe, negotiation, organisational context, future action
20	Future action	future action, future solution, information identification

Table 8.4 Demonstrating a chain of evidence over a number of cases (Urquhart 1999)

Theme	Interaction	Paragraph – analyst	Paragraph – client	Interview – analyst	Interview – client	Review
Issues to be discussed	C1, C2, C3, C4, C5, C6	C1, C2, C3, C4, C5, C6*	C1, C2, C3, C4, C5	C1, C2, C3, C4, C5,C6	C1, C2, C3, C4, C5, C6	C1, C4
Scope of system	C1, C2, C3, C4, C5	C1, C2, C4			C1,C2	C2, C5, C6
Personal sisclosures	C1, C3				C6	
Information input into system	C1, C2, C3, C5, C6	C6*		C1, C2, C3, C4, C5, C6	C5	C2, C5, C6
Processes associated with system	C1, C2, C3, C4, C5, C6	C4, C5, C6*	C1, C2, C3, C4, C5	C2, C3, C4, C5, C6	C5, C6	C5, C6
Links in information	C1, C3, C4, C5, C6	C3	C3, C4	C3		C3, C4, C5, C6
Future action	C1, C3, C6		C1, C2, C3, C5			C1, C2, C5
Problem identification	C1, C4, C5, C6	C5		C2, C4	C6	C4
Information output from system	C1, C3, C6	C5				
Analyst's understanding of processes	C3, C5	C1, C2		C1, C2, C3, C4, C5, C6		C1, C2, C3, C5, C6
Future solutions	C1, C3		C3			C2
Organisational context	C3, C5	C1,C2, C4, C5, C6*	C1	C5, C6	C1, C2, C3, C4, C5,C6	C1, C2, C3, C5, C6
Professional relationships				C1, C2, C3, C4, C5, C6	C1, C2, C3, C4, C5,C6	C1, C5, C6
Mutual understanding				C1,C2, C6	C1,C2, C5, C6	C1, C2, C3, C4, C5, C6
Note taking						C1, C3
Use of props						C1, C4, C6

*The paragraph submitted in Case 6 was a joint paragraph.

Presenting findings

A grounded theory study yields rich findings, by virtue of its method. If coding proceeds at the word or sentence level, it stands to reason that there will be a large corpus of findings to draw on. So often, the challenge of presenting findings, especially in the context of a journal article, is how best to summarise those findings without losing their richness. This issue becomes even more complex when you are trying to present a substantive theory that you have developed. So often, with the limited space afforded by a journal article (say 6000 to 10,000 words), there is an issue of trading off breadth for depth. What also complicates the presentation of findings is that this has to be done in such a way that the uninitiated (to grounded theory anyway) can follow them.

Another presentational issue is that, often, the use of GTM will have to be both explained and justified. So, the presentation of findings is not a simple exercise!

In my experience, the simplest way to present findings is to take readers through the selective codes and their components. You can start with a table that shows these codes and explain that the findings will be presented according to that table. For instance, Figure 8.6 shows how my colleague Riitta Hekkala and I (Hekkala et al. 2009) introduce a set of findings on power issues in inter-organisational projects.

After introducing the findings in this way, each selective code was discussed in turn and the open codes highlighted using italics in the narrative. We also used quotes to illustrate those codes, taking advantage of the superb chain of evidence afforded by grounded theory. Figure 8.7 is an edited example.

You can also use diagrams to show the relationships between selective and open codes and include the quotes. Figure 8.8 shows an innovative diagram by Dr Antonio Díaz Andrade (2007), which illustrates a category from his study of ICT for development in the rural Andes.

How much of a narrative of the findings you provide is up to you and determined by how much space you have to give to those findings. It will also be dictated by your research paradigm, home discipline and the style of the journal or examiner.

Figure 8.9 gives an example of some extensive quotes that I've used in my own work. One advantage of explaining the findings like this is that it gives you a chance to elaborate on the relationships between codes. Often the hard thinking about these relationships will have been done using theoretical memos. It is interesting how many times theoretical memos find their way into the presentation of findings.

In Figure 8.9 you can also see that I am weaving in some of the literature. Generally I think it's best to present the findings then discuss them in the light of the literature and do some thorough theoretical integration. We'll return to this issue later in the chapter.

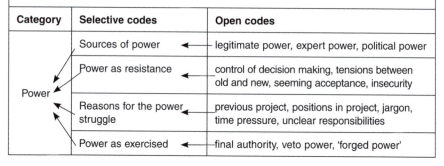

Power was one core theme that emerged during the GTM analysis and this section discusses this core theme in detail. We identified 'Sources of power', 'Power as resistance', 'Reasons for the power struggle' and 'Power as exercised' as important selective codes of the category. This table presents the open codes and selective codes that make up the category.

Category	Selective codes	Open codes
Power	Sources of power	legitimate power, expert power, political power
	Power as resistance	control of decision making, tensions between old and new, seeming acceptance, insecurity
	Reasons for the power struggle	previous project, positions in project, jargon, time pressure, unclear responsibilities
	Power as exercised	final authority, veto power, 'forged power'

Figure 8.6   Introducing some findings from a GTM analysis (Hekkala et al. 2009)

Sources of power

Expert power was also in evidence and conflicted at times with the project manager's *legitimate power*. For instance, there was a 'tug of war' between the suppliers and the project manager around various issues. The discussions were a 'little bit hostile' (Thomas, Rhoo). Supplier Cumma felt that disagreements were frequent and faults were dealt with by 'tattling' to the project manager. So, supplier Cumma sought background support for their work from other project members on the basis of their expert *power*. Later, however, the confidence in Cumma started to wane.

Thomas (Rhoo) pondered how the steering group should regard the matter, since nothing was happening. Thomas thought that the roles of 'generals' and 'officers' were not defined and, consequently, attempts were made 'to transfer war leadership on to wrong shoulders'. Thomas thought that, because legitimate power was not defined in the project, people 'took' power and that this problem was not being managed.

Figure 8.7   Example of the findings from a GTM analysis (Hekkala et al. 2009)

Presenting the substantive theory

As well as the richness that grounded theory findings afford, there is the theory itself. There is an issue with how to present the emergent theory. One possibility is to report your findings as hypotheses or propositions. Again, your decision about whether to report your findings as propositions or not will depend on the research paradigm you are working within, disciplinary norms and how

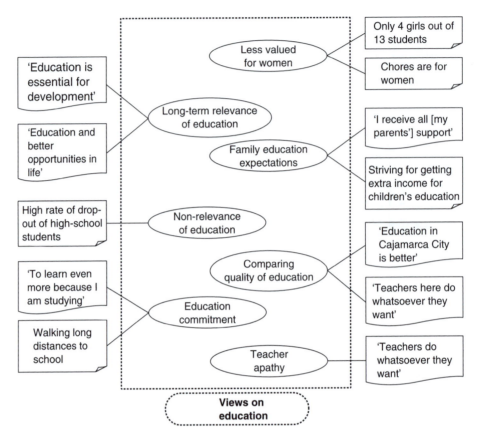

Figure 8.8   Incorporating quotes and codes into a diagram (Díaz Andrade 2007)

Later, the analyst resumes *key searching*, as seen by the following sequence of successive posits or *frames*.

Analyst: So, like each of these applicants have, like, a numerical or reference number?
Client: Yes.
Analyst: Does that get recorded on their application form or something?
Client: Yes it does.
Analyst: So you can then go back to the paper files and find out which one it talked about?
Client: So that's vital … that number … otherwise you would be powering through a host of forms looking for particular applicants.

In Case 1, the issue of whether a key was used to access an individual student recurred until the analyst used a mock-up of the form in question. Once this *prop* had been used, it was possible to establish exactly what the key in question consisted of. The fact that it took so long to resolve was probably in equal proportion to the difficulty of discussing the status of one piece of data embedded within a larger process and raises some interesting questions as to when details of information should be discussed vis-à-vis the client processes. From this perspective, it might be that analyst's framing of the problem, using a strategy of *key searching*, could have become an overwhelming conceptualisation of the problem, to the possible detriment of the problem as a whole. Schön (1983) points out that professionals tend to set problems in such a way as to make them solvable and this can sometimes result in a narrow conceptualisation of the problem.

However, the strategy of *key searching* can perhaps be seen more broadly, that of one of a repertoire of strategies that information systems professionals use to fracture apart a problem and find a solution. Given that the information system professional is generally concerned with building information systems, the establishment and formation of a key, the means of retrieving information, is an important mechanism by which information can be provided to the client. This is perhaps best illustrated by Case 6, where a key needed to be established for a register of subdivision information. This was, incidentally, not only recognised as an important strategy by the analyst but also by the client, who effectively played the role of business analyst for her section. The analyst's view of *key searching*, as expressed by her in the interaction review, was as follows.

What we were doing was discussing the key to the file or the key to the record. And that's pretty important to us, because what we want to do is eventually find out when an application ... go through a certain year and month we want to know when, and it also helps us for reporting.

Figure 8.9   Reporting findings in a narrative (Urquhart 1999)

you wish to present your theory. Figure 8.10 shows an example from my Walter Fernández (2003).

Theories, by definition, have relationships between the constructs. The easiest way to depict relationships is with a diagram. Figure 8.11 is a very detailed diagram showing lots of relationships (Sulayman et al. 2012). While there are too many categories here for this to be a parsimonious theory (it was produced as part of study extending software process factors), it does illustrate very well how categories can be related.

Of course, it's not enough to simply lay out the relationships; ideally, each relationship should be described, with reference to the findings that inspired it. Also, the idea is to get to a point where your emergent theory can be engaged with other theories, so it needs to be at a sufficient level of abstraction. Figure 8.12 gives an example from Reid's (2006) thesis. It shows three core themes and gives instances from the data of the relationship between those core themes.

The nice thing about Figure 8.12 is the level of abstraction that is evident. If the theory is at a sufficient level of abstraction, it becomes easier to engage that theory with other theories, which is the vital last stage of building a grounded theory.

In the next section, we'll have a quick look as to how theoretical integration might proceed in a thesis or a paper and how the literature can be treated, building on Chapter 7.

Interrelated concepts	Propositions
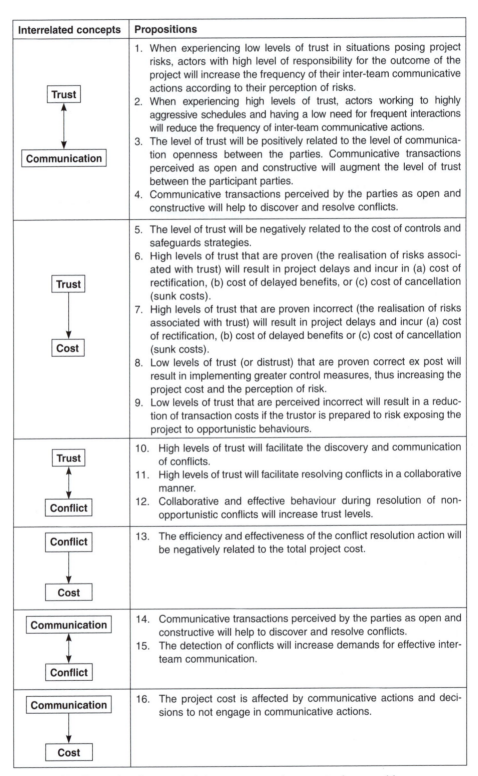 Trust ↕ Communication	1. When experiencing low levels of trust in situations posing project risks, actors with high level of responsibility for the outcome of the project will increase the frequency of their inter-team communicative actions according to their perception of risks. 2. When experiencing high levels of trust, actors working to highly aggressive schedules and having a low need for frequent interactions will reduce the frequency of inter-team communicative actions. 3. The level of trust will be positively related to the level of communication openness between the parties. Communicative transactions perceived as open and constructive will augment the level of trust between the participant parties. 4. Communicative transactions perceived by the parties as open and constructive will help to discover and resolve conflicts.
Trust ↓ Cost	5. The level of trust will be negatively related to the cost of controls and safeguards strategies. 6. High levels of trust that are proven (the realisation of risks associated with trust) will result in project delays and incur in (a) cost of rectification, (b) cost of delayed benefits, or (c) cost of cancellation (sunk costs). 7. High levels of trust that are proven incorrect (the realisation of risks associated with trust) will result in project delays and incur (a) cost of rectification, (b) cost of delayed benefits or (c) cost of cancellation (sunk costs). 8. Low levels of trust (or distrust) that are proven correct ex post will result in implementing greater control measures, thus increasing the project cost and the perception of risk. 9. Low levels of trust that are perceived incorrect will result in a reduction of transaction costs if the trustor is prepared to risk exposing the project to opportunistic behaviours.
Trust ↕ Conflict	10. High levels of trust will facilitate the discovery and communication of conflicts. 11. High levels of trust will facilitate resolving conflicts in a collaborative manner. 12. Collaborative and effective behaviour during resolution of non-opportunistic conflicts will increase trust levels.
Conflict ↓ Cost	13. The efficiency and effectiveness of the conflict resolution action will be negatively related to the total project cost.
Communication ↕ Conflict	14. Communicative transactions perceived by the parties as open and constructive will help to discover and resolve conflicts. 15. The detection of conflicts will increase demands for effective inter-team communication.
Communication ↓ Cost	16. The project cost is affected by communicative actions and decisions to not engage in communicative actions.

Figure 8.10   Example of grounded theory reported as a set of propositions
(Fernández 2003)

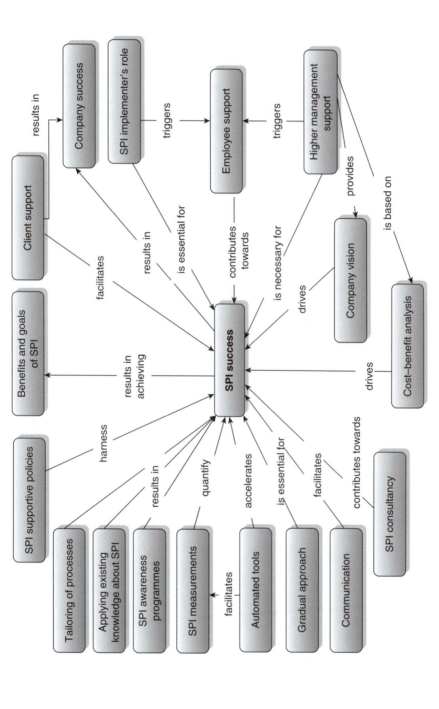

Figure 8.11   Example of a diagram showing category relationships (Sulayman et al. 2012)

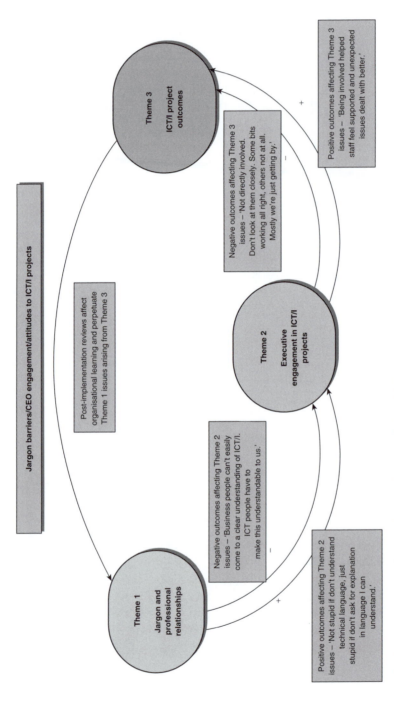

Jargon barriers/CEO engagement/attitudes to ICT/I projects

Theme 3
ICT/I project outcomes

Theme 1
Jargon and professional relationships

Theme 2
Executive engagement in ICT/I projects

Post-implementation reviews affect organisational learning and perpetuate Theme 1 issues arising from Theme 3

Negative outcomes affecting Theme 3 issues – 'Not directly involved. Don't look at them closely. Some bits working all right, others not at all. Mostly we're just getting by.'

Positive outcomes affecting Theme 3 issues – 'Being involved helped staff feel supported and unexpected issues dealt with better.'

Negative outcomes affecting Theme 2 issues – 'Business people can't easily come to a clear understanding of ICT/I. ICT people have to make this understandable to us.'

Positive outcomes affecting Theme 2 issues – 'Not stupid if don't understand technical language, just stupid if don't ask for explanation in language I can understand.'

Figure 8.12 Example of substantive theory diagram (Reid 2006)

Theoretical integration and presenting the literature

As previously suggested in Chapter 7, it is necessary to engage your emergent theory with the literature. In my view, we are not completing our jobs as scholars if we stop short of considering how our emergent theory relates to the literature. Otherwise, I think we do run the danger of being vulnerable to the 'nice story but where's the theory' accusation that I mentioned is sometimes levelled (however unjustly) at qualitative research.

There are several ways in which we can address and present the task of theoretical integration and it often depends on the nature of the emergent theory we are dealing with. First, we could simply produce a table of relevant literature and cross-reference our theory elements to it. Table 8.5, from Sulayman et al. (2012), shows how 16 software process improvement factors in a grounded theory study relate to previous literature.

Table 8.5 neatly illustrates which factors are already present in the literature, but also shows factors that are new to the literature. Thus, we can see at a glance how the theory confirms and extends the literature.

Of course, theoretical integration is not just a matter of tables. Strauss (1987) talks of the need to grapple with the literature. So, there is a very real need to discuss the emergent theory and critically relate it to existing theories, which takes up some space in the paper or dissertation. One of the interesting things about this example is that the literature being integrated is at the same substantive level, or only slightly higher, than the emergent theory, but what if we want to go further?

The second option is to view our emergent theory through the lens of higher-level, more formal theories and, in this process, start to abstract our emergent theory still further. If we are to do this, then we need to pay attention to the level of our theories. In the discipline of information systems, actor–network theory and structuration theory are all high-level formal theories that are used to explain the interaction of organisations and information technology. An early example of this in information systems is Orlikowski (1993), who related her emergent theory on software use in an organisation to larger theories about innovation.

While we are in the business of influencing examiners or reviewers that our use of grounded theory contributes to theory and makes a contribution in general, it's worth using Walsham's (1995) analytic generalisations, which enumerate the four different ways in which a case study can make a theoretical contribution. The four different types of analytic generalisation he suggested are as follows.

- Development of concepts – this is self-explanatory. Given that grounded theory studies build theory, and often discover new concepts, it would be surprising if a grounded theory study did not contribute in this area.

Table 8.5   Example of theoretical integration (Sulayman et al. 2012)

Grounded theory-based investigation/qualitative study [S1]	Replication/quantitative study [S2]	Systematic review [S3]
SPI goals and benefits	–	Increase in productivity, reduced time for development, client and development team satisfaction, operational excellence (Scott et al. 2001; Allen et al. 2003; Naidu 2003). Alignment with business goals (Allen et al. 2003).
Automated tools support	–	–
Client support	–	Client satisfaction (Scott et al. 2001; Allen et al. 2003).
Communication	–	–
Company vision	Business orientation (Dybå 2005; Sulayman and Mendes 2010)	–
Cost–benefit analysis	–	–
Employees support	Employee participation	Development team satisfaction, operational excellence, feedback from discussion (Scott et al. 2001; Allen et al. 2003)
Gradual approach	–	–
Higher management support	Leadership involvement (Dybå 2005; Sulayman and Mendes 2010)	–
SPI consultancy	–	–
SPI implementer's role	–	–
SPI measurements	Concern for measurement (Dybå 2005; Sulayman and Mendes 2010)	Feedback from discussion, project monitoring through reviews (Scott et al. 2001; Allen et al. 2003). Statistical analysis/use of metrics (Allen et al. 2003)
SPI supportive polices	–	–
Tailoring of Processes	–	–
Applying existing knowledge about SPI	Exploitation of existing knowledge (Dybå 2005; Sulayman and Mendes 2010)	–
SPI awareness	Exploration of new knowledge (Dybå 2005; Sulayman and Mendes 2010)	–

- Generation of theory – again, in a grounded theory study where a full theory is built as opposed to using the method for analysis, we would expect a contribution to be made in this area.
- Drawing of specific implications for particular domains of action, which may prove useful for other related contexts. This, again, should not be beyond the reach of a grounded theory study, because, even if extensive theoretical sampling has not been carried out, the grounded theorist will have some sense of how sampling different groups could extend and densify the theory. The principle of theoretical sensitivity should also assist with identifying other contributions to other disciplines and contexts.
- Contribution to rich insight – when the study itself gives insights that are not easily categorised as new concepts, theory or specific implications, but, nevertheless, provide insight. Grounded theory studies, because of their 'grounded' nature that has a close relationship with the data, often provide many rich insights.

Table 8.6 gives an example of how these generalisations were applied to a study of ICT in the rural Andes (Díaz Andrade 2007). I do think that spelling out the contributions like this, especially in a dissertation, is very helpful – the examiner does not have to trawl through the thesis to decide what they are. The second advantage of this approach is that if you yourself state what the contributions are, *you* are framing them and, hopefully, setting up the criteria by which you will be judged rather than allowing other people to do it for you.

A related issue to theoretical integration is how the literature in a study is reported. As discussed in Chapter 2, the GTM dictum that literature should not impose concepts on the coding of data does not act as an excuse for not engaging with the literature. It is simply a case of sequencing, with some searching done at the beginning, but much more searching done at the end of the theory development, so theoretical integration can take place.

As mentioned, for dissertation students, it is generally impossible to avoid institutional requirements that a literature review be done first. Also as mentioned, a recommendation here is to think in terms of a draft literature review, its relevance being determined by the emergent theory (Urquhart and Fernandez 2006).

Should this actual sequence be represented in a paper or dissertation? In both cases (dissertation or paper) we are talking about a *retrospective* write-up of how the research is done, so there is the opportunity to order things in a different way for ease of understanding. In a dissertation, I have seen the literature review presented as a draft literature review and new literature introduced in the discussion of findings for the purposes of theoretical integration.

In journal papers that report grounded theory studies, I have seen two configurations. The first reports the findings initially and the literature afterwards. The second uses a more conventional form of presentation, with a literature review up front, then more theoretical integration at the back. Which is best?

Table 8.6   Illustrating contribution using Walsham's (1995) analytic generalisations (Díaz Andrade 2007)

Development of concepts	Activators of information.	Individuals who not only purposefully seek information by using computers but also trigger a process of disseminating information throughout their communities using their existing connections. For instance, Alejandro in Chanta Alta, Sixto in La Encañada, Darío in Llacanora, César in Puruay Alto and Enrique in San Marcos.
Generation of theory	Computer-skilled persons, who are central individuals acting in communities with strong social texture, articulate their communal networks to their virtual networks.	Alejandro in Chanta Alta and César in Puruay Alto are remarkable examples.
Drawing of specific implications	The necessity of both strong social texture and activators of information for the ICT intervention to interact with the existing social fabric in rural areas.	Examples of strong social texture are Chanta Alta, Huanico and Puruay Alto. The activators of information in Chanta Alta and Puruay Alto are Alejandro and César, respectively. Major restrictions and extreme isolation prevent people in Huanico from accessing computers.
Contribution to rich insight	The chances of articulating both communal networks and virtual networks are hampered in the communities organised in a top-down approach.	La Encañada, Llacanora and San Marcos all have local governments who look after the community issues. The ICT-mediated information that Sixto, Darío or Enrique can obtain does not find its way to being distributed to the whole community.

Levina and Vaast (2008), to my mind are an excellent example of the second tactic. Their paper on overlapping boundaries in offshore IT out-sourcing provides plenty of literature up front, then more to integrate with the rich findings and, finally, a theoretical model, complete with relationships between the concepts. They say only that their approach is informed by grounded theory, yet it is, in fact, an excellent example of how a grounded theory study can fit the criteria of a top journal and contribute to theory building in a discipline.

Summary

- This chapter has tackled the issue of how to write up a grounded theory study from two perspectives – first, the process of writing and, second, the particular challenges involved in presenting a grounded theory study in a dissertation or journal paper.

- The actual process of writing is one that, in my opinion, is not discussed frequently enough in research methods texts. It is possible to use small, regular blocks of time efficiently to get the writing project done, if you have the right mindset. The blocks to writing are often emotional rather than practical. In this section, I introduced an 'unblocking' exercise that many of my students have used successfully to motivate themselves to write.

- The chapter identified six challenges when writing up a grounded theory study: presenting the context of the study, representing the coding procedure, presenting the chain of evidence, presenting rich findings, presenting the substantive theory and how to approach theoretical integration. The balance of these challenges will vary according to the purpose of the write-up, research paradigm and home discipline.

- How the coding procedure is represented may be of supreme interest to examiners of a dissertation, but of less interest to reviewers of a journal article. That said, explaining the coding process in a journal article is a valuable (and often the only) source of information on application of GTM for fellow researchers. It was suggested that a diagram may be the answer to showing the process within strict word limits. Several examples were given, courtesy of my wonderful former PhD students.

- Whether the representation of the coding process should be truthful or not was also discussed, given that all write-ups are retrospective. Personally, I welcome different adaptations of GTM and would rather see these discussed and debated with fellow scholars than us adhere to a 'pure' GTM.

- The chapter then went on to present different ways of showing the chain of evidence that is afforded by GTM. Given that GTM does give a very extensive chain of evidence, it seems a shame not to use it. Again, in journal articles this may be harder to do because of space restrictions, but tables can represent the chain with some economy and can be put in an appendix. For dissertations, I would always recommend showing the chain of evidence. Finally, the degree to which demonstrating a chain of evidence is important to you will depend on your philosophical position.

- The next issue tackled was how to present the rich findings of a grounded theory study. Different examples were given here from dissertations and papers. Key things to note are that the detailed level of grounded theory findings allow us to report in a narrative form with rich quotes; also that a table showing code groupings can act as a framework to guide readers as to how the findings will be reported. Relationships between categories need to be reported, too, otherwise the job of theory building will not have been done. I also gave some examples of how this can be achieved.

- The next section talked about theoretical integration. While the importance of theoretical integration was discussed in Chapter 7, this section talked about how it might be achieved in a thesis or journal paper. Some examples were given. With the notion of theoretical integration also comes the idea of contribution – how can the theoretical contribution of a grounded theory study be demonstrated? A suggestion here was to use the four types of analytical generalisation suggested by Walsham (1995).

EXERCISES

1 Access some GTM dissertations/and or journal papers in your discipline area. How do they compare in their presentations of findings? How much theoretical integration takes place and how is it achieved?

2 Take a journal paper that uses GTM and identify in which places you would present the methodology and findings differently. Why did the writers present their studies in this particular way? Can you think of reasons for them having gone for a particular mode of presentation? Suggest some different ways the findings could have been presented.

3 Research analytic generalisation. Are there other ways to generalise to theory? What are the standards for generalisation in your discipline area?

WEB RESOURCE

http://cgi.stanford.edu/~dept-ctl/tomprof/posting.php?ID=900 This provides a quick link to the article by Richard Felder and Rebecca Brent (2008), 'How to write anything'.

FURTHER READING

Cameron, J. (1995) *The Artist's Way: A course in discovering and recovering your creative self.* London: Pan Macmillan.

Felder, R. and Brent, R. (2008) 'How to write anything', *Chemical Engineering Education*, 42(3): 139–40.

FREQUENTLY ASKED QUESTIONS

I am completely baffled as to how to write my thesis. How do I know that the structure of the thesis is correct?

First, if you look at example dissertations from your institution and others, both good and bad, you will see that the structure varies quite a lot, depending on the study. Some elements, though, are consistent. You will need an introduction, based on your research proposal. You'll need a literature review, whether it is introduced before or after the findings (I have seen both). Remember, too, that the thesis write-up is a retrospective one, so you can have your literature review in the traditional place in a thesis (Chapter 2), but explain that this is a non-committal one. You'll also need a methodology, traditionally in Chapter 3 (but not always), explaining your use of grounded theory. Generally, these chapters can be started on while or before you are collecting your data. How you present your findings and the structure of those chapters will depend on disciplinary considerations and potential examiners. Ideally this should be discussed with your supervisor.

I'm completely overwhelmed by my findings. I've written them up, category by category, but now my supervisor has asked me to discuss my 'key' findings. How do I do this?

The problem you have here is balancing the richness that a GTM study gives and the need to abstract and focus on what is important. Your key findings should be obvious, in that they should be around your core categories, and the relationships between them. If they are not obvious (and sometimes writing up is a messy business), try this tactic. Organise your write-up around the categories and their constituent codes, using a table to guide the sections. For each section of minor and major category findings, include a summary of the key points for that category. In this way, you can start to 'distil' the findings by successively summarising and abstracting your findings. Don't forget to illustrate those findings with examples when you discuss them in the discussion section and integrate those findings with the literature. The more abstracted your concepts are, the easier it will be to do this.

9

The contribution of GTM – some reflections

This chapter:

- summarises some key insights from the book
- introduces some (non-prescriptive) guidelines for GTM studies
- discusses the current and potential contribution of GTM in a range of evolving contexts.

Introduction

This book comes largely from my own experience of using GTM as an academic. It is very much a personal view of GTM and, as such, will be bound to offend some and delight others. This is bound to be so, because GTM shows all the characteristics of a contested concept, as has been so insightfully pointed out by Bryant and Charmaz (2007). They applied Bryant's (2006) explanation of Gallie's (1956) characteristics of a contested concept to GTM. These ideas are worth examining in detail and Table 9.1 is my own interpretation of how they play out in GTM.

One of the delights of GTM is that it has a vigorous and complex intellectual tradition, and there is a continuing debate about its use. It will be interesting to see where the debate goes next, given the sidelining of the coding paradigm in Corbin and Strauss (2008). As the coding paradigm introduced by Strauss and Corbin (1990) was the cause of the splitting of GTM into two strands, where will grounded theory go now that the use of the coding paradigm is no longer mandatory?

Certainly, in my own discipline, the coding paradigm has not been much applied – a search (Seidel and Urquhart 2012) could find only 9 out of 85 top journal articles following the Straussian strand for the period 1990–2010 in which the coding paradigm was applied as intended.

Table 9.1   GTM as a contested concept

Gallie's characteristics as adapted by Bryant (2006)	As they play out in GTM
The concept should be significant and valuable.	GTM is seen as a significant and valuable method in the social sciences and other disciplines.
It must have an internally complex character.	GTM is internally complex, as evidenced by the number of books and articles written about it.
Its complexity leads to a variety of descriptions.	There are several different descriptions of GTM, notably the Glaserian and Straussian strands, but also constructivist and postmodern views (Clarke 2005; Charmaz 2006).
There has been considerable modification in the light of changing circumstances that could not be predicted.	Strauss and Corbin's (1990) book represented a considerable modification of the original book by Glaser and Strauss (1967). Glaser's (1978) book represented an extensive elaboration on the procedures in the 1967 book.
People who use the concept know that their specific use is contested by other parties and recognise that their own use of it has to be maintained against other uses. The concept is used 'aggressively and defensively'.	It is certainly true to say that both the Glaserian and Straussian strands have their passionate adherents. Glaser in particular feels that his version of grounded theory is closer to the original and calls it classic grounded theory.
There is an original exemplar, the authority of which is recognised by all users of the concept.	The original exemplar, of course, is *The Discovery of Grounded Theory* (Glaser and Strauss 1967).
Continuous competition for acknowledgement should enable the original exemplars' achievement to be sustained and or developed in optimum fashion.	This is perhaps one of the most interesting aspects of grounded theory – the continued level of debate around usage and the different adaptations in many fields.

So, the only remaining difference between the two strands is the sequencing of the coding steps. In the Straussian version, the sequence is open coding, axial coding and selective coding. Axial coding includes the application of the coding paradigm and grouping of categories. If we eliminate the first part of axial coding, then it becomes much more like selective coding. If relationships are not considered via the axial stage, then they hopefully will be considered in the next stage of the Straussian procedure, selective coding. So, perhaps it's possible to hope that the two strands will merge some time in the future. In any case, as a living method, GTM will continue to evolve. The next section summarises what I consider to be the key insights from this book.

Key insights

I have learnt a lot from writing this book. It is very much an attempt to explicate what is largely tacit knowledge from using GTM over an extended period.

The other thing I realised is that the process of postgraduate supervision is still somewhat of a dark art, in that there are many rules of thumb I use in postgraduate supervision which are not explicated in textbooks anywhere.

In short, this is the book I want to be able to hand to my students as a basis for our discussions and for teaching qualitative analysis using GTM. So, these insights are not only about GTM but also the process of using GTM in postgraduate research.

Insight 1: GTM is infinitely adaptable as a method, but any adaptation should always be explained

One thing I have learnt from both writing this book and using the method for so long is that the adaptations of GTM are many and various. The issue, then, is not so much how people adapt GTM but how they present those adaptations.

Because GTM has such well-established coding procedures and, indeed, is almost the only well-known qualitative coding method, it is tempting for researchers to wrap themselves in the respectability of GTM and call what they are doing GTM when it is not. Cue angry editors and reviewers from all sides of the contested terrain of GTM!

As an editor of journals myself, I gradually came up with a simple solution to this. Researchers should acknowledge their debt to GTM and explain what the adaptation is. In this way, they contribute to the scholarly debate about GTM in all its forms and we all get to learn more about the decisions colleagues make when deciding to apply a coding strategy to their data.

Insight 2: Theory is important

I often wonder if, in leveraging GTM procedures for data analysis, people lose sight of the eventual goal of GTM – producing theory. We need to remember that, for Glaser and Strauss, the whole point of the method was to produce theory grounded in everyday contexts that could then be progressively formalised. In my own discipline, information systems, which is very much an applied discipline, there are debates about theory and the fact that we do not generate our own theories. This is despite the fact that we freely borrow and adapt theories from other reference disciplines such as sociology and management. What GTM has given me, and my postgraduate students, is a good appreciation of what a theory is and, in particular, for different levels of theory. If we think about the relationships between constructs, we are so much better able to theorise about the phenomena we are researching.

There are definitely practical problems involved in building a bridge from the substantive theories produced by GTM to larger, more formal theories, but the rewards for doing so are enormous as it helps us increase the theoretical integrity of our particular discipline area. Our findings in the form of emergent theory can be abstracted and tested in successive studies. Being conscious of what a theory is, how theories are used and how we can contribute to theory building helps all of us as scholars and it is these insights that using GTM brings with it.

Insight 3: The nature of GTM does not fit well with the PhD process, but that's not an argument for not using it

Over the years I've had many discussions with colleagues and students about the pros and cons of using GTM in Masters and PhD dissertations. It's a wonderful method, why would you not want to use it? The barriers to its use can be divided into two types: practical and institutional. Perhaps we can add a third: the researcher's own temperament.

Let's take each of these in turn. The practical barriers can be circumvented with a little thought. The most significant practical barrier to GTM use in a dissertation is that of the normal institutional requirement of having under-taken a literature review as a marker of progress, whereas GTM requires that the researcher does not impose theoretical concepts on the coding process. As previously stated, the best way to deal with this is to do a non-committal literature review (Urquhart and Fernandez 2006), where its relevance is deter-mined by the emergent theory. The important thing is to not actually impose theory on the coding. The philosophy behind this is to say that we approach coding with 'an open mind, not an empty head'(Dey 1993: 63).

Another possible practical barrier is the one of the amount of time availa-ble for fieldwork. Within a Masters programme of one year, it may be hard to arrange enough time in the field in order to overlap data collection and analysis for the purposes of theoretical sampling. That said, even with a short time in the field it should be possible to do some form of theoretical sampling by, for instance, adding useful questions to the interview schedule based on what emerges from the interviews.

Another practical barrier that is often claimed is the time it takes to do the analysis. There is no doubt that the line-by-line coding discipline required by GTM takes time, but, in all the supervisions I have undertaken, candi-dates seem to finish on time. Why? One possible explanation might be that, although the time it takes to do the analysis of the data is greater (it certainly seems so at the time), writing up the findings is much easier and takes less time than usual because the write-up already has the foundation of an exten-sive analysis.

Candidates for Masters and PhDs do sometimes encounter institutional barriers when they wish to use GTM. The commonest of these by far is that the supervisor is unfamiliar with the method, perceives it as very different and is therefore unwilling to supervise a thesis that uses the method.

There are solutions to this dilemma, such as ensuring that there is someone with qualitative analysis experience on the supervisory panel or committee. It is possible to learn GTM from a book as an isolated PhD student – that was my experience after all – but it is so much better if the candidate can connect with others doing grounded theory and exemplars of grounded theory. In an increasingly connected age, opportunities exist to contact practitioners of GTM through, for instance, Glaser's website (www.groundedtheory.com) and Sage's Methodspace (www.methodspace.com).

A more insidious institutional barrier is objections to the method based on a perceived lack of rigour, often connected with a perception that GTM ignores the literature. Sometimes the objection to GTM is part of a larger bias against qualitative methods in general and/or interpretive research. If it is the latter, it should be pointed out that GTM can be, and often is, used within a positivist framework.

The fact remains that the choice of research method has a number of social implications in terms of the candidate's future, especially in terms of which research constituencies they then connect with during and after their PhD, and their future career prospects. The unfortunate truth may simply be that, in a particular department, power structures and expertise coalesce around a particular method and it may be very difficult for the candidate to do GTM if it is seen as a radical departure from the norm.

Finally, there is the issue of temperament. Detailed, painstaking analysis does not suit everyone, even if there is also a great deal of space in GTM for creative insights about the data. Researchers do have to be able to see it through and be persistent and optimistic when it seems to be going nowhere. The rewards are great.

Insight 4: GTM is a bottom-up form of coding

This may not seem like much of a revelation, but thinking of GTM in this manner helps in several ways.

First, it helps us distinguish GTM from other types of coding – top-down (the codes come from the literature) and mid-range coding (the codes come from both the literature and the data itself). It helps isolate the role of literature in general coding.

Second, we can see why it might be a challenge to scale up categories if they are generated from the bottom up, at a detailed level, during line-by-line coding.

Third, we can see that coding is also a matter of level – larger-scale codes can be grouped into themes.

The use of themes is common in qualitative data analysis, but it is emphatically not GTM. Themes can be taken from the literature or the data and applied as a framework.

This leads us on to thinking about the role of frameworks generally. The approach of most research is to build a framework from the literature, apply that framework, then extend it based on the findings – a theory-*testing* approach. GTM builds a theoretical framework or theory from the data, then relates it to the literature – a theory-*building* approach.

Insight 5: The quality of a GTM analysis is dependent on our ability to abstract concepts and think about relationships

One thing I have tried to demonstrate in the examples in this book is that the quality of the theory that emerges from applying GTM is entirely dependent, in my view, on two things: the ability to abstract concepts and think about relationships.

When we start coding, it is very easy to simply describe and, often, the open coding phase can seem, at first, a meaningless jumble of summary words for the data. It is only as we proceed with open coding and move to selective coding that we move from description to analysis and understanding the meaning behind the text. That meaning is then tested by constant comparison. Possibly one reason GTM is so successful in yielding insights is that the mode of analysis does mean researchers spend a lot of time with their data and, not only that, they are close up to that data.

We can only claim to be building theory, of course, if we consider the relationships between concepts. One of the interesting things about the process of coding is that what we think is an interesting category, somehow related to two other categories, becomes that relationship. It is also supremely helpful to write theoretical memos about how categories may relate to each other and look for sources of theoretical codes from many places, including Glaser's (1978; 2005) coding families.

Insight 6: GTM is naturally interdisciplinary

One of the most exciting things about GTM for me is that it encourages us to look beyond our disciplinary boundaries because the process of theoretical sampling leads our literature search, as opposed to what we know. This might not be such a big deal in large fields such as sociology, in that there are many subfields which may provide the literature we are looking for, but, even then, I would like to think it encourages us to look beyond what we know.

Disciplinary boundaries can also be restrictive silos and it is wonderful to think that GTM may encourage us to think more broadly because we are following the path of the concepts we are building, as opposed to well-worn paths. This, of course, makes collaboration with colleagues from different disciplines easier, too, as the principle of theoretical sensitivity enables us to understand the principles and structures of theories, wherever and in whatever discipline they may occur.

Insight 7: We need more discussion of the outputs of GTM rather than the process of theory generation

Given that GTM is such as contested concept, I find it interesting that almost all the debate occurs around how we *do* GTM, as opposed to the theories that might actually be produced. There seems to be very little discussion about theory per se in grounded theory texts. Indeed, Charmaz (2006) states that the notion of what a grounded theory actually is remains slippery at best. Yet, the paradox is that GTM is, above all, focused on producing theory – it was the focus of Glaser and Strauss' (1967) book that started it all – so I would support much more discussion on the nature of the theories we can produce using GTM.

In many disciplines, the nature of theory itself is not discussed, though it's fair to say that the Academy of Management has made many contributions to the nature of theory over the years (see, for example, Corley and Gioia 2011). In a paper I wrote about this issue with my colleague (Seidel and Urquhart 2011), we found that, in most discussions of theory in grounded theory literature, the focus tends to be directed towards how that theory is constructed rather than the nature of the theory produced. We suggested that a consideration of the intended theory's paradigm, scope, structure, constructs and relationships has an impact on the process of theory building. We also suggested that, depending on what decisions are made on these aspects, the process of theory building can be entirely different.

Guidelines for grounded theory studies

In 2010, my colleagues and I (Urquhart, Lehmann, and Myers 2010) came up with some guidelines for grounded theory studies. We did so because we felt that, in our discipline (information systems), as in other disciplines, GTM and its characteristics were often misunderstood. We also thought that they might provide good reference points against which grounded theory studies could be assessed, but in no way are the guidelines meant to be prescriptive. They are offered here to assist those who wish to gain a general understanding of what a grounded theory study might consist of.

Constant comparison

Constant comparison has been described as being core to GTM (Charmaz 2006). I see it as a very useful rule of thumb for researchers doing any type of qualitative analysis, because it is a constant process of comparing your analysis to the whole of the data.

Constant comparison is defined as the process of constantly comparing instances of data that you have labelled as signifying or belonging to a particular category with other instances of data in the same category to see if these categories fit and are workable (Urquhart 2001). Charmaz (2006) makes two points about constant comparison. First, making comparisons between data, codes and categories advances conceptual understanding because of the need to expose analytic properties to rigorous scrutiny. Second, it makes the analysis more explicitly theoretical by asking, 'What theoretical category are these data instances of?' For me, the real advantage of practising constant comparison is that there are always dozens of instances in the data to support the theory that is produced.

Iterative conceptualisation

One aspect of GTM that we felt was probably unique to GTM is what we chose to call *iterative conceptualisation* in our paper. We defined it as the process whereby theory is built in an iterative fashion by using theoretical coding, focusing particularly on relationships between categories. As discussed in Chapter 6, these relationships can be of many kinds, ranging from causal to ones that describe influences of different kinds.

One of the interesting paradoxes about GTM is that, at first glance, it offers well-signposted procedures for theory building for the novice (Urquhart 1997), yet, if procedures are followed blindly, it can lead to difficulties if researchers do not realise that theory building is an iterative process. Theory building is also a creative process, so researchers using GTM need to be alert to intuition and think beyond labels for the data.

In terms of doing iterative conceptualisation, researchers have suggested a number of alternatives. There are the coding stages described by Strauss and Corbin (1990) – open coding, axial coding, selective coding), Glaser (1992 – open coding, selective coding, theoretical coding) or Charmaz (2006 – open coding, focused coding, axial coding, theoretical coding).

Strauss and Corbin's (1990) are known to cause some difficulty for researchers (see, for instance, Melia 1996). Researchers wishing to follow the Straussian strand are advised to consider the slightly more flexible version (Strauss and Corbin 1998) or the most current advice (Corbin and Strauss 2008).

Whichever coding stages are used, the key thing is that all of them are followed to allow adequate conceptualisations, which are the basis of a formed theory.

Miles and Huberman (1994) give a useful set of characterisations about codes that are of assistance when assessing the level of conceptualisation occurring in grounded theory studies. They describe three types of codes that can be equated to analytic levels:

- *descriptive* codes – attributing a class of phenomena to a segment of text
- *interpretive* codes – when meaning is attributed with reference to context and other data segments
- *pattern* (or *linked*) codes – inferential and explanatory codes that describe a pattern.

Clearly, it is desirable that researchers reach the third stage, that of inferential and explanatory codes, because the business of theory building means understanding patterns and linkages.

Axial coding (Strauss and Corbin 1990) or theoretical coding (Glaser 1978; Glaser 2005) are essentially about relationships between categories – the very essence of theory building. Theoretical coding contributes to an understanding of relationships between the concepts or constructs of a theory. In my experience, it is in defining the relationships between categories that novice researchers often struggle to really achieve depth of theory.

Another useful way to think about iterative conceptualisation is that it helps to answer important theoretical questions concerning 'What?' and 'Why?' Whetten (1989) says that the 'What?' in a theory justifies the selection of factors and the proposed (causal) relationships. The 'Why?' in a theory attempts to explain why the factors are behaving the way they do.

Theoretical sampling

Theoretical sampling is deciding on analytic grounds where to sample from next (Glaser and Strauss 1967) and is an important aspect of GTM. While not confined to grounded theory, we identified it as an important marker in grounded theory studies, because theoretical sampling assists with iterative conceptualisation.

Through successive sampling according to the emergent theory (Glaser 1992), the research questions gradually become more refined, as dimensions of the research problem become clearer through analysis (Dey 1993). If researchers are guided by the emergent theory when collecting data, then there is very little chance of them imposing preconceived notions on the data. It is important to note, then, that this approach implies overlapping data collection and analysis.

Theoretical sampling is one of the foundations of GTM as it enables both a focus on the developing theory and ensures that the developing theory is truly grounded in the data. Theoretical sampling is a key tool that can be used to extend the scope and generalisability of the generated theory, where emerging concepts from the analysis enable us to sample other datasets to help extend and build the theory. By conscious selection of sample groups that are either similar to or very different from the original group and looking at either diverse or similar concepts in the data, we can expand and densify the theory (Glaser and Strauss 1967).

Scaling up

One of the issues we also drew attention to in our paper was that of scaling the theory up. Our collective experience with GTM told us that first-time users tend to get overwhelmed at the coding level.

The founders of grounded theory suggest word- and sentence-level coding. This literally *guarantees* rich insights and is one of the pluses of GTM. At the same time, researchers can end up mired in detail because of the bottom-up nature of the coding. The way forward here is to group categories into successively larger themes so that the emergent theory is at a sufficient level of detail. Glaser and Strauss (Glaser 1978; Strauss 1987; Glaser 1992) both recommend having one or two core categories precisely because of the need to get the theory to a reasonable level of abstraction.

Theoretical integration

Often, grounded theory studies do not go so far as to systematically relate the emergent theory to the wider literature. This was an issue that we identified in our guidelines.

Like any other theory, a grounded theory needs to be put into context by mentioning other theories in the field. The obligation (Strauss 1987: 282) to engage with theories outside the discipline is an important one, in my opinion. It means that we leverage the theory-building capacity of GTM in its widest sense and contribute to our respective scholarly disciplines by properly leveraging the method.

Glaser (1978) suggests that the substantive theory can be analysed by comparing it with other substantive theories in the area. Glaser suggests that formal models of process, structure and analysis may be useful guides to integration. For instance, in my own field of information systems, meta theories such as structuration theory (Orlikowski 1992; Walsham 2002) or actor–network theory (Walsham 1997) have been used as a lens through which to view emergent theory.

Glaser (1978) also makes the useful point that context is necessarily stripped away as one moves towards a formal theory and comparative analysis can be used to compare conceptual units of a theory.

Table 9.2 provides a summary of these guidelines.

Table 9.2   Guidelines for using grounded theory (Urquhart et al. 2010)

1. Constant comparison	Constant comparison is the process of constantly comparing instances of data labelled as a particular category with other instances of data in the same category. Constant comparison contributes to the development of theory by exposing the analytic properties of the codes and categories to rigorous scrutiny. This guideline for data analysis encourages researchers to be both rigorous and theoretical (Charmaz 2006).
2. Iterative conceptualisation	This guideline suggests that researchers should increase the level of abstraction and relate categories to each other through a process of iterative conceptualisation. In grounded theory, this is done using theoretical coding. The relationships between categories can be of many different types, not just causal. Theoretical coding contributes to an understanding of relationships between the concepts or factors of a theory. Theoretical memos are also very important to the development of theoretical coding and the whole process of iterative conceptualisation.

(continued)

Table 9.2   (Continued)

3. Theoretical sampling	This guideline stresses the importance of deciding on analytic grounds where to sample from next in the study. Theoretical sampling helps to ensure the comprehensive nature of the theory and ensures that the developing theory is truly grounded in the data.
4. Scaling up	This guideline suggests how a researcher might counter what is said to be a common problem in grounded theory – the production of a low-level theory that is then hard to relate to the broader literature. Scaling up is the process of grouping higher-level categories into broader themes. Scaling up contributes to the generalisability of the theory.
5. Theoretical integration	This guideline helps researchers deal with what we think is an obligation of grounded theorists – theoretical integration. Theoretical integration means relating the theory to other theories in the same or similar fields. It is the process of comparing the substantive theory generated with other, previously developed, theories. This principle contributes to theoretical integration in the discipline and could help in the generation of formal theories.

The future of GTM

What is the future of GTM? As a well-established qualitative analysis method with a vigorous intellectual history, there is no doubt that it will continue to thrive and debates about the nature of GTM will surely continue due to the competing intellectual traditions of Glaser and Strauss.

What has astounded me is how passionate adherents are on both sides of the argument, to the point that it almost seems like a religious dispute. While I have reached my own conclusions based on academic investigation – my sympathies are entirely with the Glaserian version – I am also incredibly grateful for Strauss' (1987) book and Strauss and Corbin's (1990) book. Without their efforts to convey the method to their students, I doubt if I would have learnt enough to attempt the same in this book.

With regard to the two strands of GTM, the removal of the coding paradigm as an obligatory point of passage for the Straussian version may make a difference. Now that use of the paradigm is no longer mandatory and has been substantially de-emphasised (Corbin and Strauss 2008), it may mean that the two strands come more closely together. That said, at the time of writing, the influence of the 1990 book remains undimmed, especially in my own discipline.

The passage of time may mean that the keepers of the flame eventually become distanced from the original dispute and attention may then spread to how we adapt GTM in the light of changing times and changing texts. So, the debate may shift from the amount of adaptations of grounded theory out there and whether or not they are legitimate to the adaptations themselves. The ones that currently exist are not only a product of confusion over the traditions of grounded theory but also of the changing demands of research in the twenty-first century. We now have to contend with digital texts, such as chat messages, the content of websites, e-mail threads and so on. Visual images have become more and more important, too, and accessible with the advent of digital photography – many more people record their lives in many more photographs. There is no reason, in my view, for grounded theory to not be applied to visual images and, indeed, a colleague of mine has already demonstrated this (Díaz Andrade and Arthanari 2009).

One interesting question about digital texts – as we increasingly study sources from the internet, chat threads and website content – is how we deal with the lack of context these texts have. If we follow an e-mail thread, for instance, we are not aware of the context in which that text was produced. There will also be many more instances of data to study, which grounded theory is well positioned to deal with because of the philosophy of sampling 'slices of data'.

So, there will be increasing, and interesting, challenges in qualitative data analysis generally and in grounded theory in particular as more and more of our research is carried out using internet sources. I predict that GTM will be more than up to the challenge.

Summary

- This final chapter has looked at the contested nature of GTM and summarised some key insights from the book. These insights are personal and the product of my attempts to distil the knowledge I have gained, in both teaching and doing GTM, as well as in the process of writing this book.
- The first insight is that GTM is littered with adaptations of the method. There are many reasons for this, but, for me, the main issue is whether or not these are indeed GTM. If they are, these adaptations contribute to GTM as a living breathing method.
- The second insight is about the value of theory. One of the remarkable things about applying GTM is how frequently it does *not* result in a theory, despite that being the aim of the method. The process of building theory helps us understand theory and the role of other theories in our respective disciplines.
- The third insight is that various barriers to using GTM in a dissertation do exist, but they are, in themselves, no argument for not using such a wonderful method. A lack of people doing GTM in their dissertations leads to a lack of future supervisors familiar with the method, so, for me, as an academic, this is a significant point about the future of GTM.
- The fourth insight relates to the phenomena of GTM as a bottom-up method – which is both its strength, in terms of the wonderful insights that can be gained by detailed engagement with the data, and a possible weakness because low-level theories need to be scaled up in order to engage with other theories.
- The fifth insight is that a good grounded theory analysis depends on two things: the ability to abstract concepts and think about relationships. This observation comes from looking at many GTM studies. It is perhaps not

surprising that, for me, a good GTM study is one that puts forward a theory which can be engaged with other theories.

- The sixth insight is that GTM, because of the principles of theoretical sensitivity and theoretical sampling, leads us towards a natural interdisciplinarity. Because we follow the concepts emerging in our theory, rather than the dictates of our discipline, when searching for literature, we gain an appreciation of other disciplines. The principle of theoretical sensitivity helps us recognise how theories are constructed, regardless of discipline.
- The seventh insight discussed the curious fact that, in GTM, the process of theory generation is much examined, but the type of theory that is output from this process is not. I suggested that questions of an intended theory's paradigm, scope, structure, constructs and relationships will have an impact on the process of theory building, so they should be considered at the outset (Seidel and Urquhart 2011)
- I then went on to discuss some guidelines for GTM (Urquhart et al. 2010). While these guidelines are in no way meant to be prescriptive, they do give an indication of the elements that we might expect to see in a GTM study – namely, constant comparison, iterative conceptualisation, theoretical sampling, scaling up and theoretical integration.
- Finally, I went on to speculate about the future of GTM. Will it continue to be a contested concept? How will new digital texts influence our coding practices as we do more and more research using internet sources of all kinds? How will visual data influence the practice of the method? I look forward to finding out, in the company of my students and colleagues. In the meantime, I wish all those on the grounded theory journey well, and I hope they enjoy it as much as I do.

EXERCISES

1 Consider the contested nature of GTM, as described at the beginning of this chapter. How has this played out in your particular discipline? Has one orthodoxy prevailed? Can you think of any other examples in your discipline of a contested concept?

2 Discuss the seven insights about GTM listed in this chapter with a fellow student or researcher. Do you agree with the insights? Why or why not? Can you come up with any of your own and how do they relate to those insights in this chapter?

3 When it comes to research adaptations of GTM in your own discipline, are they explained or do readers have to ponder the relationship of the adaptation to GTM? Which GTM texts are quoted most frequently in journal articles in your discipline?

4 Can you think of qualitative research challenges that GTM would not be able to meet? Why? What would be most difficult to analyse using GTM? How would you deal with issues of context (or lack of) in digital texts?

WEB RESOURCES

www.linkedin.com/groups/Online-Qualitative-Research-Forum-3125683? trk=myg_ugrp_ovr This forum – the Online Qualitative Research Forum – on the professional networking site LinkedIn, contains some interesting discussions about how qualitative research can be applied to digital texts, which, in my opinion, is the next challenge for qualitative research in general and GTM in particular.

www.methodspace.com Again, this is a forum for discussing qualitative research. It is run by Sage and has lots of resources. If we are to look at the future of qualitative research and GTM, it is likely that discussions in such forums will give us a guide to future developments and concerns.

FURTHER READING

Kearney, M.H. (2007) 'From the sublime to the meticulous: The continuing evolution of grounded formal theory', in A. Bryant and K. Charmaz (eds), *The Sage Handbook of Grounded Theory*. London: Sage. This fascinating chapter looks at what attempts have been made to generate grounded formal theories since Glaser and Strauss' 1967 book and speculates on the future of GTM theorising from a postmodern perspective.

Suddaby, R., Hardy, C. and Huy, Q.N. (2011) 'Where are the new theories of organization?', *Academy of Management Review*, 36: 236–46. This article discusses issues of theory development in the management discipline and makes for fascinating reading. There is a lot of discussion about how existing theory might inspire new theory and the lack of indigenous theories in what is an applied discipline. The irony is that, while there is a lot of discussion about how to engage with other theories, there is very little detail regarding theory building from the ground up. It seems to provide a theoretical sampling, of sorts, of existing literature, which is interesting. I can't help thinking that GTM would provide an answer!

FREQUENTLY ASKED QUESTIONS

How do I defend my use of GTM to others?

This is possibly the question I get asked most frequently by postgraduates. This is a reflection on the institutional barriers to using GTM that still seem to exist in some discipline areas. It is still seen as an unusual method in some disciplines, including my own.

GTM is *very* defensible, I think, for several reasons, two of which are that it has a superb chain of evidence and it is absolutely 'grounded' in the findings. It also has a systematic set of procedures. We get to find out what the data is telling us in a particular context, as opposed to imposing a theory on it from elsewhere. Thus, it is brilliant for investigating innovations, processes and what people do in various settings. For me, though, the overriding reason for using GTM is that it helps us understand the theory-building process and how important theory is.

In terms of defending its use, there are many, many references relating to GTM – too many to detail here – but the point is that it is a well-established method that has been in use for over 40 years. So, in any defence of a PhD proposal, those references can be quoted. The method is superb for new research problems where no previous theory exists. The use of GTM can otherwise generally be justified in terms of its appropriateness for the research problem, so how the research problem is framed always matters. If we start with a general research problem and make the point that the analysis will determine the dimensions of that research problem (Dey 1993), this is also helpful.

I've just read your whole book. Forgive me for being cynical, but why is GTM so great again? Surely if it was as good and useful as you suggest, a whole lot more people would be using it? Doesn't the whole preponderance of books on GTM just illustrate how difficult it is?

This, of course, is not a frequently asked question that I encounter now, but it may be one I encounter in the future! I do, however, encounter students and colleagues who regard GTM as an esoteric qualitative research method, of needless complexity to boot. I think it *is* complex, actually, because theory building is, by definition, difficult. Analysing qualitative data is also complex. The key procedures of GTM, however, possess simplicity and elegance. GTM has a robust intellectual tradition, in no small part due to the continued writings of one of its founders, Barney Glaser, who has made, and continues to make, important advances in the method.

The reasons for people not using GTM vary from discipline to discipline and how they use it varies, too. This, to my mind, says everything about the battle to use qualitative research methods in the past 40 years or so rather than the method itself. It's obvious to me, and others, that power resides in various discourses about research methods and vested interests in certain methods sometimes trump others. Putting all that aside, I do think most people who have used GTM will attest to its power, to both analyse data and build robust theory.

Glossary

Axial coding   A stage of coding proposed by Strauss and Corbin. The codes are first dimensionalised, then the Strauss and Corbin coding paradigm is applied. This stage of coding has, in the past, presented researchers with challenges (see Kendall 1999; Urquhart 2001). It is important to note that this phase is not used in Corbin and Strauss' current version (2008).

Blank slate   Sometimes people erroneously assume that, to do GTM, researchers have to be a 'blank slate' ('tabula rasa') and forget everything they have read. In fact, the injunction is quite different – not to impose concepts on the data, but consider what the data says first. Page 3 of Glaser and Strauss' book *The Discovery of Grounded Theory* (1967) points out that researchers do not approach reality as a 'tabula rasa'. *See also* 'Non-committal literature review'.

Coding   The act of attaching concepts to data. These concepts are called codes.

Coding families   First proposed by Glaser in his book *Theoretical Sensitivity* in 1978, where he introduced 18 coding families. These help us to see how categories might be related to each other. Glaser introduced a further 25 families in another of his books in 2005. The '6Cs' and 'Strategy' families seem to have been the basis for Strauss' controversial *coding paradigm*.

Coding paradigm   The coding paradigm was proposed by Strauss and Corbin in their book *Basics of Qualitative Research* in 1990. This paradigm, and the book itself, was the cause of a split between Glaser and Strauss in 1990. The coding paradigm consists of 'Causal conditions, context, intervening conditions, action/interaction strategies and consequences'.

It was stated in their book in 1990 that it was mandatory, stressed less in the next edition in 1998 and, now, is purely optional in Corbin and Strauss' 2008 book. In my own field, it has not been much applied, but, when it has, it does seem to have been implicated in the 'forcing' that Glaser felt would occur if the paradigm was used Seidel and Urquhart (2011a).

Constant comparison	A method proposed by Glaser and Strauss that helps with qualitative analysis. Put simply, it is the act of comparing one piece of data you have attached a concept to with another piece of data you have attached the same concept to in order to see if it represents the same concept.
Emergence	This term was first used by Glaser in 1992 and I would argue that it is a key tenet of his thinking. Emergence is the idea that the theory emerges from the data, the data needs to be allowed to tell its own story. The idea of emergence is subject to some criticism (see, for instance, Bryant 2002) due to the lack of consideration of reflexivity when analysing data. It also has philosophical implications – it depends on your ontological view, if you regard the findings as an underlying structure within the data.
Forcing	This term was first used by Glaser in 1992 and encapsulates one of the key debates of grounded theory. Glaser felt that the use of the coding paradigm proposed by Strauss and Corbin in 1990 forced the data and derailed it from relevance. For Glaser, it is very important that the data is not 'forced' but allowed to tell its own story, as opposed to having a particular theoretical view overlaid on it.
Formal theory	Formal theories focus on high-level conceptual entities (Strauss 1987), such as organisational learning. Other examples of formal theories include structuration theory, theories on social capital and actor network theory. Glaser and Strauss (1967) say that it should be possible to build a formal theory from a substantive theory, by using theoretical sampling to widen the scope of the theory (see Glaser and Strauss 1967: Chapter 4). There are, however, not many examples of formal theories produced by GTM (see Kearney 2007).
Grounded theory	What is produced by GTM. The theory is said to be 'grounded' because it is underpinned by data. Each concept in a grounded theory is underpinned by many instances of the concept occurring in the data.

Grounded theory method (GTM)	This term was suggested by Antony Bryant as a useful way of making the point that grounded theory is a method and a grounded theory is the product of that method. It is used in this book for precisely that reason.
Integrative diagrams	A technique suggested by Strauss (1987). Categories and relationships are represented visually (and cumulatively) as a means of thinking about relationships.
Non-committal literature review	This is a useful mechanism for those using GTM – the idea that a literature review should be non-committal and the emerging theory will determine the relevance of the literature. Especially useful for dissertation students who don't have the option of not doing a literature review.
Open coding	The first stage of coding in both strands of GTM (Glaserian and Straussian). The data is examined line by line and codes attached to words or groups of words.
Scaling up	The process of scaling up the emergent theory to a sufficient level of abstraction in order to engage it with other theories in the field. Because the initial stage of coding in GTM is detailed, the theory can be at quite a low level, which is why the founders suggest having one or two core categories for the emerging theory.
Selective coding	The second stage of coding in the Glaserian version of grounded theory. It is when open codes are grouped into higher level categories, with the core category or categories in mind.
Substantive theory	This is the type of theory that GTM produces in the first instance. It is substantive in the sense that it pertains only to the phenomena being studied and makes no claims to generalise beyond that particular phenomenon.
Theoretical codes	A theoretical code, to quote Glaser (1978: 55), 'conceptualises how the substantive codes may relate to each other'. Theoretical codes are contained in the coding families put forward by Glaser (1978; 2005), but can also be self-generated by the researcher. Glaser warns of the possible danger of 'forcing' using a theoretical code – the theoretical code has to fit with the emerging theory.
Theoretical coding	The third stage of coding in the Glaserian version of grounded theory. Relationships are built between categories, often using *theoretical codes* from *coding families*, as first proposed by Glaser in 1978.

Theoretical integration	The task of relating the emergent theory to other theories in the same or similar field. Strauss (1987) talks of our obligation to 'grapple' with the literature once the theory has been generated.
Theoretical memos	Theoretical memos are a key tool for theorising. The idea is that, during coding, the researcher can break off to write down ideas they have about the codes they are working on. Theoretical memos were first proposed by Glaser (1978) and their use is no longer confined to GTM as others value the practice, which allows researchers space to think creatively about their data.
Theoretical sampling	A very powerful idea from GTM and one that has spread from GTM to other methods of research, such as Eisenhardt (1989). Theoretical sampling is deciding on analytic grounds where to sample from next. In this way, the theory can be quickly developed based on emerging concepts. One common way to increase the scope of the theory is to sample unlike groups, while, to increase the explanatory power of the theory, researchers sample diverse and less saturated concepts. For a full explanation, see Glaser and Strauss (1967: Chapter 4).
Theoretical saturation	Theoretical saturation is the point in coding when you find that no new codes occur in the data. There are mounting instances of the same codes, but no new ones.

References

Adam, M. (2008) 'IT capacity building in the Maldives: A study of the tourism sector'. Unpublished PhD thesis, Information Systems and Operations Management, University of Auckland.

Allan, G. (2003) 'A critique of using grounded theory as a research method', *Electronic Journal of Business Research Methods*, 2: 1–10.

Allen, P., M. Ramachandran, et al. (2003) *PRISMS: an approach to software process improvement for small to medium enterprises.* Proceedings of Third International Conference on Quality Software.

Alvesson, M. and Sköldberg, K. (2009) *Reflexive Methodology: New vistas for qualitative research.* London: Sage.

Andrew, T. (2006) 'The literature review in grounded theory: A response to McCallin (2003)', *The Grounded Theory Review*, 5: 29–41.

Annells, M.P. (1996) 'Grounded theory method: Philosophical perspectives, paradigm of inquiry, and postmodenism', *Qualitative Health Research*, 6: 379–93.

Bacharach, S. B. (1989) 'Organizational Theories: Some Criteria for Evaluation', *Academy of Management Review,* 14(4): 496–515.

Badshah, A. (2010) 'Notes from the field: Unlimited potential a catalyst for social and economic empowerment', *Information Technologies and International Development*, 6: 72–7.

Barthes, R. (1972) *Mythologies.* London: Paladin.

Baskerville, R. and Pries-Heje, J. (1999) 'Grounded action research: A method for understanding IT in practice', *Accounting, Management and Information Technologies*, 9: 1–23.

Benoliel, J.Q. (1996) 'Grounded theory and nursing knowledge', *Qualitative Health Research*, 6: 406–28.

Bhaskar, R. (1998) *The Possibility of Naturalism: A philosophical critique of the contemporary human sciences.* London: Routledge.

Bourdieu, P. (1986) 'The Forms of Capital', in J. G. in Richardson (ed.), *Handbook of Theory and Research for the Sociology of Education.* New York: Greenwood, pp. 241–58.

Brunello, P. (2010) 'View from practice: ICT for education projects: A look from behind the scenes', *Information Technology for Development*, 16: 232–9.

Bryant, A. (2002) 'Re-grounding grounded theory', *Journal of Information Technology Theory and Application*, 4: 25–42.

Bryant, A. (2006) *Thinking 'informatically': A new understanding of information, communication and technology.* Ceredigion: Mellen Press.

Bryant, A. and Charmaz, K. (2007) 'Grounded theory research: Methods and practices', in A. Bryand and K. Charmaz (eds), *The Sage Handbook of Grounded Theory.* London: Sage.

Burgess, C., Livesay, K. Lund, K. (1998) 'Explorations in context space: Words, sentences, discourse', *Discourse Processes*, 25: 211–57.

Burrell, G. and Morgan, G. (1979) *Sociological Paradigms and Organizational Analysis.* Oxford: Heinemann.

Cameron, J. (1995) *The Artist's Way: A course in discovering and recovering your creative self*. London: Pan Macmillan.

Casnig, J.D. (1997–2009) *A Language of Metaphors*. Kingston, Ontario: Knowgramming.

Charmaz, K. (2006) *Constructing Grounded Theory: A practical guide through qualitative analysis*. Thousand Oaks, CA: Sage.

Clarke, A.E. (2005) *Situational Analysis: Grounded theory after the postmodern turn*. Thousand Oaks, CA: Sage.

Coe, K. and Reitzes, M. (2010) 'Obama on the stump: Features and determinants of a rhetorical approach', *Presidential Studies Quarterly*, 40: 391–413.

Corbin, J. and Strauss, A.L. (2008) *Basics of Qualitative Research: Techniques and procedures for developing grounded theory*. Thousand Oaks, CA: Sage.

Corley, K. and Gioia, D. (2011) 'Building theory about theory building: What consititutes a theoretical contribution?', *Academy of Management Review*, 36: 12–32.

Cresswell, J.W. (1998) *Qualitative Inquiry and Research Design: Choosing among five traditions*. London: Sage.

Crotty, M. (1998). *The Foundations of Social Research*, CA: Sage.

Day, K.J. (2007) 'Supporting the emergence of a shared services organisation: Managing change in complex health ICT projects'. Unpublished PhD thesis, Information Systems and Operations Management, University of Auckland.

Dey, I. (1993) *Qualitative Data Analysis: A user-friendly guide for social scientists*. London: Routledge.

Dey, I. (1999) *Grounding Grounded theory: Guidelines for qualitative inquiry*. CA: Academic Press.

Díaz Andrade, A. (2007) 'Interaction between existing social networks and information communication technology (ICT) tools: Evidence from rural Andes'. Unpublished PhD thesis, Information Systems and Operations Management, University of Auckland.

Díaz Andrade, A. and Arthanari, T. (2009) 'An unorthodox interpretive approach in information systems research: A picture is worth 1000 words'. Paper presented at the 30th International Conference on Information Systems (ICIS): 'Doing IT Research that Matters', Phoenix, Arizona, 15–18 December.

Dudash, E. (2007) 'International appeal in the presidential inaugural: An update on genre and an expansion of argument', *Contemporary Argumentation and Debate*, 28: 47–64.

Dybå, T. (2005) 'An Empirical Investigation of the Key Factors for Success in Software Process Improvement', IEEE Trans. of Software Eng, 31(5): 410–24.

Eisenhardt, K.M. (1989) 'Building theories from case study research', *Academy of Management Review*, 14: 532–50.

Emrich, C.G., Brower, H.H., Feldman, J.M. and Garland, H. (2001) 'Images in words: Presidential rhetoric, charisma, and greatness', *Administrative Science Quarterly*, 46(3): 527–57.

Felder, R. and Brent, R. (2008) 'How to write anything', *Chemical Engineering Education*, 42(3): 139–40.

Fern, E. (2008) 'The implications of how social workers conceptualise childhood, for developing child-directed practice: An action research study in Iceland'. Unpublished PhD thesis, School of Health and Social Studies, University of Warwick.

Fernández, W.D. (2003) 'Metateams in major information technology projects: A grounded theory on conflict, trust, communication, and cost'. Unpublished PhD thesis, School of Information Systems, Australian National University, Canberra.

Fernández, W. and Lehmann, H. (2011) 'Case studies and grounded theory method in information systems research: Issues and use', *Journal of Information Technology Case and Application Research*, 13(1): 4–15.

Fever, P. (2010) 'What can Obama say about Iraq?', *Foreign Policy Magazine*, 29 August.

Frank, D.A. (2009) 'The prophetic voice and the face of the other in Barack Obama's A "A More Perfect Union" address, March 18, 2008', *Rhetoric and Public Affairs*, 12(2): 167–94.

Galal, G. (2001) 'From contexts to constructs: The use of grounded theory in operationalising contingent process models', *European Journal of Information Systems*, 10: 2–14.

Gallie, W.B. (1956) 'Essentially contested concepts', *Proceedings of the Aristotelian Society*, 167–98.

Glaser, B.G. (1978) *Theoretical Sensitivity: Advances in the methodology of grounded theory*. Mill Valley, CA: The Sociology Press.

Glaser, B.G. (1992) *Basics of Grounded Theory Analysis: Emergence vs. forcing*. Mill Valley, CA: The Sociology Press.

Glaser, B.G. (2005) *The Grounded Theory Perspective III: Theoretical coding*. Mill Valley, CA: The Sociology Press.

Glaser, B.G. and Strauss, A.L. (1967) *The Discovery of Grounded Theory: Strategies for qualitative research*. Chicago, IL: Aldine.

Gorton, A. (2010) 'Language techniques of effective speech making', 7 April.

Gregor, S. (2006) 'The nature of theory in information systems', *MIS Quarterly*, 30: 611–42.

Guinan, P. (1988) *Patterns of Excellence for IS Professionals: An analysis of communication behaviour*. Washington, DC: ICIT Press.

Hansen, B. and Kautz, K. (2005) 'Grounded theory applied: Studying information systems development methodologies in practice. Paper presented at the 38th Hawaii International Conference on System Sciences, Big Island, Hawaii, 3–6 January.

Heeks, R. and Molla, A. (2009) 'Impact assessment of ICT-for-development projects: A compendium of approaches', Development Informatics working paper series. Development Informatics Group, Institute for Development Policy and Management.

Hekkala, R., Urquhart, C., and Iivari, N. (2009) 'Who is in charge and whose rules are being followed?: Power in an interorganisational project'. Paper presented at the European Conference on Information Systems, Verona, 8–10 June.

Hirschheim, R. and Newman, M. (1991) 'Symbolism and information systems development: Myth, metaphor and magic', *Information Systems Research*, 2: 29–62.

Holton, J.A. (2007) 'The coding process and its challenges', in A. Bryant and K. Charmaz (eds), *The Sage Handbook of Grounded Theory*. London: Sage.

Jeffrey, C., Jeffrey, P. and Jeffrey, R. (2005) 'Reproducing difference?: Schooling, jobs, and empowerment in Uttar Pradesh, India', *World Development*, 33: 2085–101.

Jick, T.D. (1979) 'Mixing qualitative and quantitative methods: Triangulation in action', *Adminstrative Science Quarterly*, 24: 602–11.

Jones, R. and Noble, G. (2007) 'Grounded theory and management research: A lack of integrity?', *Qualitative Research in Organizations and Management: An international journal*, 2: 84–103.

Kearney, M.H. (2007) 'From the sublime to the meticulous: The continuing evolution of grounded formal theory', in A. Bryant and K. Charmaz (eds), *The Sage Handbook of Grounded Theory*. London: Sage.

Kendall, J. (1999) 'Axial coding and the grounded theory controversy', *Western Journal of Nursing Research*, 21: 743–57.

Klein, H.K. and Myers, M.D. (1999) 'A set of principles for conducting and evaluating interpretive field studies in information systems', *MIS Quarterly*, 23: 167–94.

Kuruvilla, S., Erickson, C.L. and Hwang, A. (2002) 'An assessment of the Singapore skills development system: Does it constitute a viable model for other developing countries?', *World Development*, 30: 1461–76.

Layder, D. (1993) *New Strategies for Social Research*. Cambridge: Polity Press.

Layder, D. (1998) *Sociological Practice: Linking theory and research.* London: Sage.

Lehmann, H. (2010) *The Dynamics of International Information Systems: Anatomy of a grounded theory investigation.* Springerlink.

Levina, N. and Vaast, E. (2005) 'The emergence of boundary spanning competence in practice: Implications for implementation and use of information systems', *MIS Quarterly*, 29(2): 335–63.

Levina, N. and Vaast, E. (2008) 'Innovating or doing as told?: Status differences and overlapping boundaries in offshore collaboration', *MIS Quarterly*, 32(2): 307–32.

Lings, B. and Lundell, B. (2005) 'On the adaptation of grounded theory procedures: Insights from the evolution of the 2G method', *Information Technology and People*, 18: 196–211.

Lockheed, M.E. (2009) 'Evaluating development learning: The World Bank experience', *Evaluation,* 15(1): 113–26.

Madill, A., Jordan, A. and Shirley, C. (2000) 'Objectivity and reliability in qualitative analysis: Realist, contextualist and radical constructionist epistemologies', *British Journal of Psychology*, 91(1): 1–20.

Martin, V.B. (2006) 'The relationship between an emerging grounded theory and the existing literature: Four phases for consideration', *The Grounded Theory Review*, 5(2/3): 47–57.

Maylor, H. and Blackmon, K. (2005) *Researching Business and Management.* London: Palgrave Macmillan.

McCallin, A. (2003) 'Grappling with the literature in a grounded theory study', *Contemporary Nurse*, 15(1–2): 61–9.

Melia, K.M. (1996) 'Rediscovering Glaser', *Qualitative Health Research*, 6(3): 368–73.

Miles, M.B. and Huberman, A.M. (1994) *Qualitative Data Analysis: An expanded sourcebook.* Newbury Park, CA: Sage.

Mio, J. S., Riggio, R. E., Levin, S., Reese, R. (2005) "Presidential leadership and charisma: The effects of metaphor." *Leadership Quarterly* 16: 287–94.

Myers, M. (2008) *Qualitative Research in Business and Management.* London: Sage.

Naidu, R. (2003) Software Process Improvement of Small & Medium Organizations. MSc thesis, Department of Computer Science, University of Auckland, New Zealand.

Nathaniel, A. (2006) 'Thoughts on the literature review and GT', *The Grounded Theory Review*, 5(2/3): 35–41.

Olesen, K. (2006) 'Technological frames and practices of use within an organisation over a 10 year period'. Unpublished PhD thesis, Information Systems and Operations Management, University of Auckland.

Orlikowski, W. (1992) 'The duality of technology: Rethinking the concept of technology in organizations', *Organization Science*, 3(3): 398–427.

Orlikowski, W. (1993) 'CASE tools as organizational change: Investigating incremental and radical changes in systems development', *MIS Quarterly*, 17: 309–40.

Orlikowski, W. and Baroudi, J. (1991) 'Studying information technology in organizations: Research approaches and assumptions', *Information Systems Research*, 2(1): 1–28.

Ramiller, N. C. (2001) 'The "textual attitude" and new technology.' *Information & Organization* 11: 129–56.

Reid, G. (2006) 'Non-ICT executive perceptions of, and attitudes toward, ICT infrastructure projects'. Unpublished PhD thesis, Information Systems and Operations Management, University of Auckland.

Rowland, R.C. (2002) *Analyzing Rhetoric: A handbook for the informed citizen in a new millennium.* Dubuque, IA: Kendall Hunt.

Ruth, S. R. (2000) 'Measuring long term effects of technology transfer in developing nations: the case of Internet training at the Romanian Academy of Science', *Information Technology for Development*, 9: 105–21.

Saldaña, J. (2009) *The Coding Manual for Qualitative Researchers* London: Sage.

Schön, D. (1983) *The Reflective Practitioner: How professionals think in action*. New York: Basic Books.

Schwandt, T. (1994) 'Constructivist, interpretivist approaches to human inquiry', in N. Denzin and Y. Lincoln (eds) *Handbook of Qualitative Research*. Thousand Oaks, CA: Sage.

Schwandt, T. (1997) *Qualitative Inquiry*. London: Sage.

Scott, L., Jeffery, R. et al. (2001) Practical software process improvement-the IMPACT project. Proceedings of Australian Software Engineering Conference, Australia.

Seidel, S. and Urquhart, C. (2011) 'Characterising grounded theory development in information systems: A framework'. Working paper.

Seidel, S. and Urquhart, C. (2012) 'Strauss and Corbin's grounded theory in IS top journals from 1993 to 2010: A case of emergence or forcing?', *Journal of the Association of Information Technology* (submitted).

Sen, A. (1999) *Development as Freedom*. Oxford, Oxford University Press.

Seyranian, V. and M. C. Bligh (2008) "Presidential charismatic leadership: Exploring the rhetoric of social change." *The Leadership Quarterly* 19: 54–76.

Spradley, J. (1979) *The Ethnographic Interview*. Fort Worth, TX: Harcourt Brace Jovanovich.

Stern, P.N. (1994) 'Eroding grounded theory', in J. Morse (ed.), *Critical Issues in Qualitative Research Methods*. Thousand Oaks, CA: Sage.

Strauss, A. (1987) *Qualitative Analysis for Social Scientists*. Cambridge: Cambridge University Press.

Strauss, A. and Corbin, J. (1990) *Basics of Qualitative Research: Grounded theory procedures and techniques*. Newbury Park, CA: Sage.

Strauss, A. and Corbin, J. (1998) *Basics of Qualitative Research: Techniques and procedures for developing grounded theory*. London: Sage.

Suddaby, R. (2006) 'From the editors: What grounded theory is not', *Academy of Management Journal*, 49:4 633–42 .

Suddaby, R., Hardy, C. and Huy, Q.N. (2011) 'Where are the new theories of organization?', *Academy of Management Review*, 36: 236–46.

Sulayman, M., Urquhart, C., Mendes, E. and Seidel, S. (2012) 'Software process improvement success factors for small and medium Web companies: A qualitative study', *Information and Software Technology*, 54(5): 479–500.

Sulayman, M. and Mendes E. (2010) 'Quantitative Assessments of Key Success Factors in Software Process Improvement for Small and Medium Web Companies'. 25th Symposium for Applied Computing, ACM, Switzerland.

Trice, H. and Beyer, J. (1984) 'Studying organizational cultures through rites and ceremonials', *Academy of Management Review*, 9: 653–889.

Urquhart, C. (1997) 'Exploring analyst–client communication: Using grounded theory techniques to investigate interaction in informal requirements gathering', in A.S. Lee, J. Liebenau and J.I. DeGross (eds), *Information Systems and Qualitative Research*. London: Chapman & Hall.

Urquhart, C. (1999) 'Themes and strategies in early requirements gathering'. Unpublished PhD thesis, Department of Computer Science, University of Tasmania, Hobart.

Urquhart, C. (2001) 'An encounter with grounded theory: Tackling the practical and philosophical issues', in E. Trauth (ed.) *Qualitative Research in IS: Issues and trends*. Hershey, PA: Idea Group Publishing.

Urquhart, C. (2002) 'Regrounding grounded theory – or reinforcing old prejudices?: A brief reply to Bryant', *Journal of Information Technology Theory and Application*, 4(3): 43–54.

Urquhart, C. and Fernández, W. (2006) 'Grounded theory method: The researcher as blank slate and other myths', in *ICIS 2006 Proceedings*. Paper 31.

Urquhart, C., Lehmann, H. and Myers, M. (2010) 'Putting the theory back into grounded theory: Guidelines for grounded theory studies in information systems', *Information Systems Journal*, 20(4): 357–81.

Walker, D. and Myrick, F. (2006) 'Grounded theory: An exploration of process and procedure', *Qualitative Health Research*, 16(4): 547–59.

Walsham, G. (1995) 'Interpretive case studies in IS research: Nature and method', *European Journal of Information Systems*, 4(2): 74–81.

Walsham, G. (1997) 'Actor–network theory and IS research: Current status and future prospects', in A.S. Lee, J. Liebenau and J.I. Degross (eds), *Information Systems and Qualitative Research*. London: Chapman & Hall.

Walsham, G. (2002) 'Cross-cultural software production and use', *MIS Quarterly*, 26(4): 359–80.

Watzlawick, P., Weakland, J. and Fisch, R. (1974) *Change Principles of Problem Formation and Problem Resolution*. New York: W.W. Norton.

Weick, K. E. (1989) 'Theory Construction as Disciplined Imagination', *Academy of Management Review*, 14(4): 516–31.

Whetten, D.A. (1989) 'What constitutes a theoretical contribution?', *Academy of Management Review*, 14:4 490–5.

White, H. (2010) 'A Contribution to Current Debates in Impact Evaluation', *Evaluation*, 16.

Yin, R.K. (2009) *Case Study Research: Design and methods*. Thousand Oaks, CA: Sage.

Index

Tables and Figures are indicated by page numbers in bold.

abstraction, 89
Academy of Management, 182
action research, 63, 68
Adam, M., 72
adaptability of GTM, 178
agenda setting, 111, **112–13**
aim of
GTM, 4, 5, 16
Allan, G., 30
Alvesson and Sköldberg, 71
analytic coding, 36–7
analytic generalisations, 169, 171, **172**
Annells, M.P., 31
approaches to coding, **44**
axial coding, 25–6, 177, 184, 191

Badshah, A., 141, 142
Barthes, Roland, 28
Benoliel, J.Q., 15
Bhaskar, R., 60
'blank slate' myth, 7, 29–30
bottom-up coding, 38, 44, 180
Brunello, P., 141, 142
Bryant, A., 31, 176, 177
building blocks of theory, 132–4, **133**
Burrell, G. and Morgan, G., 57, 58

Cameron, J., 150, 174
case study, 63, 67, 68
cases, selection of, 61
categories, 9, 103, 108
    core categories, 133
    grouping, 185
    see also relating categories; theoretical coding
chains of evidence, 159–**61**, **160**
Charmaz, K., 104
    coding, 24, 28, 50
    constant comparison, 182
    data collection, 8, 65
    neutrality of GTM, 32
    theoretical memos, 113, **114**
    in vivo codes, 96

Clarke, A.E., 71
coding, 3, 9, 21–8, 35–54
    approaches, **44**
    axial, 25–6, 177, 184
    bottom-up, 38, 44, 180
    conditions, 25, 26
    and context, 69
    definitions, 35, 36, 191
    descriptive and analytic, 36–7, 41, 81
    dimensionalised, 25
    discussion with colleagues, 54, 60, 124
    families, 27–8, 108, **109**, 118–19, 191
    and language translation, 105
    line by line, 24, 38, 46–8
    middle-range, 39, 44
    open see open coding
    presentation of, 154–9, **155**, **156**,
        157, **158**
    procedures, 9–10, 19, **23**, 45–51, **155**
    selective see selective coding
    thematic, 39–41, 44, 180
    theoretical see theoretical coding
    and theory, 179
    as theory building, 41–4
    tips, **103**
    top-down, 38–9, 44, 53, 180
    types of codes (Miles and Huberman), 183
    using literature, 53
    validity, 54
    variations in approaches, **40**
    visual materials, 69–70
    in vivo codes, 96, 103
coding paradigm, 19–20, 25–6, 176,
    186, 191–2
Coe, K. and Reitzes, M., 138
components of theories, **6**, 106
conceptualisation, 131–**2**
consent of participants, 70
constant comparison, 5, 17–18, 22–3, 181,
    182–3, 186
    definition, 9, 192
    with theoretical sampling, 63

constructs in GTM, 106
constructs, relationships between, 6
context, 153, 187
Corbin, J. and Strauss, A.L., 6
   coding paradigm, 20-1, 176, 192
Corley, K. and Gioia, D., 146
corroboration, 62
Cresswell, J.W., 4
critical research philosophy, 59
Crotty, M., 57

data analysis, 5, 8-9, 67
   software, 101-2
data collection, 5, 8
   commensurable methods of, 62
   how much?, 72
   methods, 69-70
   overlapping analysis and, 64, 67
   phases of, 65
   and preliminary analyses, 64-5
Day, K., 68
defending use of GTM, 190
descriptive coding, 36-7, 183
Dey, I., 4, 11, 29, 39, 41
Díaz Andrade, A., 67, 74, 162, 164
digital texts, 186, 187
dissertations see PhD studies; writing up
Dudash, E., 138

Eisenhardt, K.M., 67, 74
emergence, 7, 17, 60, 192
Emrich, C.G. et al, 138
epistemology and ontology, 56-62, **57**, **59**
   paradigms of social theory (Burrell and
      Morgan), **58**
ethics, 70
ethnographic methodology, 63, 67

Felder, R. and Brent, R., 150, 174
Fern, E., 74
Fernández, W., 165, 166
Fernández, W. and Lehmann, H., 75
focused coding, 50
forcing, 18, 19, 22, 125, 192
formal theories, 131, 192
frameworks, 6, 28, 30, 40, 180
Frank, D.A., 138, 139

generalisability of a theory, 60-1, 169, 171
Glaser, B.G., 6, 24, 104, 127
   Basics of Grounded Theory Analysis,
      19, 22
   coding, 23, 24, **27-8**, 49, 88, 108, 118-19,
      128, 191
   dispute with Strauss and Corbin, 18-21
   Doing Grounded Theory, 22
   Grounded Theory Perspective III, 22

Glaser, B.G. cont.
   literature review, 16-17
   philosophical stance of GTM, 31
   relating categories, 107
   substantive theories, 185
   theoretical memos, 90, 110, **111**, 113
   Theoretical Sensitivity, 15, 22
   theory development, 31
Glaser, B.G. and Strauss, A.L., 3, 5, 16, 21
   'blank slate' myth, 29, 191
   slices of data, 18
   The Discovery of Grounded Theory, 14-15,
      22, 177
   theoretical sampling, 64
   theory development, 31, 64, 131, 143-4
Gregor, S., 6-7
Grounded theory method (GTM)
   as a contested concept, **177**
   definitions, 4-5, 16, 192-3
guidelines for GTM, 182-5, **186**
Guinnan, P., 38-9

Heeks, R. and Molla, A., 141, 142
Hekkala, R. et al, 162, 163
Hirschheim, R. and Newman, M., 28
history of GTM, 3, 14-15, 18
   Glaser-Strauss dispute, 18-21
   seminal books, **22**
Holton, J.A., 38
hyperspace analogue, 60

in vivo codes, 96, 103
in/flexibility? of GTM, 30
integrative diagrams, **114**-16, **115**, 193
interdisciplinary nature of GTM, 181
interpretive codes, 183
interpretivist research, 61-2
   and positivist research, 31-2, 56-60,
      58, **59**
interviews, 10, 69
IT skills in developing countries: example
   relating theories to literature, **140**-3, **141**
iterative conceptualisation, 183-4, 186

Jeffrey, C. et al, 141

Kearney, M.H., 189
key features of GTM, 4-5, 15-18
Klein, H.K. and Myers, D., 71, 75
Kuruvilla, S. et al, 141, 142

labelling, 41
language translation, 105
Layder, D., 89
Lehmann, H., 66, 75, 134
levels of theories, 131-6, **132**, 169
Levina, N. and Vaast, E., 125, 127, 136, 172

line by line coding, 24, 38, 46–8
literature
    integration with theories, 169–**72**, **170**
    in presentation of findings, 162, **164–5**
    relating theories to, 136–43, **137**
        emergent categories example, **140–1**
        key audiences, 138
        metaphors, 138
        themes and rhetorical devices,
            137–9, **138**
literature review, 7, 16–17, 29, 34
    and development of theories, 136, 179
    non-committal, 193
    phasing, 29–30
    and PhD studies, 179
Lockheed, M.E., 140

Madill, A. et al, 31, 60
Martin, V.B., 29–30
Masters degrees, 179
means of representation, 106
Melia, K., 15, 34
meta theories, 136
methodology, 62–70
    methods of data collection, 69–70
    theoretical sampling, 63–6, **65**
Miles, M.B. and Huberman, A.M., 53, 183
Mio, J.S., 138
Myers, M., 62, 63, 67, 70

narrative framework, 5

Obama, Barack: inauguration speech:
    example
    of coding, 78–91, 116–21
    of relating theories to literature, 137–40
observation, 65
Olesen, K., 154, 155
open coding, 5, 9, 10, 23–4, **45–9**, **46**,
    105, 193
    example 1, 78–88
        1st section, **80–1**
        2nd section, **82**
        3rd section, **84**
        4th section, **85**
        5th section, **87**
        emerging themes, 81–2
        excerpt from Obama's speech, **79**
    example 2, 91–9
        1st chunk, **94**
        2nd chunk, **95**
        3rd chunk, 97–8
        data chunks, 91, 92, **93**
        excerpt from interview, **92**
        in vivo codes, 96
    example from interview, **155**
    families of codes, **109**

open coding cont.
    length of codes, 86
    line by line, 24, 46–7
    time needed, 48–9
    see also selective coding; theoretical coding
Orlikowski, W. and Baroudi, J., 57, 59, 61, 62
outputs of GTM, 181–2

pattern (linked) codes, 183
PhD studies, 55, 56, 75–6
    and institutional barriers to GTM, 179–80
    and use of GTM, 179–80
    see also writing up
philosophy of researcher, 56–60
photographs, 69, 73, 187
positivist research, 60–1
    and interpretivist research, 31–2, 56–60,
        58, **59**

qualitative research, 13, 32, 180
    as 'high risk' research, 75
quality of analysis, 181
quantitative data, 5, 8

reality, nature of, 57–8
reflexivity, 70–1
reframing, 39
Reid, G., 155, 156, 157, 158, 165, 168
relating categories, 41–4, **42**, **43**, 108, **110**,
        127, 134
    importance of, 116, 181
    presentation, 165, **167**, **168**
    see also theoretical coding
representation of theories, 6
research design, 55–77
    breadth and depth in, 72
    ethics, 70
    general designs, 68–9
    methodology, 62–70
    philosophy of researcher, 56–62
    reflexivity, 70–1
    role of GMT, 55–6
    suggested headings for, 67–8
    theoretical memos, 71–2
    and theoretical models, 76–7
    theory-building designs, 63–8
rewriting theories, 143
rhetorical studies, 138
Rowland, R.C., 138
Ruth, S.R., 141

Saldaña, J., 53
scaling up theories, 10, 30–1, 129–47, 184–5,
        186, 193
    definition, 193
    and levels of theories, 131–6
    reasons for, 130–1

scaling up theories *cont.*
  relating to literature, 136–43
    scope and generalisability, **143-4**, 145
scientific method, 56–7
scope, 6
seed concepts, 131
selective coding, 5, 10, 24, **48**, 49–50, 177
  core categories, 88–**9**, 116
  definition, 88, 193
  example 1, 88–91
    revised codes, **91**
  example 2, 99–101
    1st selection, **100**
    2nd selection, **101**
  example (Reid), **156**
  grouping categories, 100, 116–**17**, 127
  presentation
    diagram of relationship paths, **157**
semantic relationships, 108, **110**
semantic space modelling, 60
Seyranian and Bligh, 138
'slices of data', 16, 18, 69
software, 101–2
Spradley, J., 27, 42, 43, 108, 110, 119
statements of relationship, 106
strands of GTM, 18–21, 34, 177, 186
Strauss, A., 25, 31, 49, 90, 110
  integrative diagrams, 114
  Qualitative Analysis for Social Scientists, 22
  scaling up theories, 130–1
Strauss, A. and Corbin, J., 3, 25
  Basics of Qualitative Research, 15, 16,
    19, 22
  coding paradigm, **26**, 110, 176, 191–2
  dispute with Glaser, 18–21
  relating categories, 107
substantive codes, 107
substantive theories, 4, 16, 31, 61, 162, 178
  definition, 193
  writing up, 162, 163, 165, **166**, **168**
Suddaby, R., 13
Suddaby, R. et al, 189
Sulayman, M. et al, 165, 167, 170

thematic coding, 39–41, 44, 180
theoretical coding, 10, 25, 26–8, 50–1,
    106–10, 184
  definition, 193
  ample 1, 116–21
    ouping selective codes, 116–**17**, 127
    etical memo fragment, **120**
    2, 121–5
      ategories, **122**
      des for, **121**
      mo, 123–**4**
      8
      agrams, 114–16, **115**

theoretical coding *cont.*
  and theoretical memos, 110–14
  tips, **126**
  and use of families, 119
theoretical integration, 169–**72**, **170**, 185,
    186, 194
theoretical memos, 26, 50, 71–2, 90,
    110–14, 119
  example, **135**
  possibilities for, **114**
  sorting, 113
  in writing up, 149
theoretical sampling, 8, 18, 61, 184, 186
  definition, 194
  extending scope of theories, 135–6
  implications for theory-building, 65–8
  and saturation of categories, **66**, 134
  strategies for (Glaser and Strauss), 64–**5**
theoretical saturation, 9, 194
theoretical sensitivity, 16, 76–7, 136–7
theories, 4–5, 5–7, 11, 89
  building, 16, 17, 41–4, 107, 178–9, 180
    blocks, 132–4, **133**
    'wall of theory', 42–**3**
    see also integrative diagrams; iterative
      conceptualisation; theoretical coding;
      theoretical memos
  components, **6**, 106
  conceptualisaion, 131–**2**
  derived from data, 7
  emergent, 7, 17
  importance of, 146, 178
  levels of, 131–6, **132**, 169
  low-level, 30–1
  nature of, 181–2
  quality of, 181
  rewriting, 143
  scope, 106
  substantive, 4, 16, 31, 61, 162
  see also scaling up theories
theory-building designs, 63–8
theses *see* writing up
time taken by GTM research, 32, 179
top-down coding, 38–9, 44, 53, 180
triangulation, 60, 61–2

Urquhart, C., 45, 160, 161
Urquhart, C. et al, 16, 131, 182
Urquhart, C. and Fernández, W., 13, 29
uses of GTM, 8, 10–11, 75–6
  in PhD studies, 179–80

vignette (example), **153-4**
visual materials, 69–70, 186–7

Walker, D. and Myrick, F., 34
Walsham, G., 67, 68, 75, 169, 171, 172

weak constructivism, 62
web resources
  Atlas Ti, 104
  citation manager and social network, 12
  coding, 52–3
  digital texts, 189
  digitised theses, 74
  ethics, 74
  Feaver, Peter: Obama and Iraq, 126
  forum for discussing qualitative research, 189
  Glaser's site, 33, 180
  Gorton, Angela: language and speech
    making, 126
  GTM theory, 12
  information systems, 145
  metaphors, 146
  Methodspace, 180, 189
  NVivo, 104
  QDA packages, 104
  resources for novices, 12
  rhetorical studies, 145
  writing up, 174

Whetton, D.A., 132–3, 134, 146, 184
widespread use of GTM, 28, 30
writing up, 148–75
  blocks and unblocking, 150–2, **151**
  chains of evidence, 159–**61**, **160**
  coding procedure, 154–9, **155**, **156**,
    157, **158**
  description of context, **153–4**
  and editing, 150
  findings, 162–**3**
  key findings, 175
  for publication, 150
  structure of theses, 174–5
  substantive theories, 163, 165,
    166, **167**
  theories and literature, 169–**72**, **170**
  time, 149–50
  using literature, 162, **164–5**
  using quotes, 162, **164–5**
  writing process, 149–52

Yin, R.K., 61, 67